D0301178

11.1.07

The Novel Now

To Amy Burns; and to Helen and Gerard, the world's best in-laws.

The Novel Now

Contemporary British Fiction

Richard Bradford

. 1771231

LIBRARY

ACC. No.	DEPT.
36035684	
CLASS No.	

UNIVERSITY
OF CHESTER

Blackwell
Publishing

© 2007 by Richard Bradford

BLACKWELL PUBLISHING
350 Main Street, Malden, MA 02148-5020, USA
9600 Garsington Road, Oxford OX4 2DQ, UK
550 Swanston Street, Carlton, Victoria 3053, Australia

The right of Richard Bradford to be identified as the Author of this Work has been asserted in accordance with the UK Copyright, Designs, and Patents Act 1988.

All rights reserved. No part of this publication may be reproduced, stored in a retrieval system, or transmitted, in any form or by any means, electronic, mechanical, photocopying, recording or otherwise, except as permitted by the UK Copyright, Designs, and Patents Act 1988, without the prior permission of the publisher.

First published 2007 by Blackwell Publishing Ltd

1 2007

Library of Congress Cataloging-in-Publication Data

Brafford, Richard. 1957-
  The novel now : contemporary British fiction / Richard Bradford.
    p. cm.
  Includes bibliographical references and index.
  ISBN-13: 978-1-4051-1385-4 (alk. paper)
  ISBN-10: 1-4051-1385-5 (alk. paper)
  ISBN-13: 978-1-4051-1386-1 (pbk. : alk. paper)
  ISBN-10: 1-4051-1386-3 (pbk. : alk. paper)
    1. English fiction—20th century—History and criticism.   2. English fiction—21st century—History and criticism.   I. Title.

PR881.B684.2006
823'.91409—dc22

2006019317

Set in 10.5 on 13 pt Galliard
by SNP Best-set Typesetter Ltd, Hong Kong
Printed and bound in Singapore
by COS Printers Pte Ltd

The publisher's policy is to use permanent paper from mills that operate a sustainable forestry policy, and which has been manufactured from pulp processed using acid-free and elementary chlorine-free practices. Furthermore, the publisher ensures that the text paper and cover board used have met acceptable environmental accreditation standards.

For further information on
Blackwell Publishing, visit our website:
www.blackwellpublishing.com

Contents

Preface   vi
Acknowledgements   viii

Part I: Realism Versus Modernism: Win, Lose or Draw?   1
1 Before Now. A Brief Account of the Pre-1970s
   British Novel   3
2 Something Unusual: Martin Amis and Ian McEwan   12
3 The Effects of Thatcherism   29
4 The New Postmodernists   47

Part II: Excursions From the Ordinary   79
5 The New Historical Novel   81
6 Crime and Spy Fiction   100

Part III: Sex   113
7 Women   115
8 Men   141
9 Gay Fiction   151

Part IV: Nation, Race and Place   159
10 Scotland   161
11 England, Englishness and Class   177
12 The Question of Elsewhere   191
13 Wales   219
14 The Troubles   225
15 Epilogue: The State of the Novel   242

Select Bibliography: Recommended Further Reading   248
Index   250

Preface

Readers of contemporary fiction tend to fall into two categories: those whose opinions upon the novel are a function of their predispositions and for whom pleasure plays a large part in evaluative judgement – aka the general reader – and those for whom their choice of reading and their response to the novel are compromised by other commitments – the latter tend to exist within the education system. One objective of this book will be to show that enjoyment and critical scrutiny are not mutually exclusive activities; it is designed to appeal both to ordinary readers and their university-based counterparts.

I have borrowed the title from a book by the late Anthony Burgess but, given that his 'Now' occurred almost half a century ago, I feel confident that he would not have taken this as an affront. The subtitle is misleading, but not in a mischievous or pernicious way. The book deals with Ireland but only to the extent that it covers novels which address themselves to the events of the past three decades in Northern Ireland. I have excluded Irish fiction per se because it involves political, social and cultural trajectories which reflect a nation and a state of mind that have matured into confident separateness. To attempt to deal with these alongside a study which focuses upon the tense, fragmentary nature of Britishness would create a thematic imbalance; it would, in effect, involve the forced intermeshing of two books.

The rationale for the four-part division will I hope be self-evident. Part I examines how fiction of the past three decades has absorbed and obscured the distinction between modernism and realism. It also looks at how developments in the structure and perceptions of British society – particularly those brought about during the 1980s when

Thatcherite Conservatism set the agenda for all subsequent British political activity – have influenced the progress of the novel. Part II deals with the new historical novel and crime and spy fiction, two quixotic and flexible subgenres which raise questions regarding the relationship between mainstream and popular writing. Parts III and IV fix, respectively, upon sex and our sense of national, racial and socio-cultural identity. To allow such considerations to override attention to the essential qualities of novels would be an affront to their authors, so I have concentrated particularly on how well, or otherwise, novelists execute a balance between polemic and literary craftsmanship.

My decision to eschew the conventional format of dealing with separate authors chapter by chapter is based upon my contention that while there is a putative hierarchy of major contemporary figures a book planned around such a 'canon' deliberately obscures our aware-ness both of broader trends and less established figures. For those of you who wish to locate those parts of the book which deal in detail with well-known writers, go to the index. If you are keen to learn of newer figures in the landscape read the book.

There are no footnotes. Publication details of cited critical works are provided in the body of the text. The bibliography comprises recent critical work which addresses issues similar to those dealt with below.

Acknowledgements

Thanks are due to Rosemary Savage of the University of Ulster and I am also indebted to Karen Wilson and Emma Bennett for their patience and help. Jenny Roberts has provided matchless assistance. Amy Burns toiled heroically in the early stages and ultimately made it possible.

Part I

Realism Versus Modernism: Win, Lose or Draw?

Chapter 1

Before Now. A Brief Account of the pre-1970s British Novel

In 1971 David Lodge invented the now famous image of the novelist at the crossroads. The main road to this junction had been taken by the 'realistic novel', beginning in the eighteenth century and 'coming down through the Victorians and the Edwardians'. At that point the modernists – notably James Joyce, Virginia Woolf and Dorothy Richardson – had begun to chart significant byways. In 1971, at least in Lodge's view, realism was still the principal route chosen by the majority of novelists. There had been exceptions – writers who, after Joyce et al., had kept the torch of modernist experiment alight – but more frequently contemporary novelists would simply 'hesitate at the crossroads' and then 'build their hesitation into the novel itself' (*The Novelist at the Crossroads*, Routledge, 1971, p. 22). To decode Lodge's metaphor: the radicalism of modernism had by 1971 become an accoutrement, a decorative feature of the mainstream, realist novel. Twenty years later Lodge reframed the image as a question, 'The Novelist Today: Still at the Crossroads?' (in *New Writing*, ed. M. Bradbury and J. Cooke, British Council, 1992), and conceded that the situation of the novelist in 1992 bore less resemblance to a figure standing at a junction than a person in an 'aesthetic supermarket' facing an unprecedented abundance of styles, techniques and scenarios; the novelist/customer could now select and combine these in any way they wished. What had once been the stark contrast – often antagonistic conflict – between realism and modernism had been sidelined; hybridity now occupied the centre ground.

One of the objectives of this book will be to test Lodge's thesis, and to give an account of what has happened to the novel from the

1970s to 2005. In order to do so, however, we need to look briefly at the writers and trends which predated the 1970s and any such investigation must focus upon the opposition that bestraddles all of twentieth-century literary culture: modernism (also known as radicalism, the avant-garde, experiment, self-referentiality et al.) versus realism (aka traditional, naturalistic, conventional or orthodox writing).

In *Adam Bede* George Eliot digresses briefly on the nature of her task as a novelist and offers what could stand as the manifesto for classic realism, the mode of writing that evolved during the eighteenth century and dominated fiction until the beginning of the twentieth. She concedes that she could 'refashion life and character entirely after my own liking' but this would be an 'arbitrary picture'. Her duty, her task, is to 'give a faithful account of men and things as they have mirrored themselves in my mind'. She will, she adds, minimalize any distortions in this mirror image by striving 'to tell you as precisely as I can what that reflection is, as if I were in the witness box narrating my experience on oath'. This seems to be a watertight ordinance for what the novel is supposed to be and do, but it raises questions, questions which would inspire and inform the writing of the modernists.

James Joyce's *Ulysses* (1922) is cited by most as the quintessential modernist novel. The story, such as it is, involves the relatively mundane activities and experiences of Stephen Daedalus, Molly and Leopold Bloom and a cast of secondary characters of their acquaintance during one day (6 June, 1904) in Dublin. The text shifts unpredictably between the chaotic interior monologues of each principal character, more objective conventional narrative methods, journalistic reportage, operatic collage, theatre-style dialogue and in one famous passage an account of stultifyingly ordinary events via a sequence of styles borrowed from virtually every period of the history of English prose from the middle ages to the present day.

It is routine but misleading to treat *Ulysses* – along with related but by no means identical pieces by Virginia Woolf and Dorothy Richardson – simply as radical deviations from realism. Certainly in manner and technique they bemused readers who had become accustomed to the trustworthy, dependable presence of the nineteenth-century narrator, but it is a mistake to perceive modernism as founded upon an anti-realist aesthetic. Its practitioners were offering an alternative form of realism, something which exposed the naturalistic techniques of the nineteenth century as hidebound and self-limiting, capable only of offering a socially and culturally acceptable 'mirror image'. Joyce and Woolf, albeit in different ways, treated the world not simply as something composed predominantly of prelinguistic states and objects to be articulated and represented by language – the premise of the classic realists – but rather as a condition and an experience that are, at least in part, dependent upon and modified by language. Moreover, the modernists challenged what had become the pre-eminent – some would argue the defining – characteristic of fiction since the eighteenth century: the demand that the novel, irrespective of its accuracy as a 'mirror', should tell a story. A narrative in which a succession of events and their effects upon characters operates as the structural core of the book is the mainstay of traditional fiction. Modernist writing, however, inferred that storytelling, involving deference to an ever-present question of 'what-happens-next?', involves a reshaping of life and experience according to an arbitrary system of fabulation. In the novels of Joyce, Woolf and Richardson, very little tends to happen; instead the focus shifts toward the process of representation and to conditions and states of mind. Whether this or the conventional reliance upon a cause-and-effect narrative backbone enables fiction to best fulfil its role as combination of art and a means of recording the world is the question that has divided advocates and practitioners of modernism and realism for almost a century. Few would deny that the attraction of having our disbelief suspended, of being drawn into the mindset of a character or a group of characters and following them through a sequence of compelling episodes has maintained traditional fiction writing as far more popular than its experimental counterpart. This, however, raises the question of whether the pre-eminence of a story indulges a populist taste for fantasy, and that other means of writing should be employed to bring the book closer to the random unpredictabilities of life. By inference this question informs the work of novelists who sustained the modernist project beyond its heyday of the 1920s and 1930s.

Samuel Beckett's 1950s fiction, including *Watt* (1953), *Molloy* (1956), *Malone Dies* (1958) and *The Unnameable* (1960) (all dates refer to Beckett's own English translations from French) are extensions of the pioneering work of his friend and associate James Joyce. None involves a story or even a recognizable context beyond the imprisoned, self-referring mindset of a speaking presence. If they can be said to have a subject it is language, specifically the undermining of the assumption that reality can exist independently of the strangeness of language. Similarly, in Malcolm Lowry's *Under the Volcano* (1947) Geoffrey Firman, alcoholic depressive British Consul to Somewhere, is less a character than a witness to the novel's unbounded concern with the cyclic and unfathomable nature of truth and its quixotic confederate, writing.

Another postwar writer within this general tradition – referred to by some as postmodernism – is B. S. Johnson. Johnson's novels are frequently cited as archetypes of metafiction – fiction whose principal topic is its own status as fiction. *Travelling People* (1963) extends the moderately experimental technique of the chapter-by-chapter shift in narrational perspective – already used by Aldous Huxley, amongst others – to include a more radical blend of foci, such as film scenarios, letters and typographical eccentricities. In *Alberto Angelo* (1964) the author steps into the narrative to discuss his techniques and objectives, in arguably the most bitter and angry example of stream of consciousness yet offered. Johnson's most famous piece is *The Unfortunates* (1969). This 'novel' is unbound, leaving it up to us to read 25 of the 27 loose-leaf sections in whatever order we may wish to do so: the 'story' becomes as a consequence a mutable, dynamic intermediary between the processes of writing and reading.

In Christine Brooke-Rose's *Such* (1966) the book occupies the three minutes between the main protagonist's heart failure and his return to consciousness, during which his past is recalled in a singularly unorthodox manner. David Caute's *The Confrontation* (1969–71) comprises three texts: a play, a critical essay (by one of the characters of the play) and a short novel. Each shares themes, characters and perspectives with the others and by implication poses the question of whether identity is a condition of the various conventions of representation. Gabriel Josipovici in *The Inventory* (1968) and *Words* (1971) takes up the challenge of Caute's experiment in genre-interweaving by writing exclusively in dialogue, obliging the reader to construct a context and, to a degree, a story from their interaction with recorded speech. One could add to this list Ann Quinn's *Berg* (1964), John Berger's *The Foot of Clive* (1962) and Alan Burns's *Celebrations* (1967), all of which do self-consciously unusual things with narrative sequence, description, perspective or dialogue.

These constitute the vast majority of the postmodern novels written between the Joycean heyday and Lodge's contemplation of a cross-roads, and they are accurate exemplars of what modernism involved after Joyce. At the top of their agenda is the apparently unsteady relationship between linguistic representation and actuality, what goes on within a text and what exists outside it. Their watchword, if they had one, would have been self-referentiality: that the familiar cliché of 'suspending disbelief' should be challenged, even forbidden, in the writing of fiction and replaced with an engagement with the very nature of language and identity. In short, novels should not so much tell stories as be about the telling of stories.

In 1954, less than a year after Beckett's *Watt* came out and shortly before his *Waiting for Godot* was first performed in London, Kingsley Amis's *Lucky Jim* and John Wain's *Hurry on Down* were published, for each their first novel in print. Both are regarded as embodying a new wave of postwar realism – intelligent, reflective of contemporary mores and habits, amoral and contemptuous of the class distinctions and ethical norms that the likes of Evelyn Waugh and Anthony Powell had carried forward from the nineteenth century. These novels might have been unconventional in manner and outlook – and in this regard they are frequently cited as exemplars of the 'Angry' mode of 1950s writing – but their formal characteristics were uncompromisingly orthodox.

There have been an enormous number of works on the postwar trends in English literature (see particularly R. Rabinovitz's *The Reaction Against Experiment in the English Novel, 1950–60*, Columbia University Press, 1967 and Blake Morrison's *The Movement*, Oxford University Press, 1980) and all tend to rehearse the standard postulate that Amis, Wain, William Cooper, C. P. Snow, Pamela Hansford Johnson, Philip Larkin et al. felt threatened by modernism and were involved in an attempt to reinstall nineteenth-century classic realism as the institutionalized mainstay of fiction writing. This is misleading, in two respects. First the idea that the countermodernists felt in some way besieged by the encroachments of the prewar avant-garde is a flawed myth. Book sales alone testified to the fact that, as Kingsley Amis put it, 'believable stories' were a great deal more attractive to the general reading public of 1950s Britain than novels which, sentence by sentence, challenged the conventions of reading and representation. Indeed those realist novelists who had begun their careers at the same time as the arrival of modernism – figures such as Anthony Powell, Evelyn Waugh and Graham Greene – and had as a consequence been obliged to function in its more powerful cultural presence remained, after the war, far more popular than Joyce or Beckett. Secondly, the postwar realists certainly did not see themselves as mid-twentieth-century versions of Thackeray, Dickens, Trollope or Henry James. In purely stylistic terms there were similarities but these were outweighed by the manner in which these were used by the 1950s writers. In truth the postwar novelists were involved in a counter-revolution against both the modernists and the classic realists. They rejected the mannerisms of the former as the obtuse, inaccessible preserve of an intellectual elite while they saw George Eliot's notion of the Victorian novel as a 'mirror' to society as purblind hypocrisy. In the 'Books of the Year' survey for *The Sunday Times* of December 1955 W. Somerset Maugham senses the coming of a cultural apocalypse:

> They do not go to university to acquire culture, but to get a job and when they have got one scamp it. They have no manners and are woefully unable to deal with any social predicament. Their idea of a celebration is to go to a public house and drink six beers. They are mean, malicious and envious. They will write anonymous letters to fellow undergraduates and listen to a telephone conversation that is no business of theirs...they are scum. They will in due course leave the university. Some will doubtless sink back, perhaps with relief, into the modest social class from which they emerged; some will take to drink, some to crime and go to prison. Others will become schoolmasters and form the young, or journalists and mould public opinion. A few will go into parliament, become Cabinet Ministers and rule the country. I look upon myself as fortunate that I shall not live to see it.

Maugham's almost obsessive use of 'they' indicates his inability to distinguish the apparently threatening presence of the authors from their unseemly creations and the irony of the elder statesman of Edwardian realism being so appalled by the new generation of traditionalists points to the essential difference between the 1950s writers and their predecessors.

Maugham's unease was caused by the fact that many of the new novelists – and he was particularly distressed by Amis and Wain – were able to execute clever, unnervingly realistic portraits of contemporaneity while showing a disdainful indifference to the cultural and ethical values with which fiction, as an art form, had associated itself since the eighteenth century. Not only did they refuse to judge their characters, they seemed in some instances to actually endorse bad behaviour. The novels of Alan Sillitoe, David Storey, John Braine, Stan Barstow and Nell Dunn sustained and extended this unapologetic warts-and-all coverage of people and society. In Sillitoe's *Saturday Night and Sunday Morning* (1958) Arthur Seaton is rebellious, contemptuous of all types of authority – government, management, army, police – but he has no concern for an alternative moral or political agenda. Instead he unleashes his energy via drink, womanizing, fishing and fist fights.

The countermodernist trend in postwar fiction was neither simply a reaction against the aesthetic of experimentation nor a continuation of techniques refined through the nineteenth century. Rather it was a new, unprecedented form of realism in which the author no longer felt beholden to any fixed or determining set of social or ethical mores. This, as we will see, is significant because these writers can be regarded as establishing a precedent for a considerable number of later twentieth-century novelists who present society and its ills as little more than a patchwork of hopeless grotesques to be treated with nerveless, sometimes comedic, scrutiny.

Aside from the torch-carriers for fundamentalist modernism and the new realists, there were a number of writers who from the mid-1950s onwards are more difficult to classify in terms of their relationship with established precedent. William Golding's fiction is accessible and stylistically conservative while shifting between historical periods, dealing with apocalyptic themes and continually blending the specific with the symbolic. Muriel Spark combines a mood of detached observation evocative of Greene and Waugh with an antithetical inclination to allow her novels to become reflections upon the process of writing novels. Anthony Burgess indulges a more sceptical recognition of metafiction in *Enderby* (1963); Enderby is a writer whose obsession with the unreliable, tactile nature of language mirrors his prurient fascination with sex and his own insides. A similarly arch, satirical engagement with modernism's close relative – structuralism – occurs in his *MF* (1971), a novel self-mockingly enraptured by codes and anthropological riddles. Iris Murdoch's 1960s fiction is imitative in that the personae and settings are recognizably contemporaneous, but Murdoch seems determined to endow each character with a symbolic presence more closely associated with Renaissance drama or the epic poem than the mid-twentieth-century novel. Doris Lessing in *The Golden Notebook* (1962) nods allegiance toward modernist radicalism by offering a multi-perspective upon the temperament and experiences of Anna Wulf via four different notebooks, but each involves a conservative, naturalistic sense of authenticity. These writers are what Lodge refers to as 'the hesitators', allying themselves neither with the pure avant-garde nor the gritty transparency of the new realism, yet invoking both. The most famous contribution to this quasi-genre was John Fowles's *The French Lieutenant's Woman* (1969). At one level this appears to be an exercise in historical ventriloquism, creating as it does a fabric composed of the styles and mannerisms of Victorian writers, literary and nonliterary. Fowles himself complicates this issue by continually interrupting the story to remind the reader that it is indeed a fiction and by implication the product of a subjective idiosyncratic presence – one John Fowles. Just to make sure that we don't insist on suspending disbelief he offers us two different endings, of equal plausibility. Its insistent play upon truth as a relative, elusive entity prompts comparison with Joyce's *Ulysses*, yet in terms of accessibility Fowles's novel is soundly traditional.

The French Lieutenant's Woman is treated by many as a landmark, but it should in truth be regarded as such principally because of its isolation within a landscape of fiction that was still predominantly conservative in its manner and frame of reference. Within 18 months either side of its publication date novels by long-established scions of traditional writing appeared, notably Anthony Powell's *The Military Philosophers* (1968), Graham Greene's *Travels With My Aunt* (1969), and C. P. Snow's *The Sleep of Reason* (1968) and *Last Things* (1970). The countermodernists of the 1950s were still turning out solidly mimetic engagements with contemporary life: John Braine's *Stay With Me Till Morning* (1970), Simon Raven's *Places Where They Sing* (1970), Alan Sillitoe's *Guzman Go Home* (1968), Stan Barstow's *A Raging Calm* (1968), Kingsley Amis's *I Want It Now* (1968) and *The Green Man* (1969), John Wain's *A Winter in the Hills* (1970), Elizabeth Jane Howard's *Something in Disguise* (1969) are symptomatic of what can be regarded as the norm. None of them played self-consciously perplexing games with the nature of writing; none caused the reader to question the experience of reading and none subjugated reflections of contemporaneity to broader metaphysical concerns.

The novelists who began their careers in the 1940s and 1950s had rejected modernism not because they were possessed of some inbred or socially inculcated reactionary aesthetic. Rather, they had been confronted with a new Britain, a complete transformation of the economic and social infrastructure set in train by the policies of the postwar Labour Government and over the next 15 years driven by factors such as new levels of social mobility, the explosion of unprecedented types of popular culture – in radio, TV, cinema, popular music – all heavily influenced by America. Realism seemed to many to be the method demanded by these phenomena because the events themselves were so unusual. Modernism, it should be remembered, had evolved as a reaction against an apparent alliance between a society whose structures and perceptions of itself had remained largely unchanged for more than a century and novelistic conventions which seemed complicit in this sense of conservatism bordering on complacency. After the war, however, social change was so rapid and varied that the logical response, for the novelist, seemed to be to attempt to record it, to incorporate its particulars and incidentals as guilelessly as possible; mimesis rather than experiment became the preferred technique.

When Lodge assessed the state of the novel at the turn of the 1960s he was addressing as much a socio-historical as a literary issue. All of the radicals, the conservatives and the 'hesitators' were, at their youngest, in their late thirties. For them modernism was, whether espoused or abjured, the new aesthetic – even during the 1940s and early 1950s *Ulysses, To The Lighthouse* and *Finnegans Wake* were being debated as if they had only just been published. Similarly World War II and the social, cultural and technological transitions of the decades that followed it carried for such writers, irrespective of their effect upon their ideas and techniques, a sense of communal immediacy. What Lodge did not, indeed could not, take into account was the incoming generation of potential writers: those for whom modernism was a fascinating but antiquated phenomenon, the war and its socio-cultural aftermath a remembrance from their parents.

These are the novelists who began to establish the territory of contemporary fiction, the ones who started their careers in the 1970s and who have made their presence felt over the past three decades.

hing Unusual:
Amis and Ian McEwan

Martin Amis's first novel *The Rachel Papers* (1973) was published when he was 24 and is frequently cited as evidence of Martin's indebtedness to his father, Kingsley. There are similarities certainly: irreverent, crudely confident wit is ever present; Martin catches the mores, concerns and conversational mannerisms of the early 1970s with the same unnerving accuracy as his father had caught those of the 1950s; and the 'hero', Charles Highway, could be a younger precociously acerbic version of Jim Dixon. At the same time, however, there are a sufficient number of differences to raise questions regarding the claim that Martin Amis is perpetuating the standardized model of satiric realism. The plot – principally involving Highway's pursuit of the eponymous Rachel and his distracted reflections on his family and prospects beyond his late teens – becomes a self-sustaining excuse for something else: Highway's ability to keep the reader variously amused, affronted and enviously engaged with his presence as a storyteller. Sterne's Tristram Shandy is arguably the most idiosyncratic, affable narrator in the history of fiction and one is often caused to wonder what kind of novel would have resulted from him actually telling something resembling a story. Charles Highway enacts this hypothesis. He shows off. He turns the most mundane and insignificant occurrences into launch pads for finely crafted, sometimes unsettling anecdotes. We never quite lose track of the narrative but it soon becomes evident that the novel is not so much an account of what has happened to Highway as a show-piece for his ability to give verbal substance to otherwise hollow events.

The third-person narrator of Amis's second novel, *Dead Babies* (1975) offers a somewhat grotesque picture of near-contemporary life via a group of undergraduate-age bon vivants, gathered for a long weekend at the country house of the patrician Quentin Villiers. For a few chapters one might easily mistake it for a late twentieth-century version of Evelyn Waugh's *Vile Bodies*, incorporating an appropriately updated excess of sex, drug taking and alcohol abuse. Then, however, sinister events begin to occur and by the end each of the hedonists – who range from the clever through the tragic to the laughably pitiable, and with Amis's brilliant versatility for dialogue seem very real – has been killed. The killer is the mysterious intruder known only as 'Johnny', who turns out to be Villiers himself. No moral, symbolic or allegorical subtext is even hinted at. Villiers is certainly not mad. He seems indeed to be the most stable, intelligent, self-possessed figure in the book. He derives no particular pleasure from extinguishing his associates – wife and close friends included – but implies, with characteristic hauteur, that it was something that was inevitable. The only other person in the novel to whom he bears any resemblance is the narrator. Without the latter the events and many of the characters would prompt little more than irritation or abhorrence but the narrator weaves them into a narrative texture of mordant elegance, brilliant timing and choreography. We know we ought to feel unsettled, even disgusted by the unfolding chronicle but despite ourselves we submit to various states of literary gratification and guilty laughter. Villiers and the narrator share the ability to at once animate, control yet stand outside the particulars of the novel. They might be dimensions of the same presence; both are manipulative craftsmen, Villiers applying his skills to the unwitting cohabitants of the book and the narrator doing something similar with the reader. The double-act is beguiling, irritating and effective, but one detects throughout that it is driven by its own sense of inappropriateness, that Amis the anonymous stylist would like to be a little more involved with the characters and that Villiers kills everyone to mark out his territory as a kind of narrator-manqué.

The most controversial and celebrated of Amis's unifications of character and chronicler occurs in *Money* (1984). John Self, producer of self-evidently crass TV commercials, is a literary paradox – one of the best ever created. He is definitely not the kind of person with whom most readers of intelligent fiction, indeed any kind of fiction, would wish to spend time. For John Self's life is composed mainly of sordid excess, whether involving sex (pornographically witnessed, purchased or forcibly obtained), cigarettes (a 60-a-day habit), alcohol consumed by the gallon, drugs selected and self-administered with impressive versatility, or artery-clogging junk food disposed of with fantastic speed. He has a grudging acquaintance with Orwell's *Animal Farm*, but this is the totality of his literary, indeed his cultural, experience. The paradox is that the more we learn of this apparently odious individual, and of the equally repellent world he inhabits, the more we become transfixed by him; he even, on some occasions, seems able to procure sympathy. We face this dilemma because as a first-person narrator he is a genius. Like his anonymous predecessor in *Dead Babies* he is able to invest the vile, the grotesque, with something that resembles artistic shape. His account, for example, of his brief excursion to a New York live pornography emporium is symphonic in the way that levels of humiliation and degradation are segued toward an apogee:

> Finally I devoted twenty-eight tokens' worth of my time to a relatively straight item, in which a slack-jawed cowboy got the lot, everything from soup to nuts, at the expense of the talented Juanita del Pablo. Just before the male's climax the couple separated with jittery haste. Then she knelt in front of him. One thing was clear: the cowboy must have spent at least six chaste months on a yoghurt ranch eating nothing but ice-cream and buttermilk, and with a watertight no-hand job clause in his contract. By the time he was through, Juanita looked like the patsy in the custard-pie joke, which I suppose is what she was. The camera proudly lingered as she spat and blinked and coughed...Hard to tell, really, who was the biggest loser in this complicated transaction – her, him, them, me. (*Money*, Penguin, 1985, p. 47)

Reviewers and subsequent academic commentators have been unsettled by Self, mainly because he is an overreacher. Bad, abhorrent people had of course been written about before – though none of them was quite as unapologetically monstrous as Self – but only as the subjects of novels. Self takes charge, and despite his indifference to anything vaguely literary he does so with skill and verve.

Late in the novel he meets Martin Amis and hires the novelist to help him out with the screenplay for a film. Amis gets on reasonably well with Self and often appears concerned with his personal problems, but he never seems able to prevent himself from discoursing on the nature of contemporary fiction and artistic representation per se. For example:

> The distance between the author and narrator corresponds to the degree to which the author finds the narrator wicked, deluded, pitiful or ridiculous [...] the further down the scale he is, the more liberties you can take with him. You can do what you like with him really. This creates an appetite for punishment. The author is not free of sadistic impulses. I suppose it's the – (pp. 246–7)

At this point he is interrupted by Self (who is bored and more concerned with his toothache), but Amis has made his point, which for the reader is deliberately, mischievously, confusing. Self is obviously well 'down the scale' but Amis's implication that the more uncultivated and unpleasant the narrator the more the author can take 'liberties' should not be regarded as licence for the author to appear superior to his subject. Self, while not sharing his creator's sophisticated frame of reference, can write as well as Martin Amis. What, then, should be made of the strange contrast between Self's proud loutishness, and his stylistic abilities? Self and Amis consider this.

> 'Do you have this problem with novels, Martin?' I asked him, 'I mean is there a big deal about bad behaviour and everything?'
> 'No. It's not a problem. You get complaints, of course, but we're pretty much agreed that the twentieth century is an ironic age – downward looking. Even realism, rock bottom realism, is considered a bit grand for the twentieth century.' (p. 248)

As creative manifestoes go this one seems enigmatic, almost self-contradictory, at least until one looks at the novel that contains it. *Money* involves matchless, consummate irony in which repulsive activities and states of mind are made crisply, horribly amusing. It outdoes the most transparent realism by causing the reader to feel a kind of complicit involvement with Self and his world.

Amis has not abandoned realism in the manner of what by the 1970s and 1980s had become virtually the complacent conventions of postmodernism. He does not, like Fowles, enter his own text and reflect upon the puzzles and self-contradictions of fiction; rather he does so as a mildly indifferent observer. For Amis it is the text itself that subtly rethinks realism, not his self-conscious participation in it.

If Amis's fiction has a recurrent, if implicit, watchword it is probably guilt. He is sometimes celebrated and just as often derided and caricatured as perhaps the most expansively gifted prose stylist of his generation. Even his father Kingsley – who himself took over from Waugh as the guardian of the crisply executed apothegm – paid him the backhanded compliment of finding a 'terrible compulsive vividness in his style [...] that constant demonstrating of his command of English' (*Esquire*, January 1987, p. 111). With more economy, if similar intent, *Private Eye* took to calling him 'Smarty Anus'. None of his critics seemed willing to make clear, however, what exactly he was doing wrong. He was never accused of actually overwriting, of stylistic hyperbole or unnecessary floridity and one is left to assume that his alleged flaw lies in the mismatch between style and substance; the writing is too good for the material. Although he never addresses the issue one suspects that Amis himself is aware of a curious inconsistency between what he is able to do with words and the raw material of life outside the novel.

The Prologue to *Other People* (1981) begins:

> This is a confession, but a brief one.
>   I didn't want to have to do it to her. I would have infinitely preferred some other solution. Still, there we are.

Even the reader disinclined toward, or bored with, the potentialities of metafiction would know that this is a double-edged declaration, pertaining both to the commission of a crime and the process of writing about it; in novels you can't have one without the other. In *London Fields* (1989) the narrator eventually discloses that he is both terminally ill and the murderer of Nicola Six. The novel's posthumous endpapers are addressed to Mark Asprey, aka Martin Amis, with whom Samson Young, the narrator, has exchanged flats, and to an extent roles. He ends his note to Asprey: 'PPS. You didn't set me up. Did you?' Of course he did, but Young too played his part in setting up the cast of characters and retinue of events that comprise the novel. The most memorably evocative of the former is Keith Talent, compared with whom John Self could easily make a claim to sainthood.

Talent inhabits, indeed animates, a world of hellishly black comedy never before witnessed in English fiction. He beats up an unfortunate fellow-lowlife who has tampered with his darts prior to one of the games which feature for Keith as a kind of ongoing quest motif. The onlookers in the pub approve admiringly, as does the brother of the girl who has given him venereal disease when Talent decides to visit similar damage upon her, so much so that he joins in; male solidarity at its finest. The scene during which Talent becomes enraged as his drunken wife attempts to hand him their baby daughter while he is trying to eat his dinner should, like practically every incident in which he features, possess the reader with competing levels of disgust, outrage and horror. The fact that they don't testifies to the skill of the narrator, Young, who causes us to laugh; hilarity is followed very rapidly, on the part of most readers, by unease. We know we shouldn't be laughing at such things and Young knows that his ability to catch the reader between unbidden instinct and good taste is one of the powers of fiction writing. Another is his ability to kill people and, as he discloses at the end, he has done that too.

It would be at once inaccurate and convenient to treat Amis's endeavours as postmodernistic. Keith Talent and John Self leap from the page with a gargantuan authenticity that would have made Dickens shudder, but Amis's is a discontented mimesis. He never allows the reader to become content with their response to the text. His father's generation, or at least most of them, would maintain a balance throughout the novel between its conventions and the world beyond it. The authorial tone might be urbane, sardonic or satirical and this would inform other dimensions of the book. Consequently, even though different readers might have different opinions about the nature of the world and about the qualities of the novel, these differences would encompass a collective mean. For Martin Amis, however, the opportunity offered by fiction to set in train separate apparently incompatible trajectories of documentary-style mimesis versus grotesque caricature, brilliantly choreographed slapstick versus metafictional experiment, to name but four, overrides what had even 20 years earlier been a straightforward set of obligations. His methods bring vividly to mind Lodge's image of the fiction-supermarket, with a plethora of techniques, devices and effects available, and the question raised is whether Amis's use of them testifies to an overabundance of choice and collateral lack of self-control or whether his baffling dalliance with and undermining of realism embodies a more serious intention to reshape the novel as a token of its era.

Ian McEwan is a near contemporary of Martin Amis (b. 1948 and 1949 respectively) and both are regarded as having made formative contributions to the landscape and tempo of fiction writing during the past three decades. On first reading their novels seem to have very little in common. McEwan, and his narrators, maintain a modest, learned elegance of manner; their style is unobtrusive yet quietly, sometimes frighteningly, evocative. Often, an accumulation of detail and descriptive registers – not an overaccumulation but an accretion that is deceptively routine – will create for the reader a sense of the very ordinary and familiar as possessed of something potentially discomforting. How different this is from, say, John Self's rampant litanies of self-destructive excess. McEwan's novels are eclectic in theme and subject but there is a persistent element that can best be described as tectonic, a sense of two strata or planes of existence coming together, perhaps through an accident, with consequences that are numinous with significance but rarely explained. In *The Comfort of Strangers* (1981) we encounter Colin and Mary – an English couple of outstanding ordinariness, intelligent and dutifully concerned with a standard retinue of intellectual and political issues, comfortably off, still more or less in love but no longer with passion – on holiday in Venice, where they meet Robert and Caroline, residents of the city. The foursome seems at first to be an exercise by McEwan in exposing the mindset of leftish, thirty-something Britain as a fabric of complacencies. Robert, for example, perceives feminism as an opportunity for fat and ugly women to take revenge on their better-looking counterparts who have, for several millennia, been enjoying the atavistic attentions of powerful handsome men such as Robert, and Caroline seems fully satisfied with his thesis. Mary, a biddable card-carrying feminist, is lost for words but the fact that her sex life with Colin is suddenly rejuvenated indicates the effectiveness of Robert's notion of animalistic anti-intellectualism, albeit second-hand. So far the novel seems to be making claims upon territory left vacant by D. H. Lawrence 50 years earlier, with a hint of Iris Murdoch's taste for the acceptably macabre. Quite soon, however, Robert turns out to be a murderous psychopath so obsessed with the easy-going, almost feminine, manner of Colin that he decides to combine sexual fantasy, sadism and the assertion of power by torturing him, kissing his blood-smeared lips and killing him by slashing his wrist. Mary, drugged, looks on while Caroline assists with compliant, appropriately vicarious (for she is a woman) satisfaction.

For any novelist a shift from the mildly unsettling – Mary's and Colin's meeting with Robert and Caroline is tinged with eerie fatalism, for example – to the mind-numbingly horrific would be difficult to achieve without glaring discontinuities of tone or a suspicion of thematic gratuitousness. McEwan's ability to do so with unnerving ease is in many of his novels his authorial signature. In *The Comfort of Strangers* the transformation is executed with grisly verisimilitude, in that its effect upon the reader is comparable with what Colin and Mary must have felt as they realized the sort of person Robert is and the nature of the trap into which he has so cunningly lured them. The pace and mood of the narrator's account does not change. Movements and facts are recorded and feelings indicated but with a kind of indifference that suggests inevitability stripped of significance. We learn, during Colin's last moments, that Robert 'drew the razor lightly, almost playfully, across Colin's wrist, opening the artery. His arm jerked forward, and the rope he cast, orange in this light, fell short of Mary's lap by several inches'. One feels that it is only the narrator's third-person status that prevents him from informing us of the precise number of inches. The old legalistic cliché that 'the devil is in the detail' appears to have become manifestly refreshed in the texture of the novel. The closeness of the rope to Mary's lap, the indication that the razor was drawn 'lightly, almost playfully' across Colin's wrist typify the neo-photographic documentary mode of the account, to the exclusion of any real indication of what each of the characters actually feels or what in truth prompts them to behave as they do: the latter are left to the surmise of the reader, based mainly upon reported speech and the choreography of action and reaction.

At no point is there an indication that McEwan is prompting the reader to interpret the events as allegorical, symbolic enactments of victimhood, evil or any other generality or abstract. True, in a 1985 interview he stated that '[some] people collude in their own subjections' and conceded that 'there was a sense in which Colin and Mary had agreed about what was going to happen to them' (John Haffenden, *Novelists in Interview*, Methuen, 1985, p. 181), but this could quite easily be an account by Barbara Pym of her tales of subservience to the tired codes of middle England, not middle-English persons subjected to blood-drenched humiliation and slaughter in Northern Italy. No reason is offered for what happens in the novel but if one looks back to McEwan's first full-length piece of fiction, *The Cement Garden* (1978) one can discern continuities, if not explanations. It is, to say the least, a Gothic tale, one of bizarre though not violent internecine activities. It begins with Jack, the 14-year-old narrator, achieving his first ever ejaculatory climax while masturbating in his bedroom. At the same moment his father, who has been labouring outside to concrete over the garden, suffers a terminal heart attack and collapses face first into the wet cement. Some time later the mother of Jack and his three siblings dies in bed after a long painful illness, and the children decide to bury her in the basement in the father's trunk along with his remaining mementoes. Conveniently there is enough unmixed sand and cement left over from the late father's garden-covering project for them to securely entomb mother and trunk. Thereafter the children engage in a versatile dance of incest, transvestism and regression to infantilism, interrupted occasionally by disconcerting smells and noises from the cellar as the mother's body produces gases of decomposition and cracks occur in the concrete.

On the reader's part morbid fascination is virtually guaranteed but what else is one supposed to make of the novel? For the sophisticated, analytically inclined reader there appear to be a proliferation of signposts marked 'Freudianism', most obviously the Oedipal myth of the death of the father – in this case not killed literally but departing with heavy-handed symbolism – and the interment of the mother, connoting her embedded presence in the subconscious of her offspring. The bewildering variety of gratuitously perverted activities undertaken by the children could provide sufficient material for a conference of psychoanalysts, but there are two problems here. First a novel whose principal function is to incite a proliferation of Freudian interpretations is at best a curiosity and, by virtue of its self-defining limitations, deficient in value and range. Moreover, McEwan raises the question of plausibility. Irrespective of one's opinion on the validity of Freudianism are we expected to treat the behaviour of the children, particularly with regard to the burying of their mother and their activities thereafter, as in some way symptomatic of characteristics shared by a large percentage of the teenage population?

In all probability the rather cumbersome exercise in Freudian coat trailing was a reflection of McEwan's university experience. The Sussex

University English department where he did his BA was even in the late 1960s and early 1970s enthusiastically undermining the drab academic protocols of old-fashioned literary studies with such fashionable exotica as psychoanalysis. More significantly the novel as a whole exhibits a premeditated experiment with credulity, a calculated sacrifice of the normal to something arbitrarily weird and deviant. Initially, for example, the motive for hiding the mother's body seems to be the teenagers' fear of being put into care – a feeling that most would recognize, perhaps even recollect – but it is difficult to discern how and why this anxiety is exchanged for their collective creation of an isolated, surreal micro-world. The process by which, and the consequences of, the ordinary becoming the potentially unimaginable and inexplicable is the factor which sustains the novel and which would feature in different manifestations in virtually all of his future work.

In *The Innocent* (1990) McEwan excurses into recent history. It is 1955, the hero Leonard Marnham is on National Service in West Berlin and finds himself, as much by accident as design, involved in the construction of a tunnel under the Berlin Wall in which will be installed listening devices to monitor military radio and telephone communications in the East. Marnham and his story are the only inventions; everything else accords with historical fact. He begins an affair with the enchanting Maria Eckdorf and so far the plot incorporates familiar characterizations and settings. Marnham is the unadventurous British soldier inadvertently drawn into the more suspenseful world of military intelligence and espionage and Maria embodies and adds a sexual dimension to this increased sense of excitement; she has a murky past which like everything else in Germany at the time carries a resonance of Nazism and the war. Markham is forced to kill Maria's ex-husband Otto in self-defence and the most gripping elements of the rest of the novel focus upon his attempts to dispose of the body. The lengthy description of what happens as he saws up the corpse in his flat is rigorous in its determination to leave nothing out, including the 'liverish reds, glistening irregular tubing of a boiled egg bluish white, and something purple and black...' (*The Innocent*, Picador, 1990, p. 182) as the lower abdomen empties itself onto the carpet. The intersection of several potentially apocalyptic events – the Cold War forces meeting virtually head on, sexual initiation with a noirish femme fatale, killing, butchery, fear of capture and its consequences – is for Marnham particularly nightmarish since prior to all of this he was attempting simply to see out his National Service and return to normal life in England. McEwan adds an even more unfathomable dimension to the mixture, specifically the presence of one George Blake, junior diplomat, who lives in the flat above Marnham's and assists, albeit unwittingly, in the final concealment of Otto's body parts in the tunnel. The 1990 reader would know of Blake as one of a notorious group of M16 double agents who throughout their careers disclosed British Intelligence details to Moscow. Blake's presence has a multiple effect. First he reinforces the overall sense of historic authenticity – Blake was indeed in Berlin during this period – while at the same time he becomes Marnham's doppelganger. Both of them are living double lives and for each the only witness to the coexistence of these states is themselves. Blake does not know what Marnham has done and Marnham is unaware of Blake's private world of betrayals and antitheses. It is probable that had Blake not been caught no-one outside the Foreign Office and his friends and family would ever have heard of him. Marnham is not caught and at the end of the novel he returns to Berlin after having spent the previous three decades as an unremarkable lower-middle-class Englishman. Again we encounter the McEwan leitmotif, commendably refashioned, of the world as comprised of strata, levels of existence and experience which if kept apart will guarantee that the worst aspects of life can remain separate from the rational, the predictable and the routine. At some point in all of his novels these strata are caused to intersect.

Even in his most recent and relatively conventional novel, *Saturday* (2005) the plot, indeed the entire texture of the novel, is shaped by an accident. Distinguished neurosurgeon Henry Perowne sets out on Saturday morning for his weekly squash game with his junior colleague. He is held up at a street junction closed in preparation for the passage of the Anti Iraq War demonstration later that day. A policeman, hospitably, waves him through and within seconds his car collides with another causing only slight damage to each. It does however bring him into contact with the driver, Baxter, a man of sinister aspect accompanied by two equally unsettling associates. During the exchange that follows Perowne is able to diagnose in Baxter symptoms of a horrific genetic disorder which is incurable, will eat into his brain and in due course cause him terrible levels of pain and humiliation before his inevitable death. Perowne knows that he will not, himself, stand a chance if things turn to violence so he uses his expertise to throw Baxter off balance. 'Your father had it. Now you've got it too' he tells him (*Saturday*, Vintage, 2006, p. 94). Baxter is stunned, given that within minutes of their meeting a complete stranger is able to disclose to him knowledge of his exclusive secret. This is sufficient to disrupt the power balance between Perowne and the threatening trio and for him to effect his escape.

After this Perowne does not give particular attention to the encounter – no more than a standard, intelligent, busy, middle-class, middle-aged professional would – but McEwan brilliantly creates such a contrast between it and the enviable state of orderliness and mutual affection in which the Perowne family exist that we know that Baxter will at some point and by some means return. It is difficult to locate for the novel a specific subject – all of McEwan's fiction shares this at once annoying and beguiling quality of elusiveness – except that the question of 'What if?' recurs continually. In this case, what if the government had not chosen to side with the US in military action against Iraq? As a consequence the demonstration would not have occurred, the policeman would not have waved Perowne through and Baxter and his frightening potentialities would have remained in their own sphere of existence, separate from the Perownes.

Throughout the novel there is a tension between factors that might variously be regarded as rational, logical, predictable, even inexorable and an opposing network of erratic, quixotic, arbitrary and unforesee-able elements. Perowne is the embodiment of the former. He spends his working life repairing and reshaping the machinery of consciousness. He is not unemotional – indeed his love for his wife and children is unqualified, the most significant factor in his life – but he is sanguine regarding anything other than mechanics as an explanation for what makes human beings feel and act. Wryly, McEwan offers us Perowne's views on literature, particularly the novel since the nineteenth century. Tolstoy, Flaubert and classic realists of other traditions are in Perowne's opinion admirable chroniclers of what was going on around them. Daisy, his daughter, tells him that he is missing the point, that 'the genius was in the detail'. Perowne finds the details 'apt and convincing enough, but surely not so very difficult to marshal if you were halfway observant and had the patience to write them all down. These books were the products of steady workmanlike accumulation' (p. 67). As for more recent novels where representation becomes licence for experiment and reality is twisted according to the author's predilections – including the 'so-called magic realists' – these he regards as 'the recourse of an insufficient imagination, a dereliction of duty, a childish evasion of the difficulties and wonders of the real, of the demanding re-enactment of the plausible' (pp. 67–8). His observations are prompted by an encounter with his daughter's undergraduate reading list. One piece of work he finds particularly irritating includes a 'visionary' who 'saw through a pub window his parents as they had been some weeks after his conception, discussing the possibility of aborting him' (p. 67), which is of course the key passage of McEwan's own *The Child in Time* (1987). This is not a case of an author repudiating his own methods; rather he uses an embodied antithesis, of himself and his techniques, his Perowne, as a means of re-examining them. For Baxter, Perowne's sudden disclosure of his brain condition must have seemed like a form of black magic, when in truth it was based exclusively upon Perowne's meticulous command of diagnostic signals – an ability that segues into his temperamental preference for realism. In *Saturday* McEwan has not so much changed direction as perspective. The familiar ingredients are present – dissimilar levels of existence and perception coexisting and then colliding – but in this case it is not Stephen Lewis, author of children's books and hero of *The Child in Time*, who experiences a potentially life-altering moment but his opposite, the rationalist brain mechanic for whom time and physics suspend their more predictable operations and threaten to remove everything he values from his sphere of knowledge and control.

Placed on a scale whose opposing points are a naturalistic realism and radical experimentation Amis and McEwan are substantially closer to the former while electing to use precedents and techniques initiated by the latter at their own discretion. Open one of McEwan's works at random, read 500 words, and one will encounter a narrative presence disclosing events with urbane transparency and effecting an unobtrusive choreography of dialogue that is both compelling and authentic; McEwan's early work in film screenwriting apprenticed him well for the latter. The building blocks of his fiction are made up of the familiar and the conventional. It is in their assembly that he creates unsettling discordancy between the world we know and that which unfolds in the novel. Amis gives more attention to the localized stylistics of fiction. He is capable of producing figures of gargantuan absurdity, malevolence and vulgarity, creating scenarios variously horrifying and mischievous and in all instances one is constantly aware of his concern with literary sophistication. He does not, in the modernist mode, constantly disrupt expected parallels between language and meaning, but he does point up their interdependency. In, for example, *Times Arrow* (1991), his most self-consciously experimental novel, time is rewound from the conclusion of events to their inception but rather than resembling a piece of neo-Beckettian metafiction the novel uses, indeed refreshes and refashions, familiar narrative devices with uncluttered elegance.

Amis and McEwan began to earn themselves recognition as talented writers in the mid-1970s. By the end of that decade, when each had produced three volumes of fiction, neither was regarded by those who take it upon themselves to assess the state of fiction writing per se as having significantly altered a mood and landscape that had predominated since about 1950.

In 1976 Peter Ackroyd set the tone for a litany of subsequent complaints in his *Notes for a New Culture* (Vision Press). He argued that England – though by implication not necessarily Britain – had 'insulated itself' from the benefits of modernism and maintained the 'false context' and 'false aesthetic' of realism. His ideal was the French *nouveau roman*, the kind of fiction writing which constantly uses the genre to re-examine its own precarious fabric. The closing issue of *The New Review* in 1978 comprised a colloquium of writers and critics summoned to pronounce on the state of the novel. The general view was that fiction, and indeed all other literature, had suffered at the hands of electronic media – no-one read novels any more – and the British were by varying degrees self-absorbed, unambitious, complacent and reactionary in what they produced, at least compared with American, French and Third World writers. Weightier academic assessments were equally pessimistic, with John Sutherland in *Fiction and the Fiction Industry* (Athlone Press, 1978) proposing that the relationship between writers and major publishers stifled originality; the latter were concerned only with reliably saleable goods and the former, who needed either to get published or to sustain their income, complied. Bernard Bergonzi updated his 1970 *The Situation of the Novel* (Macmillan) in 1979. Both editions, particularly the second, remind one of an extended angry headmaster's report on yet another decade's group of recalcitrant idlers. The English novel was now stultifyingly, almost irrevocably 'parochial' in its range. In Bergonzi's opinion little had changed since the nineteenth century and, lamentably, the crystallization of liberal ideas and actions that made the classic realist novel valuable had now been replaced by a nugatory conservatism; traditional techniques and reactionary values appeared to be working hand in hand. The most famous contribution to this growing caterwaul of disgruntlement came from Bill Buford, an American and editor of the recently founded Cambridge-based literary journal *Granta*, who in the third issue of 1980 voiced his concerns in an essay entitled 'The End of the English Novel'. He was prompted to do so, he claimed, by an article in the trade journal *The Bookseller* by Robert McCrum 'a young editor at Faber' (25 years later a major presence in the literary establishment; amongst other things literary editor of the *Observer*). McCrum had claimed, from first-hand experience, that Sutherland's thesis was valid, and worse that the publishing houses and established writers were perpetuating bad writing. Buford accords with McCrum's and Sutherland's diagnoses. He personally has 'no quarrel' with, as he puts it, the promulgators of 'the middle-class monologue' (specifically Kingsley Amis, C. P. Snow, Margaret Drabble, Melvyn Bragg) 'or their readers' except when they conspire to 'crowd out the kinds of books I'd like to read'. He senses that something new is happening

> What it means to tell, to write, to narrate, to *make up* is changing [...] Current fiction is remarkable for its detachment, its refusal to be affiliated, its suspicion of the old hierarchies and authorities. It is not modernist or pre-modernist or postmodernist or of that debate, but managing nevertheless to be both arriving and departing at once. If I am right that we are moving into a different period of creative prose, it is characterized by a writing which, freed from the middle-class monologue, is experimentation in the real sense, exploiting traditions and not being wasted by them. (*Granta*, 3, 1980, p. 9)

What this means in practice is difficult to discern since he offers only one example, Salman Rushdie. At the time Rushdie had published a single novel, *Grimus* (1975) and it is only because of Rushdie's later more significant and controversial writings that *Grimus* is taken seriously at all. It is an incoherent reworking of several genres, most prominently science fiction, and even the most sympathetic critics have struggled to make sense of a prose narrative that is belligerently lacking in focus or continuity. So while Buford appears to be canvassing a form of creative compromise – not unlike Lodge's 1991 image of the novelist in the supermarket picking and mixing as he or she wishes – his hoped-for future actually involves the familiar premise that improvement can only be secured by radical innovation.

Two things are apparent throughout these disconnected commentaries. First, there is an implicit consensus that the novel cannot rely upon precedent, irrespective of the intrinsic abilities of a new novelist who elects to write in a comparatively conventional manner. This might seem curious, even perverse, given that it appears to have quietly replaced the notion of evaluation, the appreciation of the specific qualities of a novel, with the dictum that everything has to be new. This is, however, one of the legacies of modernism: the intuitive fear that if art does not go forward it must as a consequence be retrogressive and in some way handicapped. It is not an opinion shared by all critics but is has been and will remain the mantra of a considerable number, particularly in universities.

Secondly, few critics address the question of the predominant subject, or subjects, of contemporary fiction. The omission is not entirely surprising since the major novelists who had risen to prominence since the 1950s had rarely shifted the focus of their work very far from contemporary predominantly local issues, and the reason for this was that there was very little else to write about. The 1945 Labour Government led by Clement Attlee effectively set the political and social agenda for the next three and a half decades. The Attlee administration created the Welfare State, the most significant and enduring feature of which was the National Health Service. The blueprint for postwar social policy was compiled by Sir William Beveridge in 1942. It was effectively a programme for pragmatic socialism, making it the duty of the state to ensure that all citizens had the right to unemployment benefit, education, a pension and free health care. It was implemented between 1945 and 1951 and became the unofficial ideological constitution of Britain until the end of the 1970s, providing the anchor for such policies as the permanent nationalization of core industries and services, the introduction of the comprehensive education system and the liberal humanist legal reforms of the 1960s, including the decriminalization of homosexuality, the legalization of abortion, the abolition of the death penalty, and the Race Relations Act. Throughout this period Labour and Conservative Governments gave the impression of embodying respectively a left- and right-leaning political outlook while in effect neither made significant alterations to the consensus initiated in 1945. Postwar British society underwent changes, mostly the same as those experienced by virtually all other Western democracies: class distinctions became gradually less prominent, political protest offered a somewhat muted challenge to conventional party politics during the 1960s, apathetic secularism made further inroads into the power and influence of organized religion, and perceptions of race and gender gradually altered, mostly for the better. Beyond such localized modifications there was of course the Cold War, involving specific military conflicts in Korea and Vietnam and the anxious cliffhanger of the Cuban Missile Crisis. In all of this Britain played a junior peripheral role and despite a reluctance to forgo its image as a grand imperial presence, every Briton knew at heart that their fate would ultimately be determined by the relationship between the United States and the Soviet Union.

All of the above were addressed and chronicled in the predominantly realist fiction produced after the war, and although the so-called Angry generation created various levels of unease and anxiety among those whose values had been forged within the prewar hangover from Victorianism they were in truth recording mutations in postwar society that were at once irrevocable, enervating and innocuous. The standard of living of the population gradually improved and political activism became a matter for extremists. For everyone else political affiliation was determined by background, habit or temperament; changes of government meant little more than the replacement of one managerial team with another, with minimal alterations in the consensual status quo.

Chapter 3

The Effects of Thatcherism

One begins to appreciate why so many commentators were, by the end of the 1970s, voicing a sense of frustration. The realists seemed only able to recycle familiar formulae and subjects and the alternative, a new means of fictional representation, appeared either exhausted or practised by an ineffectual minority. The significance of what happened next is still a matter for debate and speculation, but a number of facts are beyond dispute. In 1979 a Conservative administration led by the first ever woman Prime Minister, Margaret Thatcher, came to power. Initially the Thatcher government seemed unlikely to unsettle the centre-left/centre-right consensus of British postwar politics. Certainly they had been elected mainly because they had offered the more convincing claim to be able to end the lengthy period of strikes that had culminated in the so-called Winter of Discontent, but it was not until around 1982–4, particularly with the mineworkers' dispute, that the media and the general public began to recognize that an alteration in the nature of British society unlike anything since 1945 was underway. Thatcherism is one of those terms that becomes a familiar, routine element in linguistic currency but whose meaning tends to be elastic, altering with context and the political predisposition of its user. In basic, economic terms the Thatcher administrators of the 1980s and early 1990s attempted to dismantle the legacies of 1945, to replace an ideology and a collective mindset in which the State was pre-eminent with a spirit of enterprise and singularity. In practice a widespread policy of privatization was implemented with the core elements of industry and the economic infrastructure – coal, steel, electricity, gas, telecommunications, council housing, transport, even water – changed from public to private ownership. More significantly Thatcherism became the watchword for those who diagnosed a far more fundamental change in the ideology of the nation, a sense of alteration that was perceived differently by various groups and individuals, was celebrated and loathed, but whose existence was beyond dispute. Detractors argued that it encouraged and glorified greed, material ambition and shallow self-aggrandisement, while at the other end of the spectrum it was applauded as the emancipation from a culture of dependency, an opportunity to experience a new form of liberalism which incorporated a plethora of wealth-creating choices.

There is a wry unbidden irony in the fact that the Thatcher government was elected at roughly the same time that advocates of literary radicalism were uniting in what amounted to a crescendo of complaints against the nugatory persistence of postwar realism – particularly as most of these implied a complicit relationship between literary and political conservatism – for nothing could better have provoked an inclination to write about society in a seamlessly naturalistic manner as the changes wrought by Thatcherism.

It is evident that within the mainstream of realist fiction, especially that given toward social critique and satire, Thatcherism provided a wealth of fresh material, revitalizing a subject area which had been stale since the 1950s and 1960s.

Justin Cartwright's *Look at it This Way* (1990) was written at the end of the 1980s at a time when media of all types had become conscious of British society as having been transformed, though precisely how and to what long-term effect were matters for conjecture. With commendable subtlety Cartwright manages to recreate in the very texture of his novel a combination of acceptance and perplexity. The characters inhabit a world in which capital has overruled what had once been a balance between fate and choice. Their moods, foreseeable prospects, relationships with lovers, friends and family all appear to have become conditional, subject to the rarely acknowledged all-powerful presence of money. The only figure who is given to reflect upon all of this is an outsider, Tim Curtiz, a US journalist who reports on the state of Thatcher's Britain to his American readers. About half of the book is narrated in the third person, with Curtiz coming in, first person, for alternate chapters to offer a more incisive account, at once detached and informed. For example:

> Sometimes in London you get great glimpses of enormous wealth, great piles of money [...] money which has grown by leaps and bounds in the last ten years as everything, the very fabric of the country, has reached the point of critical mass. This wealth appears to have no physical limits. Low temperature nuclear fission of wealth has taken place, on a scale which is a surprise even to the beneficiaries [...] How has it happened? Nobody really knows. It is necromancy, it is alchemy. The philosopher's stone has been found. (*Look at it This Way*, Picador, 1991, p. 59)

It is also, as the novel makes evident, a contagion that affects even those who are most certainly not its beneficiaries. Money, its lack or abundance, has taken charge of those shades and dimensions of the human condition once animated by compassion, amiability, aesthetic gratification, even lust. Curtiz is fascinated by what he witnesses, but in a distracted dispassionate way, much in the manner of an anthropologist. This is appropriate given that his other concern is a lion which eventually escapes from London Zoo and eats one of the main protagonists, Will, an avaricious share dealer. This mildly bizarre subplot might have become a modern morality tale – with the real carnivore exacting revenge upon his human usurper – except that Cartwright does not quite allow the pieces to fit into such convenient slots. He has Curtiz choreograph the killing, which he does with indifference to the consequences; he seems instead to have become part of the dehumanized web of events and causes on which he has reported. What seemed to be impartiality was a kind of crazed connivance and the book's message, if so straightforward a term can be applied to it, is that the society that informs it is too unprecedented, too peculiar, for analysis.

A novel written five years earlier in the midst of the Thatcher era does attempt to make sense of contemporary Britain. Julian Rathbone's *Nasty, Very* (1984) is the story of Charlie Bosham, scion of middle-class middle England. It begins on Coronation Day 1953 with Charlie aged 14, and charts his progress up to the second consecutive victory of the Tory government, following the Falklands War, in which he becomes a Conservative MP. Charlie is a thoroughly unpleasant individual, a ruthless businessman but without even a veneer of charm to compensate for his feral selfishness. For much of the novel, at least until the late 1970s, Charlie seems to be a grotesque, a curiosity. The people with whom he mixes and frequently exploits and the society

31

in which this occurs are certainly imperfect but he is self-evidently very much worse. With the arrival of Thatcherism, however, Charlie finds himself within a more welcoming, indulgent context. There is a passage towards the end in which Charlie is invited by a senior party grandee to his London club for a final interview to see if he is the sort of person who will sustain a Conservative majority. Charlie has rehearsed his part well. He refers to the working class as 'the elves':

> They as always are the key factor in the equation. So long as the top ones are happy, the skilled, the technicians, and those with bottle like the miners, though nukes will see them off in the end, what it comes down to is we're laughing [...] It's a matter of pride. Top eight grand a year in your pay packet and it's buy your council house, fence it with reconstituted Portland-type stone, change the front door to one of those with a fanlight and a brass knocker. Catch a bloke who's done that much for himself voting Labour, and I'll kiss his arse... (*Nasty, Very*, Grafton, 1986, p. 291)

Charlie's, and indeed Rathbone's, analysis of how and why Thatcherism could permanently seize the mandate from Labour is shrewd and, as most subsequent commentators would agree, accurate. Soon after this, when in the toilet, Charlie overhears a conversation between two Old-Party Tories in which one asks 'Who was that oick?' that Giles, Charlie's host, was entertaining. An 'aspirant from the sticks' answers his friend. Charlie, Rathbone informs us, 'is overcome by anger, frustration and humiliation', and the reason is self-evident. The upper-class Conservatives regard the likes of Charlie Bosham as a slightly improved version of the new council-house-owning swathe of the proletariat who have exchanged class solidarity for greed.

Rathbone's novel is almost Marxist in its wry chronicle of capitalism mutating and accommodating levels of materialism that had previously been treated by the old Labour–Conservative consensus with distaste. While Cartwright created an atmosphere of almost horrified incomprehension Rathbone exposes and dissects, but both, however, share an inclination to place at the heart of their picture of contemporaneity something, and in Rathbone's case someone, of unfailing repugnance.

George Crawley, the first-person narrator of Tim Parks's *Goodness* (1991), is a rare type of fictional presence: someone who can sustain a tragic story while being pitiably unaware of the part he has played in his own and everyone else's dreadful experience. His manner of discourse reminds one of Mr Pooter, a combination of idiocy and self-importance. The account of his relationship with his wife, Shirley, involves a catalogue of events that ought to provoke in the reader a degree of horrified compassion – Shirley's departure and their tearful reunion, the birth of their handicapped child and their decision, ultimately, to kill the infant – but it does not because Crawley seems incapable of disentangling emotions from a perception of the world as composed primarily of material possessions; only the latter seem capable of conferring significance upon life in general.

Bosham and Crawley bear a close resemblance to Michael Parsons of David Caute's *Veronica, or the Two Nations* (1989), the anonymous narrator of Michael Dibdin's *Dirty Tricks* (1991) and the eponymous central character of Terence Blacker's *Fixx* (1989). These men were not completely without precedent in British fiction. Amis's Jim Dixon and Wain's Charles Lumley were by degrees irresponsible and opportunistic while John Braine's Joe Lampton, Alan Sillitoe's Arthur Seaton and David Storey's Arthur Machin pressed ahead with increased levels of hedonistic self-regard. But for each there was a compensating, sometimes endearing factor – scabrous wit, anti-establishment charm, a refusal to conform to stereotypes of class or background all contributed to dividing their readership between those who disapproved and those who, often despite themselves, felt sympathetic or amused. The Thatcherite characters, however, are united in their unambiguous odiousness. While the creators of previous disagreeable, even villainous figures sometimes used circumstances for an exculpatory unravelling of their condition and acts, the post- 1979 generation are presented as innately unpleasant types for whom the political and social environment has finally provided an arena in which their nastiness accords perfectly with the prevailing ideology.

Never before in the history of English fiction had a group of writers – who might otherwise have differed in temperament and outlook – been so assiduously fascinated by the prevailing political regime and united in their unreserved contempt for it.

Dirty Tricks blends a satirical chronicle of 1980s Britain with a genre more familiar to Michael Dibdin, the crime thriller, but one should not assume from this that his treatment of Thatcherism is negligent or indulgent. The narrator's tale, which includes his virtual confession to a murder, is framed as an account to a court in a somewhat suspect country from which he is attempting to prevent his own deportation. He closes:

> There is no such thing as society, only individuals engaged in a constant unremitting struggle for personal advantage. There is no such thing as justice, only winners and losers. I have not deserved to lose, but if I do so, it will be without complaint or regret. (*Dirty Tricks*, Faber, 1992, p. 237)

The first sentence is lifted almost verbatim from an infamous speech by Mrs Thatcher in which she argued that the postwar British State had become a network of ideological restraints and impositions and should effectively be abolished. For Dibdin's character the same political thesis becomes a licence for murder.

It is intriguing to compare Dibdin's novel with Piers Paul Read's *A Married Man* (1979). John Strickland, a successful barrister, experiences a surplus of middle-aged ambition and egotism and as a consequence pursues a political career and an extramarital affair with the daughter of a wealthy banker. Gradually his self-interested pursuits spin out of control with his mistress turning out to be mildly psychopathic; along with a disgruntled criminal client of Strickland's, she plans the murder of his wife. Strickland is a member of the Labour Party, embodying the middle-class, liberal consensus which ensured a protective attitude to nationalized core industries, the welfare state and a tolerant legal system. His experiences with his mistress shock him out of his complacent notion of humanity as intrinsically virtuous and in turn causes him to turn a more cynical eye upon his fashionable bourgeois politics. The novel was set in the mid-1970s and written shortly before Mrs Thatcher's election victory of 1979. Nothing like it would, or could, be written again for the simple reason that its context – the notion of a beneficent, liberal consensus in politics and society – had ceased to exist.

Even in novels which did not address themselves directly to the post-1979 brand of Conservatism its presence can be unnervingly evident. Martyn Harris's *Do It Again* (1989) is a fable of middle-aged nostalgia for times past, specifically the radical 1960s when its main characters were students, but throughout the book the present is enshrouded with a sense of regretful completion. It appears that not only have those now in their forties opted for comfortable conformity, the option for contemporaneous twenty-somethings to do anything else has been taken away. The universities are being strangled by underfunding, which for most of the characters is seen as a means of starving dissent and making sure that the intellectual left is so wrapped up with its own complaints as to remain indifferent to the similar brutalities visited upon the health service and the welfare state. In one darkly comic passage a left-wing literary critic delivers what has become known as her 'annual George Orwell lecture'. This attracts students, lecturers from other disciplines and fans from outside the university who have heard of its ritualistic status. Vivien, the lecturer, offers the equivalent of a bitter funeral oration for the kind of literary culture capable of addressing injustice and inequality. In her view it has not so much been killed by Tory ideology as committed complicit suicide (*Do It Again*, Penguin, 1990, pp. 87–91).

The British 'University Novel' was founded as a subgenre with Amis's *Lucky Jim* (1954) and its two most robust practitioners thereafter were Malcolm Bradbury and David Lodge. In their earlier campus-based works (such as the former's *The History Man* and the latter's *Changing Places*, both published in 1975) the university functions as an eccentric microcosm of society per se with the routine menu of human characteristics and idiosyncrasies exaggerated or comically inverted by the detached, perversely unreal environment where academics live and work. Thatcherism changed this too. Much of Bradbury's *Cuts* (1987) concerns Henry Babbacombe, an academic in a small provincial university, who decides to move beyond his scholarly activities to the glitzy, profit-driven world of screenwriting. The decision is not so much his as a symptom of the political environment in which departments are being closed and unproductive academics obliged to take early retirement. It is probably Bradbury's worst novel, in which he exchanges his once incisive satirical nuances for heavy-handed farce. It becomes difficult to seriously undermine in fiction the lofty assumptions of academia when the government appears to be pursuing a similar and much more frightening policy in actuality; hence Bradbury opts for a damage limitation exercise and creates figures who are bumbling, and of course affectingly blameless in their predicament.

Lodge in *Nice Work* (Secker & Warburg, 1988) addresses the same issues with a little more astuteness. In response to the prevailing government opinion that universities should reattach themselves to an economy, indeed an ethos, dominated by enterprise, a scheme is created whereby an academic and the managing director of a local engineering company spend time in each other's daily working environments. It seems at first to be a meeting of antithetical stereotypes. Dr Robyn Penrose, feminist semiotician, and Vic Wilcox, hard boss, pragmatist and man who has a vague knowledge of the Brontë novels – 'women's books, aren't they?' he enquires guardedly at one point (p. 141). The pair grudgingly begin to see the world from each other's perspective and eventually have an affair. The message seems to be that estranged polarities of opinion are bad for everyone, but as with all novels which carry an admonitory subtext there is a consequential depreciation in quality. Again satire is replaced by a defensive action against a hostile environment and in both novels a sad urgency of tone invests itself.

Hardly any fiction which addressed itself to contemporary Britain during the 1980s and early 1990s remained immune from the effects of Thatcherism. These are tangible if rarely predictable, and a particular conundrum is created by Martin Amis's *Money* (1984). John Self is consumerism personified and gloriously exaggerated. His life is a catalogue of excesses while whatever might once have invested pleasure with a degree of significance has long since departed from his and everyone else's existence. It would, however, be simplistic to claim that Self is a critique of the values underpinning Thatcherite Conservatism and their social consequences. He is, rather, an extension of characteristics close to the core of Amis's previous novels, all but one published before 1979. Unlike the majority of his contemporaries Amis was not perplexed or horrified by political developments, post-1979. He had always treated the mindset and behaviour they were accused of engendering as, in truth, propensities that most people shared and practically all denied: with Self and Talent he was not so much caricaturing as disclosing.

A more intriguing contrast between how novelists respond to shared circumstances would be difficult to find than in Amis's and Ian McEwan's work. *The Child in Time* (1987) has been condemned by Adam Mars-Jones (*Venus Envy*, Chatto, 1990, p. 33) as an opportunistic paean to feminism and by D. J. Taylor (*A Vain Conceit. British Fiction in the 1980s*, Bloomsbury, 1989, pp. 55–9) as a grossly exaggerated Orwellian exercise in political prognosis. Its plot and its apparent central theme involve childhood and the child–parent relationship, beginning as it does in McEwan's characteristically jarring manner with the kidnap of the main character's daughter. The child and her captors are never found but throughout the novel there are sufficient layerings of the sinister to suggest that it is in some way symptomatic of the prevailing political climate. He projects a Thatcher-style government into an even more extreme, authoritarian version of its mid-1980s manifestation, 10 years hence in its fifth term. This administration issues childcare handbooks which are designed to indoctrinate in parents and offspring an acceptance of the only norm available for survival in society; children should be schooled in the necessary qualities of avarice, competition and self-styled aggression. The parallel between the actual kidnap and its ideological counterpart is too heavy-handed to take seriously and too intrusive to ignore.

Charles Darke, close friend of the central character Stephen Lewis, is a glamorous publisher and Tory politician. He abandons his career and regresses to a childhood realm, relishing 'the powerlessness, the obedience, and also the freedom that goes with it, freedom from money, decision, plans, demands' (*The Child in Time*, Cape, 1987, pp. 200–1). The fantasy eventually kills him, as he sits down in the freezing cold under his tree house, unable to reconcile the basics of responsibility to his health with the desire for release. The signposts between Darke's behaviour and the demeanour and policy of a government regarding children are crude and the symbolic resonance cumbersome.

When writing *The Child in Time* McEwan said in an interview that he was 'aware of the danger that in trying to write more politically, in the broadest sense [...] I could take up moral positions that might exclude that rather mysterious and unreflective element that is so important in fiction...' (John Haffenden, *Novelists in Interview*, Methuen, 1985, pp. 173–4). In the novel itself we witness the consequences of this sense of creative conflict between writing which feels dutifully bound to address contemporaneous ills and injustices and that which bears no other allegiance than to its own, elected particulars of theme and character. In this instance the former does indeed 'exclude' the latter, but the fact that it does so further complicates the fascinating issue of the relationship between actuality and invention in post-1979 fiction.

Amis's cast of characters from *The Rachel Papers* up to the more recent *Yellow Dog* (2003) is dominated by despicable egotists, pitiable dupes, and soulless hedonists. He refuses to judge them and also more significantly makes it difficult for the reader to do so by investing each with an energy, charisma, and often manic eloquence. He has not been inspired or assisted by images of Thatcherism in these enterprises but from the reader's point of view there does seem an almost demonic complicity between the cruel, debased worlds he conjured up and the predominant, albeit generally left-wing, perception of the 1980s and its aftermath. McEwan is a writer whose characters are less grotesque than Amis's and more tragic, figures whose already unsettled notions of good or evil, happiness or dejection are further disrupted by unsignalled visitations of the painful and horrific occurrences. In *The Child in Time* he attempted to open out his generally private chronicles of catastrophe to a more public sphere, to incorporate political and ideological registers that his characters and his readers shared, and the result is a novel in which the symbolism is distracting and debilitating.

In precise terms the Thatcher era concluded in 1990 when Margaret Thatcher was deposed as party leader and Prime Minister by the Conservatives themselves. Most political commentators would, however, concur on the fact that irrespective of the departure of its namesake Thatcherism remains as the unceasing, perhaps irremovable, core element of the British social, economic and political fabric. Tony Blair's unofficially designated 'New Labour' party replaced the flailing Conservative administration of John Major in 1997 and at the time of writing is still present and likely to remain so for several years to come. The Labour Party first under Neil Kinnock and John Smith and then Blair had since the end of the 1980s systematically detached itself from everything that had ensured its electoral failures during the Thatcher years. Specifically it became left-wing in tone and demeanour only; all policies that could be even roughly conceived as socialist, particularly nationalization, were abandoned. The post-1997 Labour governments have presented themselves as more humane and charitable than their Tory predecessor, but in truth have preserved and in some cases pressed ahead with the fundamental policies of post-1979 Conservatism. What happened after 1945, the preservation of what Labour had done despite superficial differences between the parties, is now repeating itself, except with a largely antithetical political consensus. The effect of this upon the complex web of experiences and agenda that make up society is the subject for a different kind of book, but it has most certainly had a fascinating effect upon fiction. Most of the novels covered so far were written during the 1980s or soon afterwards. Jonathan Coe could claim with some justification to have produced fiction that takes advantage of a broader perspective upon contemporaneity.

What a Carve Up (1994) focuses upon the period between August 1990 and January 1991, during which Mrs Thatcher was replaced by John Major and Britain prepared itself for the first Gulf War. Its actual frame of reference reaches beyond this through the preceding decade which, specifically and implicitly, is treated as the cause of the ghastly state of Britain. Its chief characters are composed largely of members of the Winshaw family, minor gentry who gained their wealth in the nineteenth century and despite subsequent misfortunes are revelling in the new economic climate. They are, needless to say, vile individuals and as such the book appears to be an elaborate rerun of Rathbone's *Nasty, Very*. There is, however, a significant difference in that the only major non-Winshaw character is Michael Owen, a novelist who has been commissioned to write a history of the family. Owen bears a deliberately contrived resemblance to Coe, at least in the sense that his two published novels carry titles that are virtually paraphrases of Coe's first two novels. More subtly Coe shows us that he and his surrogate also face similar, perhaps intractable problems. Although we are not vouchsafed a glance at how Owen's history of the family is progressing as a text its nature is enacted in the novel. Chapters alternate between first person accounts by Owen of aspects of his ongoing and recent life and chapters which concentrate upon particular members of the Winshaw family. The latter comprise a variety of discourses, including extracts from journals, newspaper articles, transcripts of radio and TV interviews, letters, all threaded along a rather dry third-person narrative. This is a patchwork of the basic material that Owen would draw upon in his account of the living Winshaws. Coe creates a beguiling riddle in that throughout the book – both in the parts exclusively involving Owen and those given to the Winshaws – he allow us glimpses into a society entrapped by Thatcherism and, it is implied, its evil consequences: the encroachment of privatization and free enterprise into the National Health Service, the virtual paralysis of an independent media by private sector influences, the stock market as a licensed forum for fraud, the exchange of manufacturing industry for a more controllable service sector, the poisoning of the food chain in pursuit of profit. The novel is self-evidently a state-of-the-nation piece, yet within it we have the spectacle of a writer, not unlike Coe, who when he completes his account of the Winshaws will, we assume, have combined his novelistic skills with a merciless scrutiny of their activities and produced something not unlike the book he is in. How would it have turned out? Coe, cunningly, poses the same question. At one point Owen has an exchange with a character called Graham who contends that novels 'today' are 'an irrelevance'

> ...the problem with the English novel is that there's no tradition of political engagement. I mean it's all just a lot of pissing about within the limits set down by bourgeois morality, as far as I can see. There's no radicalism. (*What a Carve Up*, Penguin, 1995, p. 276)

Graham goes on to mention one notable exception to this alleged state of torpor and Owen is pleased because he has recently produced a hostile review article on this same novelist, a figure in his view:

> ...ludicrously over-praised in the national press. Because he made his characters talk in crudely notated dialects and live in conditions of unconvincing squalor, he was hailed as a social realist; because he sometimes played elementary tricks with narrative, in feeble imitation of Sterne and Diderot, he was hailed as an experimental pioneer [...] More annoying than any of this, however, was his reputation for humour. He had been repeatedly credited with a playful irony, a satiric lightness of touch, which seemed to me to be entirely lacking from his work, characterized as it was by lumbering sarcasm and the occasional abject attempt to jog the reader's elbow with well-signposted jokes. (pp. 276–7)

What is needed, according to Owen, are novels 'which show an understanding of the ideological hijack which has taken place so recently in this country', novels which would by necessity evolve unprecedented techniques to deal with unprecedented circumstances. Tantalizingly and irritatingly Owen does not provide clues to the nature of such novels, and nor does Coe, unless he wishes us to accept that *What a Carve Up* – generally traditional and realist in form with a slight nod towards postmodernism – is in truth the best we can hope for.

The device of placing an author within a novel, with ambitions which correspond in some way with the realized text which enables him or her to exist, is as old as Sterne but in the 1980s and 1990s the agenda for its use became a little more predictable. We have already seen how in *Look at it This Way* Cartwright uses the narrative equivalent of a split-screen effect with one half given over to Curtiz, a writer somewhat perplexed by a society in a state of transition. In Maggie Gee's *Grace* (1988) we encounter Paula who is attempting to write a novel about actual events, actual in her's and Gee's novels and outside both. Hilda Murrell, an anti-nuclear campaigner, had been preparing a paper for a parliamentary committee on the siting of a nuclear reactor on the Suffolk coast, when, in 1984, she was found dead in mysterious circumstances. Articles were written and a question raised in the House of Commons alleging that she had been killed by the intelligence services who by implication were following orders from what was perceived by many as an authoritarian administration. Paula believes that fiction should address directly the most immediate, controversial issues of its age – an opinion she shares with her author – and sets about writing a novel which will, she hopes, reinvigorate interest in what really happened to Murrell and encourage debate on the government's alleged inclination to stifle opposition by force. The Grace of the title is Paula's aunt, who becomes the subject of subtle and intrusive monitoring by a private investigator in the pay of government officials, a rather heavy-handed allusion to Toryism as obsessed with private enterprise. In short, events within the novel about the writer researching the novel about real life take on a very sinister aspect, not unlike those of the Murrell case. Quite how even the more politically motivated reader is supposed to respond to or take inspiration from this clumsy blend of artifice and polemic remains unclear.

Martin Amis in *The Information* (1995) addresses no significant political issues but he does give particular attention to the dilemma of the fiction writer in the mid-1990s. Richard Tull and Gwyn Barry are novelists. The former has published two novels. Of the first, *Afore-thought*, we are informed that 'nobody understood it, or even finished it, but, equally, nobody was sure it was shit. Richard flourished' (*The Information*, Flamingo, 1996, p. 40). He was feted as a challenging radical new presence. His second novel, *Dreams Don't Mean Anything* was published in Britain, but not in the US. His third, fourth, fifth and sixth remain unpublished; his current, most ambitious piece, unfinished and he supports himself and his family, just, by working for a vanity publisher, editing an obscure literary journal and reviewing for newspapers still prepared to pay him. Richard's friend from their university days, Gwyn Barry, succeeds magnificently with his first novel *Summertown* and is about to do even better with his second, *Amelior*. Richard treats both with the special kind of disdain that those with claims to cultural hauteur reserve for the merely competent and, even worse, the popular '...purest trex: fantastically pedestrian. It tried to be "touching"; but the only thing about *Summertown* was that it *thought* it was a novel' (p. 43).

The Information is one of the best novels about writing novels of recent years. It does not address this subject by turning in upon itself, by employing self-referring, metafictional devices; it is at once more accessible and compelling than that. The third-person narrator – in truth Amis himself – allows us into the emotional landscapes of a number of its characters but none is so intimately scrutinized as Richard's. Indeed we intuit that Richard and the narrator are two dimensions of the same person. (In fact the transparently moving passages concerning Richard's relationship with his two young children were inspired by Amis's own marriage break-up that occurred shortly before he wrote the novel.) The irony which makes the novel fascinating is generated from the curious spectacle of a writer with immense, elevated conceptions of the value of writing but who cannot write being disclosed to us by one who most certainly can. We are told that

> He was an artist when he saw society: it never crossed his mind that society had to be like this, had any right, had any business being like this. A car in the street. Why? Why *cars*? This is what an artist has to be: harassed to the point of insanity or stupefaction by first principles. The difficulty began when he sat down to write. (p. 11)

Richard's problem is that the 'first principles' which underpin his idealistic, massively ambitious conception of what a novel should do – a combination of an epiphany and a thoroughgoing analysis of the state of everything – are what ensure his failure to realize these ambitions. Barry, however, has opted for the kind of writing that improves upon reality, makes it far more agreeable for the reader. And what of Amis, one is inevitably prompted to ask? The 'information' of the title is something never properly disclosed. It is capable of causing terrible dreams, animating unease, distress and destroying relationships, but its nature is coterminous with its effects. We never learn precisely what it is, but we know that had Richard been in charge of the book he would have attempted to disclose its essence, and the novel would never have been written. Amis, the narrator, is of course ever present, with his taste for the darkly comic, his beautifully executed mixture of pathos and cruelty substituting for an attempt to expose, explain or confer meaning upon the events of the narrative.

It would be unfair to treat the novel as a creative manifesto – it is far too good a novel to be simply that – but it shares with Coe's *What a Carve Up* a puzzled, almost defensive subtext, raising the question of how the novelist is expected to deal with contemporaneity.

Coe has produced two other novels which offer a portrait of Britain since the 1970s while subtly pointing up the fact that in doing so they are, like all fiction, being playfully dishonest. The first, *The Rotters' Club*, ends with the 1979 election of Mrs Thatcher and the second, *The Closed Circle*, moves us forward to 1999–2000 with the Blair administration at its most volubly confident. But the intervening period has not been completely omitted; the former, published in 2001, tells of the 1970s with a jaundiced knowledge of what would happen next and the latter indicates that while the political party in charge and the names have changed practically everything else, post-1979, remains unaltered.

All of the central characters of *The Rotters' Club* are in their late teens as the novel ends, with their parents and other older figures playing secondary roles throughout the book. This device is mischievous because for those reading it in 2001 everything that we learn of the characters – their temperaments, ambitions, beliefs – is shot through with a supplementary knowledge of Britain after 1979 and as a consequence Coe creates a collateral narrative comprised of the reader's inevitable speculations on how full adulthood in the 1980s and 1990s will treat these people. There is, for example, Benjamin Trotter, who creates among his peers a mixture of admiration and pity with his eager, transparent nature; he works hard, wants to be a 'serious' writer, is undoubtedly destined for Oxbridge, and listens to the brand of intellectually ambitious rock music typified by the likes of Hatfield and the North and Henry Cow. His friend Doug Anderton is just as clever but given also to a precocious concoction of pragmatism and cynicism. He is fascinated by punk, not because it is art but because it seems to him to distil a selfish disregard for collective or personal responsibility. Who, we wonder, will be more successful after the narrative closes?

In *The Closed Circle* we find Benjamin married, although not to the girl with whom he was besotted in the previous book; he lives in a comfortable suburb of Birmingham not far from where he went to school, works as an accountant and is still writing his first novel. Doug too is married, to an outrageously beautiful ex-model, a woman of beguiling intellectual presence and heiress to a considerable family fortune. Doug has a successful high-profile career as a journalist on one of the more fashionable 'New Labour'-supporting broadsheets. It is tempting, indeed almost obligatory, to treat these disclosures as diagnostic, to draw conclusions on how the innate characteristics of the 1979 young adults have been shaped or trammelled by the intervening years, but while Coe encourages this game of interpretive noughts and crosses he also ensures that nothing is ever quite as predictable as it might seem. Benjamin and Doug are accompanied by about five others from the end of the 1970s to the millennium and we encounter as many surprises as confirmed suspicions. Irrespective of the ways in which his characters adapt or respond to their circumstances Coe points discretely yet unambiguously to how society has, at least in his view, changed. In both novels the particulars of the plot are set against the background of historical facts. In *The Rotters' Club* the disputes that threatened the future of the, then nationalized, Longbridge car plant affect the lives of practically all of the characters, as does a single event, the 1974 IRA Birmingham bomb which kills Malcolm, the boyfriend of Benjamin's sister Lois. Coe plays games with the reader in that he compels us to bring into the novel our own recollections or vicarious knowledge of those matters, so that the characters acquire a special degree of credibility. We find ourselves going beyond the standard response to fictional presences in which who they are and what they experience are all components of the same hypothesized fabric; instead we encounter someone in a novel who responds to events that are indisputably nonfictional, sometimes down to the exact moment, day, month and year that they occurred. We are obliged not simply to imagine what they might have felt but to compare their feelings and opinions with those that we have acquired independently of the novel regarding things that happen within it.

The Closed Circle maintains this conceit, but with a difference. The events are less significant in their particularity – several male characters fantasize about having sex with the TV chef Nigella Lawson for example – and there is a palpable sense of harsh political and social issues having in some way insulated themselves from serious scrutiny. The Blair administration is frequently referred to but unlike the late 1970s when Longbridge union disputes and the IRA campaign polarized opinion throughout the political spectrum the millennium seems to have brought with it a state of enforced apathy. Benjamin's young brother Paul was, in *The Rotters' Club*, a mildly sinister figure: clever, selfish and apparently immune from the distress that he might be capable of causing. In 2000 he is a successful New Labour MP, a chameleonic figure with no political ideals and a propensity to follow any instructions provided that they will ultimately be to his benefit.

Coe's intertwining of actuality with invention is an indulgent nod towards postmodern technique, but both novels, like the rest of his fiction, remain firmly within the traditional, realist camp. Intriguingly, Benjamin becomes Coe's acknowledgement of this. Benjamin discloses to the companionable, sympathetic daughter of a friend a project that has occupied much of his time over the previous 20 years, when not practising accountancy. His groundbreaking epic will combine prose narrative with CD, visual images and music to create a genre of its own, capable of capturing those dense layerings of immediate and objective experience which resist the linearity of standard prose fiction. While in no way mocking the enterprise itself Coe presents Benjamin as a pitiable if heroic figure; we know that the grandeur of his ambition will ensure its failure. Between writing these two novels Coe spent much of his time completing a biography of B. S. Johnson, arguably the last undeviating radical in British fiction. The biography reflects Coe's fascination with what Johnson represented and his admiration for the man but acknowledges that he is, like Benjamin, destined to remain a valiant curiosity.

In those 1980s and 1990s novels which flagged up contemporaneous social and political issues, in the sense that they maintained what amounted to a dialogue with the agenda set by the news media, conventional realism held the centre ground. For example during the year of the 1997 election, which even diehard Conservatives anticipated as their final call, novelists queued up to explore the ethics of monetarism, the effects of privatization as an ideology and the mindset of a generation who had but a slight recollection of anything before Thatcher. Ben Richards's *Don't Step on the Lines*, Geoff Nicholson's

LIBRARY, UNIVERSITY OF CHESTER

Bleeding London and Stephen Blanchard's *Wilson's Island* (all 1997) read as intelligent, updated versions of the 1950s Movement-generation mode of cautiously reflecting the ongoing milieu, but there is a difference.

In the 1950s and even into the 1960s there were still in Britain vast strata of social and political life that had remained immune from change. These were perfect targets for anti-establishment fictional heroes, and the complex layerings of a nation in an albeit very slow state of transformation offered themselves as provident fabric for writers who wished to look at things differently while maintaining a familiar, conventional style. By the 1990s however the social and political landscape had ossified into a featureless plain. Distinctions between traditional (such as Christian moralist) types of behaviour and their ethically unencumbered counterparts had ceased to be the cause for conflict; these were now exceptions, curiosities. The left versus right polarity in politics now existed only at the margins. Richards, Nicholson and Blanchard found ways of anticipating a slight, but only slight, adjustment to the political consensus by the forthcoming Labour government: Thatcherism with humane features. In Coe's view, however, continuity had been maintained.

Chapter 4

The New Postmodernists

Margaret Thatcher has rarely, if ever, been perceived as a friend or connoisseur of the arts but her effect upon the direction of British fiction since the 1970s has been immense. The vast majority of modern writers – at least until they reach grouchy middle-age – tend to gather across a spectrum from the charitably inclined political middle-ground to the radical left. As a consequence their reactions to Thatcherism and its after-effects have been vigorous and predictable: nothing energizes a novel quite so much as that confection wherein sanctimonious disquiet, closeted political evangelism and sheer distaste at the ghastly vulgarity of life vie for ascendancy. One might argue that Jonathan Coe, for example, would not be the considerable literary presence that he is were it not for Thatcherism. In his fiction and his biography of B. S. Johnson he flirts wistfully with the indulgent attractions of experiment yet in practice maintains a solid commitment to realism. The fascinating grotesquery of the Britain in which he reached adulthood has ensured that for him writing about it has been far more important than writing about writing.

There is also a case to be made for Thatcher's role in the evolution since the 1980s of a special form of postmodernism. As we shall see, there evolved after the 1970s a brand of contra-realism so flexible and eclectic as to almost defy definition. All that can be said of most of its manifestations is that they maintain a reasonable level of accessibility while continually threatening what, outside fiction, are generally regarded as the rational and the logical. One might intuit a number of reasons for this. It could be argued that over the past 20 years society, and indeed our sense of selfhood that is at least partly dependent upon society, has gradually become more amorphous, transitory and superficial and that a wilfully desensitized brand of fiction is the appropriate response. Equally, it could be contended that the New Postmodernists, as I have chosen to call them, have become complicit with the cultural fabric which most would perceive as contemptible; their radicalism tends to be attuned to the demands of the marketplace. In either instance the Thatcherite imprint is legible – though, one would guess, for the majority of writers not entirely bidden or agreeable.

Arguably the best-known practitioner of this curious compromise between the customary and the aberrant is Julian Barnes, a near contemporary of Martin Amis and Ian McEwan. His first novel, *Metroland* (1980), tells the story of two characters, Toni and Christopher, from their adolescence in the early 1960s to the present day, slightly backdated to 1977. Both men have literary ambitions. Toni, adventurously, does his best to support himself as a writer while Christopher opts for a blend of calculation and compromise, securing a job in publishing to maintain a comfortable, middle-class lifestyle while hoping that his contacts in the business will enable to him to get into print. In some respects it is a novel that reflects, with languid indifference, upon bourgeois suburban England's capacity to smother the idiosyncratic and the unconventional, yet at the same time Barnes manages to preserve within the texture of the work just a hint of the indefinite, the eccentric. While it choreographs the conflict between conformity and oddity, their copresence is far less predictable in the novel which is still regarded by many as his best, *Flaubert's Parrot* (1984).

The only dependable, reliable feature of the novel is its title; the French novelist and his stuffed bird become a persistent digression. It would be wrong, however, to regard either of them as its prevailing subject, because it does not have one. Geoffrey Braithwaite is the narrator although he causes us to reconsider what the role of a first-person narrator involves. He is a middle-class Englishman, once a GP and now a retired widower who spends much of his spare time pursuing his life-long interest in Gustave Flaubert. There is not really a story in that events do not move toward a conclusion and questions are not conclusively answered. Instead we find ourselves in the company of Braithwaite, who sometimes offers accounts of his life history – his participation in the Normandy landings, for example – and more frequently refers to his late, beloved wife. He interweaves this with a chronicle of details relating to Flaubert, some direct, some peripheral. Occasionally, capriciously, he might suspend his discursive, conversational mode and insert a chapter composed, say, of examination questions on Flaubert. Chapter 12 is called 'Braithwaite's Dictionary of Accepted Ideas', all of which are Flaubert-related, and Chapter 11 – 'Louise Colet's Version' – is apparently an intimate record by Flaubert's lover of their relationship which one assumes has been written by Braithwaite, although we can never quite be sure of this.

Such an enterprise might appear, and certainly has the potential to be, a self-indulgent excursion into the postmodernist hinterland: as much an investigation of writing as something that most people would want to read. Instead Geoffrey Braithwaite emerges as a presence as disarming and companionable as any to be found in the exemplary realist novels of, say, Dickens, Bennett or Kingsley Amis. But we are beguiled by him not because he is telling us a traditional story – digression is his trademark – but in the same way that we form a friendship with someone in the real world; presence becomes more compelling than action or narrative. The novel involves an elusive compromise between effects that we associate with realism and avant-garde idiosyncrasies.

Barnes's most self-consciously innovative novel is *A History of the World in 10½ Chapters* (1989), involving a number of different narratives whose relation to each other seems tenable only to the extent that they exist in the same volume. Perspectives – frequently on completely unrelated occurrences – range from those of the astronaut to the woodworm. In one story called 'The Survivor' an Australian woman named Kath experiences what appear to be different versions of unfolding reality – one involving a nuclear apocalypse, others less terrifying – but we are never certain which has the greater claim to authenticity. If an omnipresent feature can be discerned within the apparently random patchwork it might be the pursuit of something resembling enduring love, and Barnes seems to be testing the fragility of this notion by subjecting it to a potentially destructive abundance of conditions and perspectives.

By the standards that Barnes generally maintains regarding the reader's disposition and patience the book is aberrant, and his next, *Talking it Over* (1991), is, like *Flaubert's Parrot*, an example of experimentation made all the more effective by discretion. Stuart marries Gillian, but Stuart is a decent, circumspect, reliable and, of course, rather boring individual while his friend Oliver is overburdened with wit and a propensity for enchantingly bad behaviour. Gillian, despite herself but inevitably, is attracted to Oliver. The plotline of the love triangle is as old as literature but Barnes succeeds magnificently in recreating it in an unprecedented manner. All the characters speak directly to the reader, as if to camera, but it would be wrong to regard their accounts simply as monologues because the events that animate them are taking place as they speak. Each utterance involves the blend of puzzlement, bitterness, reflection, sometimes self-justification that one would expect if the characters were addressing each other in dialogue, but the fact that their statements are at once interdependent and isolated, addressed only to an unknown listener, creates a special degree of anxiety and candour; they hold nothing back but they can depend upon no-one but themselves for a response, be it conciliatory or discordant.

One could trace the lineage of Barnes's technique back to Joyce's interior monologue but Joyce's method was both groundbreaking and self-limiting; a novel comprising only Molly Bloom in her closing chapter mode, or a variety of characters discoursing in the same way, would be an inaccessible curiosity. With *Talking it Over* experiment has not so much been compromised as matured. The characters are unnerving in that they speak directly to us, the reader, but they also maintain a fascinating authenticity. Barnes published a sequel, *Love etc*, in 2000 involving the same characters, and if testament were required for his success in merging the innovative with the engaging and accessible then one should consult the most recent novel by one of the more popular, some might argue populist, chroniclers of contemporary life, Nick Hornby. Hornby is best known for his contributions to the subgenre generally known as 'Lad Lit' but *A Long Way Down* (2005) is a darker, more unsettling novel. Martin, Maureen, JJ and Jess are all potential suicides who, improbably, meet on the roof of a high-rise block known locally as 'Toppers Towers' because of its attraction for jumpers. The scenario is given a bizarre twist through Hornby's use of Barnes's device of having the characters speak directly to the reader.

When Barnes evokes the contemporary he does so without engaging with contentious social or political issues and his only novel to carry a persistent allegorical subtext is *England, England*, which is dealt with below (pp. 180–3).

Will Self, born in the early 1960s, is half a generation younger than Barnes, Amis and McEwan and although there is no evidence to suggest that any of them has had a direct influence on Self's writing much of it resembles a combination and exaggeration of the most peculiar characteristics of all three. His style, like Amis's, is amused, deadpan, sometimes cruel; McEwan's taste for the macabre becomes, with him, an inexhaustible catalogue of the strange and the terrible and Self's experiments with realism make Barnes's seem like polite tinkerings.

Doris Lessing, reviewing his first book, a collection of short stories called *The Quantity Theory of Insanity* (1991), wrote that 'absurdity unfurls logically from absurdity, but always as a mirror of what we are living in – and wish we didn't'. Cunningly Lessing does not explain whether our unease is generated by the world created by Self or its reflection of the one we are in, because Self's trademark is to constantly invite us into an act of recognition while almost simultaneously dispersing it. *Cock and Bull* (1992) consists of two novellas. In the first Carol, an otherwise submissive wife, grows a penis and rapes her husband Dan, and in the second John Bull, a quintessentially male rugby player, acquires a vagina at the back of his knee and is seduced by his (male) doctor by whom he – or to be more anatomically specific his leg – becomes pregnant It seems to be a book designed for readers with a particular taste for the grotesque but like all of Self's fiction it defies such straightforward categorization. At the beginning of the novel and before their anatomical transformations occur Dan and Carol are presented very effectively as normal individuals, average to the point of cliché. They are outstandingly credible and they, like the reader, are confounded by the intrusion of the unimaginable into their routine existences. The novel is addictive not because of its ghoulish characteristics but because Self visits upon people whom the reader recognizes events that are utterly incredible. The question that attends all controversial or pivotal moments in a plot – what would we do in these circumstances? – is still raised but in a way that frustrates a response based on previous experience, both for the reader and the characters.

My Idea of Fun (1993) invites comparison with novels of the same period that are vehicles for their authors' judicious reflections upon the previous decade, which as we have seen are generally censorious or melancholic. The story is told by Ian Wharton who has spent much of his life under the tutelage of a father-figure acquaintance of his mother called Mr Broadhurst but referred to more frequently as 'The Fat Controller', who is almost superhuman in his capacity for conspicuous consumption. Self appears to be willing the reader into acts of allegorical interpretation, with Broadhurst as the embodiment of the worst aspects of consumerist Thatcherism. At one point Broadhurst discloses to Ian his supernatural gift of 'retroscendance', an ability to trace the precise history of any person or object. He chooses as an example his own underpants, vast as they are, and offers a vision of cotton pickers and weavers being cruelly and pitiably exploited in their Third World countries, their product arriving via various brokers at the exclusive clothes emporium where Broadhurst shops and purchased by him at something like 100 times the original labour cost, all to the benefit of inhumane, corpulent capitalists, just like himself. This could of course be treated as visionary Marxism, except that both Broadhurst and Wharton are indifferent to the ethical implications of the spectacle. It is significant only insofar as through it Wharton gains further knowledge of Broadhurst's powers and is caught between attraction and abhorrence. In the end the former proves more compulsive and the novel concludes with Wharton himself becoming a version of Broadhurst, able and willing to conduct acts of gratuitous violence while remaining immune from the consequences, a figure with demonic powers and inclinations in a post-Christian world.

In this novel and virtually all of the rest of his fiction Self is obsessively concerned with the avoidance of predictability, precedent or classification. His debt to the innovative, experimental tradition of modernism is with regard to technique tenuous – he makes sure that his horrific scenarios are conveyed with merciless realism – but at the same time he sustains the modernist doctrine of raising fundamental questions about the nature of writing. Broadhurst and eventually Wharton are repulsive wicked figures but the conventional polarity between good and evil is disrupted and there is no obvious cause or circumstantial condition which animates the prevailing culture of malevolence. Gratuitous, unfathomable barbarity is rare if not entirely unprecedented in modern fiction – but it is generally accompanied by a thread of signals via which the reader can trace parallels between what occurs in the novel and the world outside it, the best known example being Anthony Burgess's dystopian visions in *A Clockwork Orange* and *The Wanting Seed* (both 1962). Self, however, is determined to forestall perceptions of causality and notions of plausibility. At one point in *My Idea of Fun* Broadhurst appears unexpectedly just as Wharton is on the verge of his first sexual experience. He, literally, freezes the woman and informs Wharton that had he penetrated her, his penis would have broken off; and on we move to the next encounter with the bizarre. In science fiction, or novels incorporating aspects of the supernatural, events often contradict what are agreed empirical truths, but we are also provided with plausible reasons or motivations for implausible happenings; in Self's novels they simply happen. The novel ends with Jane, who was once frozen, now married to Wharton, pregnant and asleep upstairs. He is thinking about joining her and removing the foetus with a vacuum cleaner. Why? He doesn't explain, but concludes, affably. 'Remember I may have killed, I may have tortured, I may have done all sorts of terrible things but it hurt me too. I do have feelings, as you know' (*My Idea of Fun*, Penguin, 1994, p. 304). Do we? This, like the plethora of similarly grotesque existential questions raised by the novel is unanswerable.

It could reasonably be argued that Amis and McEwan were the first to weave into their fiction elements of the inexplicable – characters whose motives, objectives, reasons for existence are unclear; frequently shocking or distasteful events executed without discernable cause, and so on – but neither allowed this to completely displace what was once called the suspension of disbelief, the novel's ability to incorporate, if not accommodate, the reader's particular sense of what the non-fictional world involves. Self has and continues to do so and there is cause to suspect that his trademark has since the early 1990s become a significant trend.

John Lanchester's *The Debt to Pleasure* (1996) won its author the Betty Trask Prize, the Julia Child Award, the Whitbread First Novel Award and Book of the Year Award and the Hawthornden Prize. Tarquin Winot, its narrator, is ridiculously erudite and never ceases to display his elegant, versatile command of prose. He is by profession a food writer and for much of the novel he condescends to instruct the reader on the equal attractions of gastronomy and high culture and does so on a journey through that country where both proudly coexist, France. He is also a serial killer, taking time to inform us of how he has despatched a variety of minor characters during his gastronomic tour. Circumstances contribute to each of the murders but there is no overarching sense on Winot's part of motivation, either sadistic or materialistic, and nor is he a psychopath. Instead the killings become part of the alluring, culturally enriching fabric of his account; his command of the narrative, his elegance and learning, cause murder to seem no less distressing than the hedonistic appreciation of art, wine or food.

The Debt to Pleasure presents a fascinating, quirky spectacle and assiduously refuses to submit to anything resembling thematic interpretation. Winot is beguilingly plausible – his mannered prose style is by equal degrees enviable and irritating – but beyond that it is impossible to assess him. He kills people and appears to enjoy it; there is no more to be said.

Lanchester's next novel, *Mr. Phillips* (2000), is an account of a day in the life of the eponymous character. He is an accountant and a person more astoundingly conventional, predictable and devoid of personality would be difficult to conceive. Initially the only interesting feature of the day is that it is based upon a lie. Phillips has lost his job, has not yet summoned the nerve to tell Mrs Phillips and sets out for work as though it still exists. Phillips is not sure how he will spend this hopeless Monday but fate, or something, soon helps out with a catalogue of wildly improbable occurrences: a bank robbery in which he plays a part in saving the life of an attractive female TV producer, an encounter with a pornographer in Battersea Park, and as sole spectator to a sexual encounter on a bus. None of these seems capable of penetrating Phillips's self-willed carapace of unresponsive dullness. As an individual he is the complete opposite of Winot, every dimension of his personality being an abject nullification of the former's abundance and excess, yet as literary devices the two of them have much in common. Their unusual lives are captured with pointillistic rigour and Lanchester is equally careful in ensuring that we can perceive them only as curiosities, figures who are fascinatingly strange but who offer no clues as to how they have become like this.

Nicola Barker announced herself as one of the new generation of post-1980s writers with a short story collection called *Love Your Enemies* (1993). The enemies are not the conventional malevolent types but presences who obtrude, sometimes by accident, into the commonplace existences of ordinary people. There is an anonymous phone-caller who insists on instructing a young mother in the basics of post-Renaissance Western philosophy, a tumour which a butcher's apprentice cuts from a cow and which seems capable of its own independent existence, an unattractive teenaged shoplifter with whom an otherwise discriminating salesgirl decides to have sex in the John Lewis store where she works, and the unbecomingly aggressive RSPCA man who calls to deal with the stray cat adopted by Rosemary, a middle-aged divorcee, and who turns out to be a satyr with 'high thighs and legs...completely covered in soft brown fur' (*Love Your Enemies*, Faber, 1993, p. 183). These figures are not loved by their involuntary hosts with passion or sympathy, more as indications of a state which the latter feel some need to mutely acknowledge. Barker's flat unintrusive prose is the perfect vehicle for the meshing of the familiar and the weird, in that representatives of the latter arrive in the narrative with stealth, and almost unnoticed become part of it. After Bill the RSPCA man has revealed himself as a satyr Rosemary asks 'Do you mind if I feel your fur?' 'Feel free' he answers. Soon afterwards she warns him against seizing her dishcloth – 'I know you goats eat just about anything' – and the story ends with a vignette of domestic contentment. 'Later they ate a delicious meal of eggs, bacon and mushrooms and drank mugs of steaming coffee' (p. 184).

It would be an injustice to Barker's talents for invention and Lanchester's stylistic poise to present them as acolytes of Self, but for whatever reason all three appear to have locked into a perversity of fiction writing which, if not entirely unprecedented, now becomes the work's predominant feature. There will be something, often a plethora of things, which defy credulity but these will stand alongside factual and representational registers that are believable and accessible. No discernable tensions appear to be generated by this pairing; it is a co-existence which is puzzling but which stubbornly resists explanation.

In one of Barker's later full-length novels, *Behindlings* (2002), we encounter Wesley, a man who steals ponds, feeds his fingers to an owl and spends a night asleep in the carcass of a horse. He attracts a band of disciples and enthusiasts who are beguiled by his unfathomable, apparently motiveless, activities. Aside from the question of how exactly one could steal a pond or what sort of owl might eat fingers, Barker does not attempt to make sense of Wesley's addictively attractive potential. One might assume that for most, sane, readers he would in the first instance be only partly believable and even if projected into imagined existence would be a man to be pitied and probably avoided. There might, of course, be a clue in his name; perhaps a nod toward an unconventional figure of the eighteenth century whose resolute dissenting ministry created several subdivisions of Protestantism? This is, however, a deliberately obfuscating trail. Barker's Wesley constantly insists that he stands for nothing and does not even understand why he behaves as he does.

Barker's more recent novel, *Clear* (2004), is narrated by an American, Adair Graham MacKenny, and concerns the jamboree occasioned by the multi-millionaire David Blaine's suspension in a plastic container above the Thames embankment adjoining Tower Bridge. This use of a verifiably true scenario as the setting for invention is as close as Barker comes to offering an explanation for her mode of writing. Blaine exists without food, water or sanitation for a longer period than most physicians would recommend as providing even a slim guarantee for survival, and in doing this as a blatantly public event he becomes a kind of living fiction – unbelievable yet observable. A fraternity of individuals from the mocking drunks and egg-throwers to the Oxford undergraduate who insists on holding up quotations to him, Paul McCartney sacking his publicist when a photographer catches him box-watching and the 11 policemen disciplined for observing when on duty (all true) acquires a curious resemblance to the 'reading public' – unpredictably diverse in background and circumstances but all drawn for different reasons to the same spectacle/text. MacKenny at one point suggests that they 'try to get to grips with all those deeply perplexing anthropological and behavioural niceties' and his friend, Bly, adds that 'Blaine is a blank canvas. He's transparent. He's *clear*. So when people look up at him they…project everything they feel on to him' (p. 311). A more astute parallel between the Blaine phenomenon and the fiction of Barker, Lanchester and Self would be difficult to locate; what used to be a deferential interpretive process is turned inward and the perverse inexplicable nature of the text causes it, potentially, to become a reflection of our own state, particularly if we feel that society, its institutions and the rituals of human behaviour are empty of significance.

Andrew O'Hagan's *Personality* (2004) belongs to the same peculiar subspecies as Barker's *Clear* in that both play games with the reader's ability to distinguish between actuality and invention. O'Hagan bombards us with evidence that his is a biographical account of the life and tragically early death of the singer Lena Zaveroni. She meets Bernie Winters, Eric Morecambe and Ernie Wise, Dean Martin,

Johnny Carson and Lucille Ball. Les Dawson, convincingly brimming with puns and seaside-postcard jokes, converses with her in her dressing-room, and Hughie Green, on whose talent show *Opportunity Knocks* she was discovered aged 13, offers lengthy passages of dramatic monologue composed of his well-known blend of show business hyperbole and censored demotic. O'Hagan even incorporates a biography-style list of sources, including references to the local news-paper for the Isle of Bute where Zaveroni grew up. What he never does is actually mention her name. The main character is called Maria Tambini. O'Hagan tempts us to speculate on what it was really like to be a child star, a 'personality', in the 1970s and 1980s and draws us into a spectrum of meticulously recreated characters and events, but at its centre is an absence. Tambini/Zavaroni exists in relation to figures who seem able to cross the line between fiction and fact but the more this causes us to search for her the more amorphous and spectral she becomes. O'Hagan has transformed that badge of postmodernism, the author-in-the-text, into an even more perplexing engagement with the nature of fiction writing, the character outside it.

Candia McWilliam would at first seem to belong in a completely different branch of fiction, her early career with the magazine *Vogue* sometimes reflected in the cloying minutiae of consumerism which surrounds her characters. Yet this same concern with insignificant detail frequently effects an alteration from an atmosphere of cheerful-ness and complacency to one of pure horror. In her 1988 short story 'The Only Only' (in *Wait Till I Tell You*, Bloomsbury, 1997) we are offered an apparently affectionate documentary account of a scene on a Scottish island; groups of locals stand around conversing about their generally agreeable lives, children play and the ferry prepares to set off for the mainland. McWilliams weaves into the passage an accumu-lation of information that at first seems gratuitous, appearing to inhibit any sense of a narrative purpose or theme, but it gradually becomes evident that in their abundance those particulars provide a special level of omniscience; every aspect of the scene is made known to the reader while its participants give attention only to what imme-diately concerns them. When the ferry arrives it is tied up with a steel rope, an act so routine as to raise no interest among those not imme-diately involved. It is only the reader who sees that as the ferry steams off the rope remains untied and we watch also as it stretches, snaps and decapitates a group of children. Suddenly their parents share the same level of awareness as the reader and the resonance is disturbing. The standard effect procured by good fiction of causing us to participate is now supplemented by a sense of powerless distress; we watch as fate gradually unleashes a terrible moment, almost wishing that we could warn the victims of what is about to occur. Intentionally or not the story brings to mind B. S. Johnson's classic postmodern work *The Unfortunates* (1969), the unbound book which offers the reader the opportunity to rearrange the narrative. Here the opportunity is mooted and denied but in both pieces the reader feels as much a participant in the text as an observer.

A similar effect is achieved, albeit in a different manner, in Ali Smith's *Hotel World* (2001). There is no governing narrative; instead each of the five sections shows a brief excerpt from the lives of five people associated with the hotel. Sometimes a character will wander from their own section to the periphery of another – a device borrowed from Will Self – but the predominant feature of the novel is its preoccupation with the discordance between language and the tactile aspects of existence. There is, for example, an almost manic listing of items stacked in the Left Behind Room – children's toys, pairs of jeans, a prosthetic limb, packs of condoms and so on. No comment is offered but the catalogue is evocative of small narratives, stories of who these items once belonged to and of how they came to be left in hotel rooms. At the other end of the spectrum from this archive of inanimate pieces we find characters struggling to make language animate feelings and conditions: the bored, dispirited journalist cannot stop herself from thinking up adjectives for every moment of her ongoing existence, which is in part a professional habit and equally a reflection of her hopeless desire to ascribe significance to her life; the swimming champion dives into the lift shaft and describes in brutally precise anatomical detail how her body is destroyed on impact, her head crushed into her torso and her heart, literally, propelled into her mouth – a meticulously truthful description of something that she could never be able to describe.

Toby Litt's pseudo-crime-thriller *Corpsing* (2000) deals with the consequences of a shooting in a fashionable London restaurant. The narrator, Conrad, witnesses the shooting and his ex-girlfriend Lily is the only fatality. We learn little of each character's background and the motives for the events which drive the narrative are cursorily sketched and left mainly for speculation. We deal instead with a catalogue of graphically recorded images, probably the most vivid being the precise descriptions of the trajectories and effects of each of the gunmen's bullets. Emotion is not completely excised but it is minimalized to such a degree that it is left to the reader to imagine what they would feel if they were placed in comparable circumstances, an imperative compounded by Litt's juxtaposition of narrative with newspaper articles, hospital reports and other inert evidential material. In *Deadkidsongs* (2001) the relationship between narrative and events narrated is stranger and more fragmented. The kids of the title are a group of teenagers who play war games – imagining a potential invasion by the 'Russkies' – in an otherwise idyllic Home Counties village. Soon the imagined violence turns actual, the participants become estranged from the adult world – with the exception of Andrew's father, a deranged, manic individual – and their story takes on an air of inchoate dreadfulness. The characters share the narrative, each dominating separate chapters. They are unreliable narrators, not in the traditional sense of employing detectable strategies of evasion or deception but as guileless agents in a story that spins out of focus. Matthew in Chapter 5 describes the onset of his distressing, unnamed, illness, his admission to hospital and his own death, up to and including the moments when his consciousness ascends from and observes his lifeless body. At no point in this does he depart from the digressive monotone that marks out all of the characters as convincing late adolescents. This excursion into the fantastic might seem gratuitous but it is quirkily consistent with the accounts by Matthew's peers who do not tell of their own deaths but maintain a disturbing indifference to occurrences that most would treat as worthy at least of some studied emotion, even guilt. They engineer or witness horrible events – causing a neighbour's dog to be run over and killed; pretending, maliciously, to Matthew's almost comatose grandparent to be his baleful ghost; discovering, along with his distressed father, the hanged body of Andrew – with a mixture of apathy and satisfaction.

The novel prompts a comparison with Golding's *Lord of the Flies* (1954) given that in both preadulthood is the point where the worst aspects of the human condition are exposed as disturbingly commonplace, but the similarities are outnumbered by the incongruities. In Golding's novel the schoolboy survivors of a plane crash create a microcosm of society and the battle between fundamental evil and the moral and ethical codes that, we wrongly assume, should overrule it is exposed as unequal. In *Deadkidsongs* Litt causes Golding's vision to seem naively optimistic. Irrespective of our opinion of Golding's or Litt's metaphysical thesis, what should be noted is that *Lord of the Flies* filters its account of dreadfulness through a narrative texture that is the 1950s version of circumspect, civilized nineteenth-century realism; the boys might in various degrees be pitiable and vile but the fact that they came to us via the presence of a mature third-person narrator allows us to maintain a stable, albeit horrified, perception of them. Litt, however, employs narrative devices that are determinedly postmodern – particularly in the detachment of each narrator from a recognition of the consequences of their actions or the significance of their feelings – and makes it almost impossible for the reader to judge the characters against their own notions of good and bad; the characters attain a disturbing degree of unfathomable independence.

Litt's fiction exemplifies a trend which though diverse in modes of execution is united in its insistence on citing and undermining precedent, and more significantly in its refusal to offer a secure rationale or justification for doing so. These novels not only make interpretation difficult, they also robustly skew the hypothetical question of why or for what purpose they have been written.

Litt's recent novel *Ghost Story* (2004) appears focused upon a particularly distressing event, a couple's experience of a stillborn child, but grief is by no means straightforwardly dealt with. Agatha, the stillborn child's mother, experiences weird sounds and movements in their new house and adopts a complicated and potentially dangerous attitude to their other child. Sometimes we perceive events via Agatha's troubled mind and then without reason the perspective will shift elsewhere, in one instance to a manic chapter-long description of the builders renovating the house, written in a single bravura sentence. Also, the main narrative is prefaced by two brief stories, one about someone who turns into a hare, another about a man whose wife gives birth to fox cubs and, perhaps most disturbingly, an autobiographical memoir in which Litt writes in harrowing detail of his girlfriend's three miscarriages. One could surmise that these discontinuities are purposive, perhaps even an avant-garde form of mimesis with the reader's undoubted experience of confusion and disquiet meant in some way to correspond with similar emotions attendant upon the characters. At the same time, however, one senses that Litt and a considerable number of fiction writers of the past two decades are deliberately attempting to curb the reader's conventional inclination to interpret the text according to any rational notion of internal coherence or correspondence with the nonfictional world.

There is evidence that among these writers a degree of mutual recognition and collective purpose has been and is being acknowledged. In 2000 Fourth Estate published a collection of short stories called *All Hail the New Puritans* (ed. Matt Thorne and Nicholas Blincoe). The resemblance between this brand of writing and religious Puritanism at first seems tenuous – there is a good deal of emotionless sex and unmotivated violence – except that all of the pieces in the collection, including one by Litt, appear intent upon destroying the effigy of fiction as high art. The new, literary, Puritanism delivers its images in a manner that is unintrusive; style is pared to a minimum so that the peculiarities, grotesques and illogic of the story are thrown into the foreground.

Cherry (2004) is a recent novel by one of the coeditors, Matt Thorne. It involves Steve Ellis, a 33-year old teacher, a bachelor whose lifestyle and circumstances are rendered in meticulous detail: he is a disappointed man with no aspirations beyond maintaining his routine of drinks in the local pub, occasional dinners with friends and TV at home. Soon, however, peculiar things begin to happen. Steve meets an old man in the pub, buys him a drink and invites him to his flat to watch a video he has made of a woman walking down the street. A few days later Steve is visited by an Indian man who asks him to fill out a questionnaire on his 'Perfect Woman'. His fantasy – demure, intelligent, beautiful and with an hourglass figure – is made real and they have a relationship. She, Cherry, eventually leaves him – after his bedroom ceiling collapses and her toenails fall off – and Steve is again contacted by the old man from the pub who informs him that if he wants Cherry back he must assassinate a person called Tom who is actually a force for evil known to some as the Fox. Does he? The ending is bizarre and unspecific, and the entire book seems designed continuously to incite and extinguish the desire to discern cause and continuity. We might assume that there is some connection between the old man and the Indian who magically procures Cherry, but what exactly this involves is left entirely for speculation. And the question of why Steve has made an apparently innocuous yet in the circumstances sinister video of a woman in the street and invited a stranger to view it remains unanswered.

David Mitchell's 2004 novel *Cloud Atlas* was shortlisted for the Man Booker Prize and came top in a poll held by the late-afternoon chat show duo Richard and Judy for their audience's favourite of those books reviewed on the show. By April 2005 its paperback sales had exceeded 150,000. Mitchell's novel seemed to have traversed the long-established chasm between the world of perverse experimental writing and the reading public. In the novel there are six narrations, the first set in the mid-nineteenth century, the last in the distant future: savage behaviour during a Pacific sea voyage in the 1850s; a composer's unsettled, poverty-stricken life between the wars; the mindset of an intelligent conscientious journalist in Ronald Reagan's California; a vanity publisher pursued by murderous villains; a semi-human waitress on death row; and innocent natives of the Pacific islands observing the end of modern civilization. As independent chronicles, with some tenuously related themes, these might function as a sprawling kaleidoscopic history of the last century and a half, but Mitchell instils an ingenious twist. Each piece appears to conclude at a moment of tense climactic uncertainty and the story is carried forward by the subsequent narrator. No explanation is offered for how, say, a 1930s composer can take up where a nineteenth-century mariner left off, and in all instances the shift from the previous to the ongoing account is seamlessly executed. The overall effect is of a deliberate though not gratuitous distortion of historical perspective. Contemporaneous writings of any past period inevitably involve two levels of recognition. Codes of behaviour and representation – particularly those involving gender, race and class – will usually be different from our own and the manner in which all events, however mundane, are recorded will incorporate conventions of grammar and idiom that can be recognized as the stylistic signatures of a particular ethos. These two registers cooperate in forming our general perceptions of specific points in the past but Mitchell, by causing them to slip out of synchronization and briefly to change places, foregrounds the extent to which our knowledge of events of which we have no direct experience is conditioned by the refractory conventions of language. The novel does not aver that the past is forever beyond our comprehension; rather it offers a sequence of moments separated by chronology but interwoven by a curious dialogue as each narrator shares part of the other's story and carries it forward.

Mitchell's *Black Swan Green* (2006) seems at first to involve a switch toward a more conventional manner. It is set in 1982 and narrated by the teenaged Jason Taylor from his ordinary existence in a Worcestershire village. Any reader with even a routine awareness of the background information that has accompanied Mitchell during his early career will soon begin to pick out autobiographical parallels. Jason suffers from a severe stammer and this seems to be the cause of his tendency to retreat to the security of his own unspoken musings and observations which, in due course, become for his adult novelist counterpart a means of dividing the narrative between private, impressionistic and historically grounded perspectives. Already Mitchell raises subtle ontological questions about what fiction is capable of doing with the disparate conditions and registers that make up our lives. Often we notice a contrast between the Jason who shares the narrative with the other people and events of 1982 – a plausibly recreated teenager of that period – and another one who communicates only with himself and us. The latter seems capable of immensely precocious observations of the sort that we would be more likely to associate with an adult able to look back to 1982 from the early 2000s: someone who sees the early years of Thatcherism and the Falklands War through a 20-year prism of debate and reflection. In other circumstances such an inconsistency might be treated as negligent, but Mitchell executes counterpoints between the two perspectives that bespeak premeditation, and from a deceptively naturalistic piece of work arise more fundamental issues regarding the very nature of memory. Do we contribute to our recollections as much as we recover from them?

Mitchell belongs within the radical compass of contemporary writing, along with Litt, Thorne, Smith, Lanchester and the other figures dealt with in this chapter, and one could argue that they are the inheritors of a somewhat disparate branch of postmodernism initiated by Amis, McEwan and Barnes at the end of the 1970s and beginning of the 1980s. Beyond the fact that they cannot be classified as solidly conservative realists these writers have only one thing in common. Each gives as much attention to the nature and potentialities of fiction as they do to the subject of their writing, and two related questions are attendant upon this: why do these novelists elect to write in this way and what, in doing so, do they hope to achieve?

The vast majority of British novelists whose literary careers began after the early 1980s are graduates, mostly in English or related subjects, and the study of English in British universities has undergone changes in focus and affiliation more turbulent than experienced by its supposed subject matter, literature, in the same period. Before the 1960s English Studies in Britain and America could not, and to a general extent did not, claim for itself a disciplinary code beyond a basic requirement for scholarly correctness and an implied respect for the aesthetics of the canon. There were some academics, known collectively as the New Critics, who produced work which treated literature as a single discourse with definitive, unifying characteristics, but they were a notable minority. During the 1960s ideas and intellectual systems that had developed largely in continental Europe since the beginning of the twentieth century began by various means to filter into British and American departments of literary studies. The 'Isms' were coming: principally Structuralism, Formalism, Post-structuralism and Deconstruction, Feminism and Gender Studies, Reception Theory, Marxist Criticism. These schools of thought were by no means united in a particular objective but all in varying degrees submitted to a general premise. Prelinguistic reality is largely, though not entirely, an unreliable abstraction; reality and representation – the latter predominantly involving language – are inseparable and inter-dependent. By the 1980s theory had become a permanent fixture of English Studies while retaining its aura of the unconventional and iconoclastic, and it is in this environment that undergraduates with creative ambitions will have found a productive interface between books they are inclined or obliged to read and a cultural environment in which radical ideas on the nature of language and truth have taken root. David Mitchell, for example, did his BA at Kent and stayed on to complete a Masters thesis on levels of reality in the postmodern novel. Self, Litt, Thorne, Smith, McWilliam, Barker, Coe and a number of other contemporary novelists studied English during a period when modernism and postmodernism as aesthetic principles, and post-structuralism as their broader intellectual counterpart, appeared to have formed a mutually supportive symbiotic relationship.

Up to the end of the 1960s literature of whatever affiliation – modernist, romantic, renaissance et al. – was treated as the object of appreciation and analysis, while the scrutineer existed in the non-literary world of the known, the actual and the rational. By the early 1980s, however, undergraduates were being introduced to modes of thinking that blurred the borderline between the unlicensed sphere of literary imagination and everything else. Consider, for example, deconstruction, a concept that will forever be associated with its most industrious proponent, Jacques Derrida, and which is all too frequently misunderstood and misused. Deconstruction addresses questions raised by the linguist Ferdinand de Saussure and a number of post-Saussurean thinkers and extends them to a point that is at once ultimate, inevitable and inconclusive. Derrida contends that Western civilization – and implicitly all others – has during recorded history been engaged in a continuous process of self-deception. Every debate regarding the fundamentals of the human condition has treated language as a functional necessity, a means of articulating or particularizing essential characteristics, such as the defining features of beneficent or malicious acts and conditions; the distinction between spiritual, intellectual or physical states; or the nature and function of a monotheistic presence. Derridean deconstruction reverses this ascendancy and presents language as the precondition for thinking rather than its vehicle. The conceits and mechanisms of language are not the means by which we distort or clarify truth; without them we would not be able to conceptualize truth.

It would be absurd to treat all experimental contemporary writers as enthusiastic aficionados or advocates of Derrida, but at the same time one cannot treat as accidental the parallels between post-structuralism/deconstruction – which like existentialism in the 1950s has become a fashionable intellectual accessory outside academia – and literary writing which seems intent upon eschewing logic and defying interpretation.

Many of the novels considered in this chapter on contemporary postmodernism could be seen as carrying a deconstructive, Derridean subtext. Lanchester causes us to reconsider not merely the reliability of the narrator but also the capacities of language to create a presence so seductive, bizarre and unbelievable; Self draws us into the world of people who we know cannot exist; Ali Smith creates linguistic bridges between life and death that are addictive and false; Mitchell has people communicate in a weird, unacknowledged manner between their different situations, contexts and historical periods. Vaginas forming on the backs of knees, dead people speaking, fantastic events occurring without warning, cause or significant explanation – the repertoire of imposture appears limitless and unclassifiable, except that what all of these works have in common is their abandonment of any obligation to explain or justify their excursions from credulity and mimesis.

Literary fantasy certainly has precedents. The folk tale or fairy story, the supernatural, science fiction, and more recently magic realism, all, as subgenres of the novel create effects and worlds out of language that do not, cannot, correspond with any rational consensus on the nature of reality. At the same time each either establishes within the text sharp contrasts between what is and what is not credible or more often indicates some purpose for its involvement in the latter, most frequently allegory. The post-1980s brand of postmodernism appears intent upon a refusal to acknowledge a distinction between normality and irregularity.

Postmodernism has itself become a blanket term, a convenience for those who seem convinced that the contemporary condition – in all its aspects, from art through consumer habits to politics and personal relationships – is irredeemably bereft of what used to be called meaning. It seems that society as a whole has become an enactment of the ideas promulgated by theorists form Saussure to Derrida. Terry Eagleton in 'Capitalism, Modernism and Postmodernism' (1985) offered a Marxist explanation of how the world had caught up with its post-structuralist augurs, claiming that 'As postmodernist culture attests, the contemporary subject may be less the strenuous nomadic agent of an earlier phase of capitalist ideology than a dispersed, decentred network of libidinal attachments, emptied of ethical substance and psychical interiority, the ephemeral function of this or that act of consumption, media experience, trend or fashion' (in Patricia Waugh (ed.), *Postmodernism: A Reader*, Arnold, 1992, p. 158). In Eagleton's model the system which emptied the product and worker of significance and buttressed capitalism is now something that informs every dimension of our lives. Jean Baudrillard said: 'And so art is dead, not only because its critical transcendence has gone, but because reality itself, entirely impregnated by an aesthetic which is inseparable from its own structure, has been confused with its own image' (*Simulations*, trans. P. Beithman, Semiotexte, New York, 1983, p. 156); which sounds like a shrewd anticipation of much of the fiction dealt with above in which the distinction between art and actuality, fiction and truth is persistently obscured. Along with other commentators on postmodernism Eagleton and Baudrillard treat the artist as an unwitting functionary in an all-encompassing predicament. However, it is evident that the

New Postmodernists, from Amis to Mitchell and Smith, execute a calculated and premeditated shift away from an implied mindset, outside the novel, that involves the plausible, the rational and the predictable; if it weren't for the self-evident contrasts between their excursions into the inexplicable and stability of a routine, ordinary existence the latter would be ineffective. There is in many of these novels abundant evidence that the writers themselves are as astutely aware of the taxonomy of postmodernism as its theorists; many will have acquired this in universities but unlike Foucault, Eagleton, Baudrillard, Lyotard and their campus-based acolytes they play to the gallery. Their novels incorporate many of the mantras that their readers, if similarly schooled, would recognize as guarantees to intellectual hauteur but while the theorists write in a manner that variously bores or alienates the ordinary reader the novelists invite them in. It may or may not be the case that we are, as participants in the Postmodern Condition, experiencing an unprecedented intellectual and cultural apocalypse, an unbidden and all-pervasive state of nihilism, but what is evident is that fiction writers have seized upon this as a saleable commodity. Their style is alluring, by varying degrees elegant, friendly and transparent, and once the reader becomes attuned to this they are offered commodified thrills: multinarratives with no cohering pattern, horrible descents into the grotesque, arbitrary switches between the plausible and the unimaginable. The New Postmodernists are in truth engaged in a programme that undermines the jargon-ridden pomposity of their academic counterparts. They create fictional scenarios that are precipitately and self-evidently bizarre and implausible and in doing so they both entertain the fashionably accomplished reader and confirm that the actuality of existence outside the novel is by implication reassuringly normal. Postmodernism is an unusual myth in that only those who have become imprisoned by its vocabulary and methodology actually believe it. Everyone else, including the novelists dealt with here, can treat it as something to be observed from a more secure, comfortable perspective. Eagleton and Baudrillard, it seems, were wrong. Novelists are not symptomatic of the Postmodern Condition; they exploit, sell it and, like many others, treat it with the Postmodern Condition sceptical detachment.

As we have seen, John Berger is a novelist who kept the flame of radicalism alight during what he perceived as the benighted contra-modernist aftermath of the 1950s. His recent novel *Here is Where We*

Meet (2005) could serve as a purist manifesto for his post-1980s market-conscious fellow travellers. It sets down the thoughts of a man who bears a striking resemblance to his author. They share the same age, background and circumstances and the character is called John Berger. During his listless but not unhappy travels Berger meets his mother in Lisbon. We are informed, perfunctorily, that she has been dead for 15 years, and in a Madrid hotel bar he encounters an old university tutor who died in the early 1950s. At one point Berger recalls an exchange between himself and Ken, a mentor from his child-hood: 'Neither of us, for different reasons, believe in literary explana-tions. I never once asked him about what I failed to understand. He never referred to what, given my age and experience, I might find difficult to grasp in these books.' This could indeed be aimed at the reader who might otherwise find it difficult to locate explanations for what occurs in this novel. 'Do not try', say Berger and Ken, which is pertinent given that the latter features in the book, in Krakow, some 50 years after having died in New Zealand.

Iain Sinclair has been publishing since the mid-1970s but has entered the critical spotlight only since the late 1990s. His work is even more perplexing than Berger's since while Berger continually raises questions about the nature of writing fiction Sinclair's books themselves stubbornly evade classification, shifting quixotically between mannerisms that we associate with the novel and nonfictional registers which are part pseudo-journals and part hallucinogenic fan-tasies. One will search in vain for a plot but a narrative, of sorts, is sustained by Sinclair's twin fascination with London, its routes, land-scapes and environs, and transplantations of the past into the present. In *White Chappell, Scarlet Tracings* (1987) and *Downriver* (1991) any reliable notion of perspective or point of view is continually skewed by the difficulty of being able to distinguish between the narrator and the character Joblard, who dominate the 'fictional' aspects of the books, and their almost identical counterparts, Sinclair and the writer and artist Brian Catling, both indisputably real presences. This coales-cent quartet conducts us on a tour of a London whose present-day condition is gradually subsumed by a vast, digressive patchwork of mini-narratives from the past. The unifying feature of these is their incidental relationship to specific places encountered on the tour: Holmes and Moriarty, Jack the Ripper, Lewis Carroll, Aboriginal cricket teams from the nineteenth century, Victorian boatmen; these and a gigantic cast of other real and invented presences flicker briefly into the narrative and suddenly disappear.

Similarly, in *Slow Chocolate Autopsy*, subtitled *Incidents from the Notorious Career of Norton, Prisoner of London* (1997), the focus shifts between the experiences of Norton the convict, who amongst other things witnesses the murder of Christopher Marlowe, and 1990s London presented in language by Sinclair and photographs by Dave McKean.

These books have been treated by most commentators as novels while other pieces, such as *London Orbital* (2002), are perceived to belong in the more amorphous zone of 'nonfiction'. One assumes that *London Orbital* is excluded from novelistic status because Sinclair remains as Sinclair through the 592-page journey around the M25. However, the fact that he apparently encounters – rather than 'imagines' – John Clare watching Byron's funeral procession, nineteenth-century lunatic asylums and legendary figures from the criminal underworld of the 1950s and 1960s causes one to wonder if Sinclair is set upon disposing of that cosy bourgeois separation between literary and nonliterary writing and by implication the aesthetic and nonaesthetic dimensions of language. The device of causing real people to crop up in fiction is not entirely without precedent – David Garrick the actor appeared in several eighteenth-century novels – but Sinclair, and indeed Barker in *Clear* and O'Hagan in *Personality*, cause us to question the security of the real world outside the book by unapologetically appropriating it as a dimension of fiction. Such a policy is not simply a case of idiosyncratic licence. It returns us to the Derridean contention that the distinction between language and everything else is a falsity; in Sinclair's work the borderlines between imagination, representation and actuality have virtually ceased to exist.

Naturalization occurs when we enter a generally one-sided monologue with a literary text. In most respects we naturalize a text by explaining it, by bringing its aberrant imaginative and linguistic features into line with the world of the tactile, the logical and the verifiable in which we live. Berger and his late friend Ken seem to speak for a whole generation of postmodern novelists in their contention that such a procedure is reductive, completely at odds with the aesthetic principle that informs the book. To try to make sense of novels such as this is not so much incorrect as unappreciative of what they offer, specifically the possibilities made available when literary writing refuses even to acknowledge a norm of representation and communication from which it might deviate. In an essay on Sinclair, Julian Wolfreys happily acknowledges that he is, as a literary critic, faced with precisely this dilemma; '...no critical language is adequate to Sinclair's excessive texts,' and as a consequence '[I] do not propose to do anything amounting to a reading' ('Iain Sinclair's Millennial Fiction', *British Fiction of the 1990s*, ed. N. Bentley, Routledge, 2005, p. 195).

In a 2004 collection of tendentious criticism, appropriately entitled *Hatchet Jobs: Writings on Contemporary Fiction* (New Press), Dale Peck offered an assessment of the present condition of US and British fiction. 'There are' he maintained 'two strains of literature currently in vogue...recherché postmodernism and recidivist realism'. Evidently things have changed since the early 1980s when the chorus of complaints blamed realism exclusively for the dismal state of the novel. Now, according to Peck, postmodernism equals realism in the marketplace and also in its capacity to inhibit originality. Obtusely and unintentionally he makes a significant point. It is an indisputable fact – but one that few practitioners of the avant garde would concede – that postmodern writing is the victim of a self-created paradox. Through its collective programme of anti-realism involving the persistent avoidance of standardized mimesis and an obsessive concern with the nature of writing and representation it has become what its practitioners sought and seek to avoid, a classifiable field and subgenre of literary writing. In a collection called *New Writing 13* (Picador 2005) the editors Ali Smith and Toby Litt, both ardent producers and exponents of radical fiction, lament the fact that so many of the submissions they rejected were disappointingly unadventurous, and state that their preference, their principal criterion, was for 'writing which renews language itself', a mantra which were it not for its commendable accessibility could have come from Derrida. The collection is typified by pieces which are about writing but say little. Lawrence Norfolk offers what might be an essay but could equally be a short story about choosing the correct music for writerly inspiration. David Mitchell's story of a stammering schoolboy is comprised largely of wordplay, charts and tables, and A. S. Irvine's satire 'A Novel' is made up predominantly of doodles. Sterne, resurrected, would have felt at home. There is a pungent irony here in that one notices a parallel between volumes such as Litt's and Smith's and a number published in the mid-1950s, albeit composed mostly of verse. In both cases there is a sense of unity, except that in the 1950s this involved the anti-modernist factions known as the Movement and the Angry Young Men. Now, it seems, postmodernists are experiencing a similar sense of common purpose and mutual recognition; they are unified in their avoidance of something else, realism.

It is certainly the case that postmodern writing receives rather more intensive and enthusiastic scrutiny in the literary media than its realist counterpart, but this should not be regarded as a conscious or deliberate policy of prejudice: provocative, challenging techniques and bizarre scenarios generally incite more interesting copy than seamless, representational pieces. One might argue that the mannerisms evolved by the likes of Joyce and sustained in the works of Beckett, Berger et al. are now as much part of the literary establishment as those which they sought to undermine, and yet what we habitually refer to as experimental fiction is as much prone to derivative repetition as conservative methods. Books which meditate upon their own function as refractory lenses, as centrifuges of meaning, irrespective of their subject, tend paradoxically to be both radical and self-limiting. However, such writings still carry a distinct cache of newness and present themselves more as intellectual challenges than merely stories. Numerically the realists are still present in force, but for most critics and literary journalists their best representatives merit respectful attention to craftsmanship and guile, but little more. Consider the number of collections of new writing, comparable with Smith's and Litt's, which proscribe experiment and encourage brilliantly executed refashioning of verisimilitude, mimeses in which the mechanisms of logic and causation in the story correspond with those generally agreed as operating outside it: none.

Justin Cartwright, who we have already looked at as a chronicler of the Thatcher years, has more recently produced a work which tries to capture the mood of Britain in the early twenty-first century. *The Promise of Happiness* (2004) deploys members of the Judd family as delicately nuanced reflections of contemporaneity. The parents, Charles and Daphne, have taken early retirement in Cornwall, each behaving as though the decision was their own and never mentioning that in truth Charles had effectively been made redundant, an old-fashioned accountant now surplus to the requirements of the new, rapacious, multinational entity in which he had once been a junior partner. They have three children. Juliet, or Ju-Ju, is the star, the beautiful Oxford-educated art historian, a high flyer in the moneyed, celebrity-dense New York world of antique dealing, until she was arrested and, wrongly, imprisoned for assisting in the sale of a Tiffany window stolen from a cemetery. Charlie has created his own small empire of Internet sales: sockscribe.com specializes in underwear and will soon be bought by a German company for several million pounds. Sophie, with half-hearted literary ambitions, is mildly dysfunctional, given to occasional drug-taking and disagreeable men, one of whom is her married boss. The narrative focuses upon the imminent release of Ju-Ju, her return to England and the prospect of the family together for the first time in years at the wedding of Charlie to his pregnant, farcically exotic fiancée.

The book is boldly indicative of lives and states of mind which both retain their independence yet compellingly intersect. It might seem unlikely that Daphne, struggling hopelessly with a fish recipe recently acquired during her time at Rick Stein's summer school, would have much conception of the ongoing experiences of her daughter 3,000 miles away in a US state prison, yet Cartwright causes each of them to share the third person narrative in such a way that we recognize parallels, the linguistic equivalent of seeing a facial resemblance between daughter and mother. And so it is with each of the other members of the family; gradually, almost subliminally, we begin to notice how their differences are matched by their quiet, peculiar similarities. The world, British and US, in which the Judds attempt to reconcile themselves to their private reflections and to each other is presented as neither prepossessing nor alien; instead it is seen to comprise individuals and circumstances that are forgivably unpredictable. It would do Cartwright a gross injustice to classify him simply as a twenty-first-century classic realist – like all good writers he has a singularity of presence that rises above genre or abstract technique – but he is nonetheless a novelist who treats prose and reported speech as representational media rather than the means of raising questions about the nature of representation. It would be intriguing, therefore, to consider how a writer more disposed toward the postmodern might deal with a similar fictional scenario, and with commendable timing Ali Smith actualized this hypothesis in 2005 with *The Accidental*.

There are manifest differences but the same core element, a middle-class family in contemporary Britain, animates and informs the narrative of both. Eve Smart, the mother, is working on the latest of her best-selling books, fashionable blends of history, biography and fabrication, while Michael, her second husband and stepfather to her children, is an Eng. Lit. academic, content with his routine of seducing female students and anyone else who might fall prey to his ostentatious displays of sophisticated lechery. Magnus and Astrid, the children, are beset by a standard retinue of hectic adolescent anxieties. Much of the book has them all together for summer in a slightly run down holiday cottage in Norfolk, which sounds like a perfect recipe for realism, even perhaps of the quirkier variety once practised by Iris Murdoch and more recently by Piers Paul Read. Smith, however, sets about demolishing such expectations, in two ways. First, each of the characters informs the narrative with a psychological extension of a particular, and particularly troubling, aspect of their personality. Magnus is for much of the book beset by a feeling of guilt regarding a prank played upon a girl at his school which might have led to her eventual suicide. While he is able to communicate normally with others, the point at which he is the subject of the third-person narrative gives access to his private unspoken meanderings. His thoughts are rendered in clipped, often two-word verb phases. There is an evident reluctance to complete a descriptive sentence, which presumably is symptomatic of his private turmoil. Astrid's discourse is replete with bolshie adolescent plays on language and when faced with the world of adult responsibility she reverts to messy attempts at precociousness (she tags virtually everything as 'typical and ironic'). Outside Smith's attempts to make linguistic shape coterminous with character there is Amber, a woman of thirty or so years and indeterminate origin who simply arrives without explanation and becomes the *deus ex machina* for the entire family. They do not know how to respond to this uninvited guest – being decent middle-class sorts they can hardly just throw her out – and in a bizarre variety of ways she take each of them over. Michael, for example, no longer seems in control of his seductive, learned sophistry – Amber has him babbling in Byronic octava rima. The relatively secure borders between each character's third-person space begin to break down with voices echoing in and out of each other, changing in idiom and register. At one point the book itself appears in danger of fragmenting, as words and letters collapse out of regular typeface and scatter across the page.

73

Through their differences Cartwright and Smith show how fiction has changed over the past 25 years. Both were reviewed very favourably in the broadsheet literary pages and although pieces on Smith tend to flag up her wilfully adventurous manner – the *Daily Telegraph* of 21 May 2005 for example calls it a novel 'grounded on the idea of fracture – a fissiparous splintered artefact...' – none treat this as in any way gratuitously inaccessible or unusual – it is a choice she has made, as acceptable within the critical consensus today as, say, a novelist of 50 years ago favouring first rather than third-person narrative.

Realism, particularly that robustly British variety in which poised irony, satiric resignation and a reliance upon comedy as an avoidance of despair are variously present, is still alive within the broader fabric of contemporary fiction. Ferdinand Mount, D. J. Taylor, Michael Frayn, Nigel Williams, Simon Mason, Howard Jacobson, A. N. Wilson and Elizabeth Jane Howard are a few of its best-known practitioners and each is something of an heroic anachronism. Mount, for example, completed a loosely connected six-volume chronicle of late twentieth-century Britain in 2005 with *Heads You Win*. Each of the chief characters, including Gus Cotton, a redundant senior civil servant, Joe Follows, an entrepreneur recently recovered from a stroke and financial disgrace, and Keith Trull, out of prison and no longer producing 'magi fiction' (surely a wry nod towards Amis and Self), becomes a magnet for features of society and its effects that most would recognize as characteristically 1990s and British. The novel blends acerbic wit with elegiac charm, but what it does not do is create arbitrary incursions upon the narrative, offer kaleidoscopic blendings of style or deliberately disrupt plausibility. Today novels which do all of these things are uncommon and extreme manifestations of the postmodern but at the same time fiction which eschews all of them, like Mount's, is equally rare.

Consider A. L. Kennedy's *Paradise* (2004), a novel assembled very loosely from the first-person narrative of Hannah Luckraft, in her late thirties, intelligent, middle-class and alcoholic. It is a first person narrative in which the narrator's addiction creates a bizarre disjunction; on the one hand we are offered precise accounts of minutiae – the colour, shape and distressing pointlessness of a key-ring for example – while at the same time we are unsure of what exactly Hannah did the previous day or why she is in the airport terminal where the novel begins and ends: realist or nonrealist? One would suggest a blend of both with a slight leaning toward the former. In a similar vein we encounter Daren King's *Boxy An Star* (1999) and *Tom Boler* (2005). The eponymous Tom is in his teens in the first novel while the second backtracks to his experiences, aged nine, when his mother effectively abandons him. In both instances he is the controlling narrative presence and the following is an example of the nine-year-old's interior monologue as he comes home to find the house empty. 'She aint under the bed. Aint be hind the curtain…Me lookin in her war drobe. At her dresses. They are blue but. They are gone' (p. 24). In the earlier novel, aged 14, his prelinguistic registers and command of syntax are scrambled by his continuous intake of amphetamine-like substances. Both novels are self-evidently indebted to that originating moment of modernist fiction writing, the employment of the interior monologue by Woolf and Joyce, while at the same time they use this device to serve an objective that would once have been treated as the territory of realism: a brutally honest account of what it is like to be an abandoned, poor working-class child in an environment where drugs and violence are the commodities of everyday life. The early manifestations of the interior monologue and their offshoots in the wilfully discontinuous prose of, say, Beckett, were tied to a complex agenda regarding the very nature of consciousness and linguistic representation. In the hands of King and the mind and voice of Tom they have become primitivist realism, a lens for the observation of how innocence is dismantled by an indifferent, unpleasant world.

King's blend of Joycean technique with a working-class transparency reminiscent of Barry Hines's *Kes* shows that the borderline between realism and postmodern has become vague and elastic and it is intriguing to compare his work with a recent piece by Hilary Mantel. The style of *Beyond Black* (2005) is resolutely conservative. Its two principal characters, Alison and Colette, are rendered with unforgiving clarity, as are the dismal London landscapes, mostly the suburbs, in which they are obliged to exist. Alison has had a foul, battered childhood, her mother is a prostitute and she has to put up with being a size 22; Colette, her conniving leech-like companion, is an equally dispiriting figure. Alison's profession? She's a medium, a communicator with the spirit world, but before expectations of this as symptomatic of dim credulous desperation are realized, Mantel begins to populate the novel with dead people, or more specifically their nonphysical yet vividly realized presences. Mantel's visitors from the other side are in varying degrees as seedy, ugly, boring and down-right uninteresting as their living counterparts; mostly they are thoroughly unpleasant, and possessed of a malicious animus that, disclosed as a common element of the afterlife, would be equally surprising to agnostics, atheists and believers.

The traditional ghost story or tale of the supernatural was driven by a contrast, a counterpoint between the known world and the fascinating oddness of whatever might lie beyond it. Presences from the latter, whether benign or evil, were generally granted a pseudo-aristocratic state of otherness; even in Will Self's *How the Dead Live* (2000) they take on a mildly elevated role of aloof puzzlement. Mantel, however, causes their supernatural curiosity value to be eclipsed by their sheer loathsomeness. Morris, for example, Alison's spirit guide, is a vulgar, smelly, violent character most frequently encountered slumped against a wall fiddling with his flies.

Supernaturalism has long been tolerated as an engaging subgenre of serious fiction with some pieces, notably Henry James's *The Turn of the Screw*, elevated almost to classic realist status. But none can compare with Mantel's creation of the other world as a simulacrum of the more dull and unpleasant features of the known.

Mantel announced her membership of the fiction-purloins-reality club – joining Barker, O'Hagan and Sinclair – in a mischievous reflection on the novel in the *Guardian*. She informs us with a deadpan absence of irony that she herself first 'received a message from the dead' via a psychic 'wearing an obsolete spangled garment of the kind that used to be known as a cocktail dress' and plying her trade in the 'function room' of a local hotel. Throughout the article she maintains the same pitch of caustic transparency that informs the novel so that we never know if she believes or expects us to believe that there was a message from the other side. Instead she offers coy indications of why she refuses to do so.

> How did [the psychic] stop the dead chattering in her ear when she stepped down from the stage?
>
> I was not immune from fellow feeling. Which other self-employed persons stand up in public to talk about non-existent people? Novelists of course. (*Guardian*, 28 January 2006)

In *Yellow Dog* (Cape, 2003) Martin Amis appears also to have been drawn toward a collective fascination with provoking the reader's credulity while holding their attention. The book involves several interlinked stories. Principally, we spend time with Xan Meo (who despite his name is a white Anglo-Saxon), a middle-ranking actor turned overambitious writer whose gangland background revisits him, literally, with a duffing up in a Camden Town bar. As a consequence of this Xan sheds his liberal new-mannish persona and regresses to what we are caused to suspect is his genuine state, combining misogyny, aggressive lust and disturbing thoughts about what he might like to do with his four-year-old daughter.

Next we encounter Clint Smoker, repulsive flatulent columnist for *The Morning Lark*, a downmarket version – if such could be envisaged – of the *Daily Star*. Clint is humiliatingly poorly endowed and conducts a virtual relationship with a quiescent woman on the Internet. Alongside Clint we come upon the memorable presence of Henry IX, monarch of this crackpot kingdom who bears a close resemblance to the Prince of Wales with shades of Wodehousian absurdity and *Private Eye*-style satirical hyperbole thrown in. Simultaneously we learn that flight CigAir 101 from London to Houston is, probably, about to go into nosedive due to the weird machinations of its most unusual passenger Royce Traynor who happens to be dead, probably, and coffined in the airliner's hold. Also it is likely that an apocalypse-sized meteorite is heading towards the planet. In case one is not already too distracted by the menu of narrative oddities so far Amis then takes us, for no obvious reason, on a tour of the California pornography industry.

Amis has written a novel which seems designed to infuriate anyone expecting to find connections between its parts. Yet at the same time he procures from this apparently indifferent state of chaos an enduring claim upon even the most begrudging reader's attention. How? Irrespective of the fact that the particulars of the book are variously implausible and repulsive in their nature and appear randomly discontinuous we are aware of a controlling presence; we know that the portrait of Clint the irredeemable grotesque comes from the same hand as the moment when Xan and his daughter see a fox on the roof of a garden shed and share the experience of its 'entreating frown with its depths of anxiety'. *Yellow Dog* is a mischievous, radical piece of work in that it at once invokes and undermines the burdensome presence of Joyce's *Ulysses*. Joyce demonstrated that 24 hours of wearisome ordinariness could be turned into a stylistic and epistemological mosaic and Amis reverses the formula. He assembles a patchwork of uncooperative mini-narratives, scenarios and portraits and without compromising their fantastic independence informs each with the same stylistic signature. The effect is comparable to viewing, in sequence, a set of paintings each with a different synoptic content and mood by an artist whose technique is inextinguishably unique.

The battle between realism and modernism/postmodernism is now, in the early twenty-first century, effectively over. Neither side is victorious but the middle ground of fiction is shared by hybridized versions of both. At the extremities we encounter the likes of Ferdinand Mount and John Berger, but the vast majority of present-day writers, particularly those who have risen to prominence over the past two decades, are, as Lodge predicted, like shoppers in an aesthetic supermarket, faced with an unlimited variety of stylistic opportunities and cultural brand names. Advocates and practitioners of realism can, however, feel satisfied in a pyrrhic triumph because technical innovation and the avant-garde are now misnomers; what were once transgressive reactions against the norm have become the norm. This has not occurred because of some seismic shift in the broader cultural fabric, with *Finnegans Wake* routinely purchased as holiday reading, but because experiment has become more accessible and domesticated. It still, of course, carries a radical cachet but in the hands of Mitchell, Smith, Kennedy, Mantel et al. the groundbreaking legacies of Joyce and Woolf have been made consumer-friendly. I will return to this matter in the Epilogue but for the time being let us turn our attention to an ongoing obsession that further skews our perception of what is and is not conventional writing, the fictionalization of history.

Part II

Excursions From the Ordinary

Fiction achieved respectability as a literary genre in the nineteenth century and then only grudgingly. Suspicion has always surrounded its innate ability to both replicate and transform the world in which we exist; novelists were, and are, a little too much like conjurors, talented gatekeepers between the known, the accountable and the fantastic and unobtainable. Aspirations to aesthetic quality brought with them mechanisms of self-limitation. Indeed the competition between the techniques evolved by the modernists and the realists testifies to an equal desire to seem the least inclined toward that terrible shortcoming, the distortion of actuality. And yet fiction as an industry is dominated by what the high cultural literati treat as subgenres, those which do indeed provide for the reader's innate desire not to be reminded of the world they are in but to be taken somewhere else. The romance novel has existed as a reliable brand of escapism since the eighteenth century and science fiction has more recently fed the dispositions of some who want the novel to shift them a little beyond the inventive potential of modern technology and others who are gratified by spectacles of things and beings 'out there'. Both are engaging in their own right and often executed with stylistic acumen by their practitioners but I have chosen to concentrate on the historical novel and crime for a number of reasons. Each, more than romance or science fiction, raises questions about the consensually presumed aesthetic superiority of mainstream fiction. As we have seen many of the New Postmodernists clothe themselves in the respectable garments of metafiction and the avant garde while pandering to the reader's most prurient instincts and inclinations. This, of course, causes one to ask why supposedly serious, mainstream literature feels able to diverge from all the rational and, dare one say, civilized inclinations that might obtain in the real world – without explanation – while crime fiction with its implicit licence to follow suit seems, as we shall see, largely reluctant to do so or apologetic when caught. The historical novel has proved to be the most popular and fascinating subgenre of the last 25 years. It is fascinating because it too, like the New Postmodernism, dresses itself very respectably – often nodding toward the end of the 'Grand Narratives' of conventional history – while repackaging and selling the past as a fantasy, a means of escape to somewhere, however dreadful, that releases us form the pointless drudgery of the present.

Chapter 5

The New Historical Novel

The historical novel flourished as a subgenre during the nineteenth century with Sir Walter Scott acknowledged as its most influential and popular practitioner. Scott's novels cover iconic episodes in English and Scottish history from the medieval period to the eighteenth century and usually set individuals against thrillingly adverse circumstances. A similar formula emerges in Dickens's *A Tale of Two Cities* (1859) and Charles Kingsley's *Westward Ho!* (1855) and *Hereward the Wake* (1866). In virtually all nineteenth-century historical fiction the past is used as a convenient canvas for presentations of epic and patriotic themes – particularly courage, generosity of spirit and endurance against palpably unjust and evil agencies. History is not so much rewritten as reshaped according to the conventional nineteenth-century notions of justice and heroism.

For much of the twentieth century the historical novel's status as a vehicle for, sometimes misguided, idealism caused it to be treated with respectful disdain by most writers with aspirations toward serious recognition. It was relegated to the substatus of popular fiction with the likes of Georgette Heyer recreating the Regency era as a blend of Jane Austen and periodized Hollywood-style romance and George MacDonald Fraser's long-running *Flashman* series offering a balefully satiric glance at the nineteenth century via the improbable escapades of his anti-hero. Innovative treatments of history – such as William Golding's spare, oblique exploration of the medieval mindset in *The Spire* – were for much of the century notable for their rarity. Since the 1970s, however, the historical novel has attained a status which outranks its nineteenth-century manifestation and which has involved the transformation of its established conventions. John Fowles's *The French Lieutenant's Woman* (1969) set the precedent for much of the writing of historical fiction of the succeeding three decades. Fowles recreates and undermines the nineteenth century's image of itself with his playful mimicry of the stylistic registers of its best-known 'realistic' novelists set alongside material from Darwin and Marx.

Peter Ackroyd draws upon and further explores issues raised by Fowles in a number of novels produced in the 1980s and 1990s. His first, *The Great Fire of London* (1982), is a reworking of Dickens's *Little Dorrit* and the device of anchoring the past to a familiar theme or network of ideas and then disrupting expectations has become the predominant feature of most of his subsequent fiction. In *The House of Doctor Dee* (1993) the narrative shifts between the world of the eponymous Dee, an Elizabethan alchemist, and that of Matthew Palmer, a contemporary academic researcher who inherits from his father the house in Clerkenwell once occupied by Dee. In various ways the two figures become obliquely aware of each other's presence and aside from the supernatural resonance of the plot – which turns upon the discovery that Palmer is actually a recreated 'homunculus', a human being invented by Dee – Ackroyd seems intent upon provoking comparisons between a state of mind that we take for granted, that of twentieth-century rationalism, and its sixteenth-century counterpart. Ackroyd surrounds Dee with an accurate recreation of sixteenth-century discourses and ideas but he also has Dee and Palmer drawn toward a similar troubling question as both reflect upon their respective notions of identity, and this involves language. Palmer often feels that he is close to a hardly describable form of mental breakdown, as though he is composed exclusively of the words he utters, while Dee, more dispassionately, comes to imagine both the self and the world as inscriptions in a single overarching book.

Ackroyd's earlier novel *Hawksmoor* (1985) involved a similar conceit. Hawksmoor the architect (1661–1736) is renamed Dyer and shares the narrative with a late twentieth-century police detective, called Hawksmoor, who is investigating a series of murders committed at London churches designed by the former. This mischievous play upon names and coincidences signposts the more perplexing effect of the two characters and their respective periods blurring and intertwining: eventually the borderlines between the eighteenth and the twentieth century virtually disappear. In *Milton in America* (1996) the eponymous poet takes refuge from vengeful royalists with sympathetic Puritans recently settled in the nascent colony. *Paradise Lost* and *Paradise Regained*, those epic explorations of the origin and nature of the human condition, will never be written. Instead Milton becomes involved in a crude, chaotically misguided attempt to recreate something of our unfallen state in the real world of seventeenth-century America. Ackroyd has since his time as a postgraduate student (resulting in *Notes for a New Culture: An Essay on Modernism*, 1976) been an advocate of radical, unconventional writing and he has combined this with an almost compulsive interest in the past to create an iconoclastic brand of historical fiction. The conventional history novel used and still uses traditional perceptions of history as a backdrop for, sometimes romanticized, invention. Ackroyd continually creates collisions between our sense of the past and our notions of ourselves. He plays with orthodox conceptions of history – Dee, Dyer/Hawksmoor and Milton tally with what we believe to be authentic paradigms of their periods – and then creates a spiral of questions: the past and the present begin to become unnervingly similar and our notion of the present as a secure and, by implication, superior perspective is undermined.

A near contemporary of Ackroyd's who has cultivated a similarly unconventional brand of fictive revisionism is Robert Nye. His best-known novels from the late 1970s onwards (*Falstaff*, 1976; *Merlin*, 1978; *Faust*, 1980; *The Memoirs of Lord Byron*, 1989; *The Late Mr Shakespeare*, 1998) focus upon figures who have attained cult-like status. Much debate has surrounded Falstaff, an invention of Shakespeare, whose presence adjacent to a very real figure of vast historical importance, Henry V, has created its own mythology. Nye exploits the uncertain relationship between verifiable truth and invention and confers upon his own version of Prince Hal's ribald companion a magnetic sense of immediacy; he appears to be speaking to the twentieth-century reader of pivotal events in British history. Nye's trademark is the exploitation and despoiling of historical mythologies, the creation of someone unnervingly, sometimes disagreeably, real from a fabric of possibilities.

Neither Ackroyd nor Nye saw themselves as initiators of a literary renaissance but it is certainly the case that since the 1970s the historical novel has become fiction's most prominent and enduring subgenre and has, moreover, unshackled itself from its earlier image as a somewhat lowbrow cousin to serious writing. Two other writers who treat the conventional relationship between the past and the present as uneasily coerced are Iain Sinclair (discussed above, pp. 68–9) and Lawrence Norfolk. Norfolk's *In the Shape of a Boar* (2000) shifts from ancient Greece to Romania on the brink of World War II, and then to 1970s Paris. More significant than the events recounted is Norfolk's preoccupation with records and methods of representation that either obscure such events or enable them to outlive their actual occurrence; hence the abundance of scholarly footnotes that continually draw our attention from the main narratives of the stories from Greek mythology and his emphasis upon how the Nazi officer, active in Romania, virtually reinvents himself, postwar, as a poet.

With some writers – notably Ackroyd, Nye, Pat Barker, Sebastian Faulks and William Boyd – the majority of their best work is historical, but virtually every other contemporary novelist of any significance has made significant contributions to this new current in fiction. For example, Martin Amis in *Times Arrow* (1991) causes time to literally take us back to the Holocaust; Julian Barnes in *Staring at the Sun* (1986) has a woman record her experiences of the twentieth and twenty-first centuries from her childhood in the 1930s to advanced old age in 2021; in *The Innocent* Ian McEwan offers a meticulous evocation of 1950s Cold War Europe.

Pat Barker is a writer of immense skill and virtuosity and her reputation is founded principally upon her trilogy of novels *Regeneration* (1991), *The Eye in the Door* (1993), *The Ghost Road* (1995), which explore the emotional and psychological consequences of being on active service in World War I. In *Regeneration* we encounter two very real presences whose writings did much to shape perception of the war for decades to come, Siegfried Sassoon and Wilfred Owen. While the novel is based partly upon known biographical occurrences, including Sassoon's sessions with the psychoanalyst Dr Rivers, a Freudian whose reluctant duty it is to restore Sassoon to a mental condition that will enable him to return to the Front, there is also a good deal of invention. She uses, for example, post-Freudian concepts of amnesia – specifically the reappearance of the past, both experienced and imagined, in the present – as a symptom of the effects of continuous bombardment and the persistent immediacy of death. Barker's knowledge of World War I was more than speculative – her grandfather fought in the war and spoke to her of his experiences

– but it was not first-hand. When she grew up during the 1950s and 1960s questions were for the first time being raised in public regarding the moral and political legitimacy of the war and what actually happened on the notorious Western Front. Up until then the conventional account of what the war involved – a costly, tragic but necessary response to German aggression – was rarely encroached upon by the private experiences of those involved. The sense of there being hidden, private narratives that might well run against both official accounts and unofficial yet totemic histories involving the like of Sassoon becomes the predominant theme of the second volume of the Regeneration trilogy, *The Eye in the Door* (1993).

Billy Prior, who plays a significant role in *Regeneration*, here moves to the centre of the novel. That he is a product purely of Barker's imagination corresponds with her use of him as an avatar, whose presence questions standard perceptions of what the period involved. Prior, a decorated soldier of working-class background, is promoted from the ranks to a commission and after each leave sets aside his growing sense that the war is futile and unjust and returns to France to share the horrific burden with his comrades. At the same time, he feels no antagonism towards the pacifists and conscientious objectors that he meets at home and whose activities he is asked, by his superiors, to undermine. Indeed he sympathizes with them, but he is unable to abandon his commitment to his associates at the Front, most of whom are equally disillusioned with the nature and purpose of the conflict. As the survivors of World War I became by the end of the twentieth century a small, fragile unit more attention was paid to subjective, first-hand accounts and while Barker is clearly offering a fictional counterpart to these one cannot help but wonder if she slightly overplays this opportunity for revisionism. Prior's alliance with the pacifists veers toward a heavy-handed polemic, constantly promoting the rubric that no-one wanted the war and, given the opportunity, most would have stopped it by refusing to participate. Persistent reference to Prior's sexuality gives one further cause to suspect that the novel is more a prismatic reconstruction of the period according to late twentieth-century expectations than a sympathetic attempt to recover the truth. He is as openly bisexual as it was possible to be at the time without risking prosecution and although one can be confident that there would have been as many bisexuals serving on the Western Front as there are among a similar number of men randomly selected from the general population circa 2005, Barker supplements this familiar treatment of the theme of hidden sexual orientation and historical change with another exercise in heavyweight psychoanalytical theorizing. Prior's bisexuality seems to symbolize his shifting perception of himself as a soldier split between a person at odds with immutable circumstances and another ghostlike presence over whom he has little or no control. Barker's dealings with events and their effects so horrible as to almost defy description are admirable – often the prose seems strained and harrowed by its self-appointed burden – but there is also the sense that her clear sympathy for the people she has reinvented is accompanied by something close to intellectual condescension. She appears, somewhat presumptuously, to be visiting upon the poor victims of an early twentieth-century act of idiocy and horror the smug wisdom of their late twentieth-century counterparts.

Sebastian Faulks, on the other hand, edges a little more toward respectful authenticity, tinged with romanticism. *Birdsong* (1993), his most celebrated and popular novel, begins with the Englishman Stephen Wraysford visiting Amiens in 1910 to work and stay with the Azaire family, owners of a local textile business. He has an affair with Mme Azaire, which concludes with her departure to live with her sister and his return to England. Faulks's use of this as a prelude to the novel's core narrative – Wraysford's experience as a serving officer in World War I in the Amiens region – is at once manipulative and problematic. It offers the reader a vignette of provincial fin de siècle European society and culture. The easy complacency of life is largely undisturbed by matters such as Wraysford's affair with Mme Azaire – a classic example of elemental desire disrupting the routines of bourgeois existence, with predictably hyperbolic descriptions of sex – and the ongoing labour dispute at the textile factory. But of course the late twentieth-century reader is fully aware that soon after 1910 something unimaginable, almost apocalyptic would occur. It is the equivalent of setting a mini-narrative on family life in the suburbs of Hiroshima or Nagasaki during the early summer of 1945. We, from our enlightened historical perspective, are placed in an unusual position as readers: whatever the author might choose to do with the characters we are certain that in due course there are specific events that will certainly affect their lives. Hence Faulks is able to weave into his prewar prelude moments that for the participants are circumscribed by immediacy but which for us carry a nasty extra-textual resonance. There is for example an episode when Wraysford and the Azaires visit the languid summer countryside to the east of Amiens. The descriptions burgeon with a blend of lazy innocence and sublimated sexuality but he also leaves the reader with enough clues – even if our own knowledge of World War I history is insufficient to warn us – that quite soon a very different form of blending of the human body with the natural world – mud, bones, tissue and blood – will occur in this same place.

Faulks counterpoints the main story, involving the war itself, with a briefer narrative set in the late 1970s in which the adult English granddaughter of Wraysford's affair learns from her mother of who her grandparents were and what they experienced. Her perceptions of and presumptions about herself are as a consequence altered and there is an indication that Faulks is using her as an apologist for his enterprise: this novel, by showing you history within an almost remembered period, will cause you to re-examine your complacent notions of the present.

The most frequently cited text in current debates surrounding the nature and impact of our perceptions of history is Francis Fukuyama's 'The End of History' (1989; expanded and included in the 1992 book *The End of History and The Last Man*, Hamish Hamilton). Despite the mythology of radical tendentiousness that still surrounds the essay, its conclusions are quite straightforward and difficult to refute. The conflicts between monoliths of power and ideology that had, since the Renaissance, divided much of the world against itself have now ceased, with the effective and largely bloodless victory of liberal capitalism over its last significant opponent, Soviet-bloc communism. Irrespective of Fukuyama's accuracy as a historical diagnostician the significance of his essay as, intentionally or not, a reflection of a much broader intellectual and cultural mindset was immense. For many, history did seem to have come to an end. The prevailing norm had become the kind of liberal, largely democratic, free-enterprise state pioneered in Europe and the US from the nineteenth century onwards. There were and are plenty of aberrations from this norm – for example, dictatorships of no particular ideological designation and the predominance of Islamic law and principle in some states – but they are just that, aberrations; the face-to-face political and military tension between NATO and the Warsaw Pact, capable of annihilating most of the planet, has gone away.

There was certainly no straightforward causal relationship between Fukuyama's prognosis and the tenor of fiction writing but a case can be found that his claims reflected a broader, collective intuition that history as we knew it was about to enter an unprecedented phase. The new fashion for the serious historical novel, which used the devices of fiction to explore elemental relationships between our self-perception and our notions of the past, began in the 1980s when the Cold War seemed to become gradually more of a costly abstraction than a threat and the closing years of which saw the dismantling of the East–West divide.

Although few treat the cessation of the Cold War as their principal subject it is notable that a large number of the most celebrated, respectable, examples of historical fiction appeared toward the end of the 1980s and in the early 1990s. In 1982 William Boyd published *An Ice Cream War*, a well-researched, historically credible story set in East Africa during World War I. What took place there was a rather shambolic, almost endearing, encounter in which two colonial powers, Britain and Germany, felt obliged to mount occasional military assaults upon each other. Boyd's broader implications are clear enough: this war is surreal, farcical, pointless; it is a perverse echo of its horrible counterpart in Europe. If the book can be said to carry an ideological resonance it is that of left-of-centre scepticism about the past, particularly Britain's notion of its imperial past. Boyd's *The New Confessions* (1987) was more ambitious, with its main character, John James Todd, born in 1899 and thereafter encountering and recording some of the pivotal and most contentious periods in twentieth-century history: World War I, postwar British bohemianism, Berlin in the 1930s; World War II, Hollywood and the McCarthy era and back to Britain for post-1950s Cold War stagnation. Todd is a sagacious amiable figure. His particular chronicle of the twentieth century is a careful amalgam of wit, puzzlement and, where appropriate, horror. At the same time, however, one senses Boyd as an intercessionary presence making sure that the reader does not lose track of exactly what is happening in the world at various points in Todd's subjective account. For instance in 1922 he meets in a pub his prewar school friend, Hamish, and the conversation soon turns to Hamish's ongoing academic obsession: 'Theories of relativity, I think he said. I could make nothing of it, but I was strangely affected by his passion'. But Boyd is fully aware that the reasonably well-educated 1987 reader would indeed make something of it and would nod in recognition as Hamish explains to a bemused Todd that 'Astonishingly things are happening, John. The most amazing revelations. Everything is changing. Science is changing. We look at the world differently now' (*New Confessions*, Penguin, 1988, p. 208).

Again we encounter the intermeshing of an attempt at unpremeditated authenticity with a textbook litany of historically significant moments. Hamish's obsession with relativity as a provable revolutionary concept speaks directly to a late twentieth-century reader while Todd broods uncomprehendingly upon his friend's comments, much as he does as a mute, bemused witness to many other occurrences whose significance is much clearer to us in our retrospective wisdom. The closing paragraph of the novel points up the intent of its preceding 500 pages:

> As I stand here on my modest beach, waiting for my future, watching the waves roll in, I feel a strange, light-headed elation. After all, this is the Age of Uncertainty and Incompleteness. (p. 528)

Todd is our guide through the twentieth century; he embodies and speaks to us of a century that is convulsed by unprecedented events, which cannot predict its own future, but which has moved to a point where uncertainty can almost segue into optimism. The book was written during the period of Gorbachev's governance of the Soviet Union, when it was evident to anyone who read or watched the news that the Cold War was coming to a close.

Within months of the Berlin Wall coming down Adam Thorpe began work on *Ulverton* (1992), his first and best-known novel. The place, the village of the title, is a conceit; its real topic is the enigma of historical change. The chronicle of Ulverton from the seventeenth century onwards becomes almost magically infused with questions about why and how individuals indulged, resisted or animated the mutations of history.

In 1989 Rose Tremain published her most celebrated historical novel, *Restoration*, the story of Robert Merivel, a courtier to Charles II, enjoying the rampant hedonism of 1660s London that followed the puritan restraints of the Cromwellian republic. The novel is a magnificent example of researched minutiae – from hats through menus to sexual indecorum – strained through a gripping narrative. But one also senses that its true subject is the circularity of history.

Charles's court and Merivel's experiences would for most 1989 readers have caught an echo of Thatcherite indulgence after Labour-dominated temperance. Although there was no witting connection between Fukuyama's work and Tremain's they seemed in the same year to have reached remarkably similar conclusions regarding the one feature of society and humanity that transcends historical change, which persists, endures and is ultimately victorious – the doctrine of personal attainment and conspicuous consumption. Tremain, like many of her peers, seemed confident in her ability to step aside and take stock of what history actually is – perhaps because all now shared an incipient sense of history as the more fascinating because of its virtual completion.

A. S. Byatt in *Possession* (1990) has two contemporary scholars researching the works of and relationship between the Victorian poets Randolph Henry Ash and Christabel LaMotte. The novel won Byatt the Booker Prize partly, it was argued, because of its brilliant exhibitions of cultural ventriloquism. Ash and LaMotte are in their writings almost perfect recreations of Robert Browning and Christina Rossetti. For those who knew and valued the works of the latter pair it was as though lost and authentic manuscripts had suddenly been discovered. Impressed and fascinated as one is by Byatt's ability to recover the past through a recreation of its art and mannerisms one is equally puzzled by the question of why the novel comprises very little else. The two modern researchers, Roland Michell and Maud Bailey, are affected by their uncovering of an unalloyed, elemental passion that existed beneath the patina of nineteenth-century restraint to the extent that their own emotional and sexual lives seem calculated and arid by comparison.

The notion of the past as an exciting, edifying point of contrast with the present is a mainstay of recent historical fiction but there is a factor that goes beyond this and which is evident in the work of Boyd, Thorpe, Ackroyd, Tremain et al., and it is this. Irrespective of gestures toward lost periods as independent worlds there is a prevailing, overarching inclination among practitioners of the new historical novel toward lofty omniscience. The past is offered up in its fascinating, beguiling, often admirable peculiarity yet such gestures are underpinned by an implicit claim on the part of the author. The unpredictable mechanisms and trajectories of history seem now to have given way to a state of irreversible stasis and torpidity, and from this secure perspective novelists assume to know the past better than it knew itself.

It is evident from the works dealt with so far that three dimensions of history – too broad and elastic to be termed 'periods' – have proved particularly attractive for historical novelists of the past two decades: Britain's coming-of-age, involving the sixteenth-century Renaissance and Reformation and the formative, turbulent seventeenth century; High Victorian Britain, with the empire at its zenith, the industrial revolution at full pelt and individuals enmeshed in a stultifying network of social and moral codes; and war, particularly the two world wars of the twentieth century. As one becomes more familiar with their fictional treatments their attractions for novelists and readers alike become self-evident.

Iain Pears's *An Instance of the Fingerpost* (1997) is in the tradition of Umberto Eco's *The Name of the Rose* and set in late seventeenth-century Oxford. The novel blends the ever-popular narrative drive of the whodunit with a more respectable element of mystery, specifically our fascination with what exactly went on in the minds of those who lived at a turning point between unquestioning medievalism and the adventurous, often dangerous, trend toward intellectual freedom that would eventually become the Enlightenment. More recently, the first two-thirds of his *The Dream of Scipio* (2002) involve, respectively, fifth-century Gaul and fourteenth-century France and again the detail and scaffolding of scholarly authenticity is shot through with an appeal to the reader's suspicion that the distant past just might involve the inexplicable, the almost magical – an allurement that has without doubt secured the popularity of one of the best-selling novels of recent years, Dan Brown's *The Da Vinci Code* (2004).

Havoc in its Third Year (2004) by Ronan Bennett shows us England in the 1630s, shifting inexorably towards civil war. Bennett does not deal with the high politics of the period but his picture of the lives of a small number of inhabitants of a northern provincial town is equally evocative of the divisions, suspicions and tensions which beset the country at the time. This spectrum involved the closed mindset and political-religious intolerance of the hard-line Calvinists and Puritans, the confused ambivalent attitude toward Catholicism as the 'old religion', and the fear of it as a hive of conspiracies based in continental Europe and feeding activists through the leaky borders with Ireland and Scotland, all intent on visiting an unimaginable vengeance upon Protestant England. The main character, Brigge, one of the town's governors, embodies a state of collective paranoia. He is a covert follower of Catholicism but in his public role is obliged to act as instrument of the State, often against those charged with similar though treasonous affiliations. Occasionally one suspects that Bennett is indulging in a rather cumbersome use of history-as-allegory. In inns, in church and in the street people are constantly, nervously alert to each other, looking for signs that someone they thought they knew might be a subversive or a government agent searching for such signals from others in order to track them down. It all smacks of familiar literary and cinematic presentations of life in Eastern Europe before the end of the 1980s, and more germanely of a region that Bennett knows personally and has written about in fiction, journalism and television drama, Northern Ireland. The atmosphere of muted division and anxiety could even be seen as prescient; his evocation of apparently dull routine public settings instilled with fear and suspicion catches perfectly the mood of London commuters following the July 2005 bombings by Islamic extremists.

What elevates the novel above listless, simplistic allegory is Bennett's presentation of the capacity for brutality, casual and enthusiastic, that sits so uncomfortably against our conventional perception of the seventeenth century as pivotal in the movement toward humanism and rationality. After every Court of Session the streets are littered with public spectacles of humiliation and pain, with the lash, the bridle, the brand, the stock and the gallows as the standard furniture of daily existence. Many, with noble exceptions such as Brigge, regard this as the norm and often derive a prurient, macabre pleasure from it, and here Bennett inserts wonderfully sly questions for the twenty-first-century reader. Are you enjoying it too? If you are, how different are you from those sad denizens of the 1630s?

The combination of grotesquery and near-romantic fascination that sustains our interest in the sixteenth and seventeenth centuries derives primarily from the fact that the period involves such a beguiling mixture of fact and speculation. We are certain that some people existed – Elizabeth I, Charles I, Shakespeare, Donne, Milton, Newton – but printed records of events were in their infancy and in the intervening four centuries hypothesis and invention have avidly occupied the gaps left by this scarcity of documentation. This has exercised an inevitable magnetism for fiction, a genre where the borders between authenticity and fabulation are ever shifting. Rodney Bolt's *History Play* (2005) reflects the addictive qualities of the period. It is a fictional account of the life of Christopher Marlowe, whom several scholars and historians have presented as the true author of several works hitherto attributed to Shakespeare, mainly because he seems more deserving of this honour, being better educated, a scion of minor nobility, a rake, a spy and victim of a gruesome murder. Bolt has Marlowe stage his own death. He flees to the continent and spends 14 years in exile writing sonnets and plays while awaiting his return as literary and political hero.

The nineteenth century holds a particular fascination for historical novelists and their readers for the simple reason that throughout the twentieth century British society was involved in a self-conscious, embarrassed dialogue between what it is and what it, quite recently, was. The very notion of Britishness was a creation of the nineteenth century. The behemoth of its class system still reverberates through all aspects of an apparently more enlightened culture, and more significantly Victorian codes of morality and ethics proved so durable as to make hapless, self-indulgent, often self-destructive behaviour the only other option. As a consequence late twentieth and early twenty-first-century novelists tend to treat the nineteenth century as a shibboleth. They take on board its self-procured mythologies and images and, sometimes as an act of revenge, sometimes out of sympathy, dismantle and reassemble them.

Jane Rogers's *Mr Wroe's Virgins* (1991), Victoria Glendinning's *Electricity* (1995), Sarah Waters's *Tipping the Velvet* (1998), *Affinity* (1999) and *Fingersmith* (2002), Michel Faber's *The Crimson Petal and The White* (2002), Iain Pears's *The Portrait* (2005), Andrew Martin's *The Blackpool High Flyer* (2004), Susanna Clarke's *Jonathan Strange and Mr Norrell* (2004) and Sonia Overall's *The Realm of Shells* (2006) all function as respectful disclosures, treatments of the conventional images of nineteenth-century society not exactly as falsifications of the truth but more as public versions of a more peculiar and unusual fabric. Sexuality, almost inevitably, is an ongoing theme. Byatt's *Possession* is a classic case of inventive prurience disguised as learned fascination. Irrespective of our respect for Browning, Rossetti and Victorian culture we are equally beguiled by the prospect of contemplating the lurid passionate subtext of a century whose public discourses treated sex as virtually nonexistent.

Misfortune (2005), the first novel of Wesley Stace – also known in his singing career as John Wesley Harding – offers a coy glance toward Wilde's *The Importance of Being Earnest*, albeit backdated several decades. *Misfortune* begins with a young musician being handed a mysterious package wrapped in tarp and rags and told to toss it into the Thames. Instead he leaves it upon a rubbish tip where it is dug out by a stray dog and transported to the aristocrat Lord Geoffrey Loveall who through some unspecified inconvenience has paused by the dump in his splendid carriage. Loveall, delicate and outstandingly rich, has for most of his life been mourning the untimely death of his infant sister and decides, on discovering that the parcel contains a living baby, that the fates have vouchsafed him her replacement. For some reason – quite possibly Loveall's distaste for baseness – he does not notice that the child is actually male and thereafter 'Rose' is raised as Loveall's adopted sister, with Loveall's associates and underlings apparently unwilling or unable to disabuse him of his illusion. The curious arrangement becomes, of course, more complicated as the fashionably skirted Rose reaches adolescence and begins to share a bed with the family friend Sarah Harrison.

The book is well researched in terms of its ability to capture the detached world inhabited by English aristocrats of the late nineteenth century but its abiding purpose is to turn the Victorian obsession with sexual obfuscation against itself. Desire and sexuality are ever present but they run against the official version of how matters ought to be, in this case a tragicomic designation of the wrong gender. That this should have been initiated and maintained by a figure whose prestige, wealth and status guarantees that no one will challenge him cements the novel's prevailing image of a society where decorum, repression and wilfully absurd falsification go hand in hand.

There is an unbidden irony in the fact that Henry James despised the historical novel, which he found implausible and populist, because there have recently been two significant examples of this genre focused exclusively upon James's life. The irony is particularly sharp in that David Lodge in *Author, Author* (2004) and Colm Tóibín in *The Master* (2004) seem obsessed with pointing up the dichotomy between James's image as a writer for whom the almost symphonic complexity of sentences was a welcome substitute for the transparent or the commonplace and the living presence behind the syntax. Lodge even gives inordinate attention to the, one assumes undeniable, fact that James was prone to belching, farting and urinating. Tóibín is more controversial in his indications that James's probable homosexuality was a formative influence upon his cultured, evasive manner as a writer. On one occasion in the novel James recalls his avoidance of what appears to be an invitation from his friend, the homosexual Paul Joukovsky, that they spend the night together. Nothing specific is stated of what James imagined he was avoiding but we are told of how in his recollection, and hypothesis, he pictures the two of them walking upstairs in silence. The passage then ceases abruptly and the focus of the narrative shifts elsewhere. Without making the point explicitly Tóibín draws subtle parallels between the character he creates – a figure who continually extinguishes those patterns of thought which might lead him to confront issues long-suppressed – and the novelist whose trademark, particularly in his later work, was a combination of circumspection and avoidance.

The attraction of James to historical novelists is obvious and unavoidable in that his art reflects the broader cultural and social propensities of his period. Both novels distinguish between those elements of existence thought suitable for contemplation or public discourse and those best consigned to the vacuum of the unwritten or unutterable. With regular modern disclosures of what did go on beneath the surface – such as the meticulously researched *A Private Life of Henry James* (1998) by Lyndall Gordon for example – there becomes available for the novelist an irresistible opportunity to work creatively in those spaces between the public and private worlds.

Two recent novels indicate that the more astute practitioners of historical fiction are beginning to tire of the assumption that the nineteenth century comprised only a limitless trove of recoverable guilty secrets. In Julian Barnes's *Arthur and George* (2005) the latter is George Edalji, half Indian, a Midlands' solicitor and vicar's son falsely imprisoned for mutilating horses and the former is Arthur Conan Doyle who privately investigated the case and eventually secured a pardon for Edalji. Barnes adheres scrupulously to the well-documented facts and never employs inventive licence to suggest that the prejudices that underpinned the case were any less or more severe than disclosed in the documentary accounts. Instead he creates a modestly elegant novel out of a very real collision of actuality and literary mythology. Doyle steps into the fiction as a figure who closely resembles his own creation, Holmes, and while this carries a trace of postmodern whimsy there is the more compelling resonance of a very real character driven by a respect for truth and justice.

In *Kept: A Victorian Mystery* (2006), D. J. Taylor achieves a hall-of-mirrors recreation of the mid-nineteenth century that is more impressive in its execution and more challenging than Fowles's *A French Lieutenant's Woman* or Byatt's *Possession*. Hardly a paragraph goes by without leaving the impression that one has strayed into a lost novel by Dickens, Gissing, Gaskell or Thackeray. But rather than use these superb exhibitions of stylistic ventriloquism as a means of exposing states of costive hypocrisy – in the manner of Fowles – he works as the equivalent of a literary psychic, allowing his colloquy of dead novelists to write not about things that ethical probity would have forced them to ignore or obscure but stories and events to which, circumstances permitting, they might easily have given their attention.

'Another week, another war novel' began James Hopkins in his review of Adam Thorpe's *Nineteen Twenty-One* (2001) (*Guardian*, 14 July 2001) and he went on to 'wonder what Adam Thorpe can contribute to the ever growing canon of contemporary fiction about the Great War'. The subtext of Hopkins's wearied enquiry points us to a parallel between the popularity of the nineteenth century as a subject for the historical novel and almost equal attention given to both world wars. In both instances there is a fruitful discontinuity between officially sanctioned histories and the accounts that these judiciously remodelled or left out. Barker and Faulks set the standard by counterposing the tendentious, unpredictable nature of personal experience and attendant emotions against the grand narratives of conflict. World War I has presented the most fertile ground for invention for two reasons. Those who were actually involved or had contemporaneous knowledge of the war had become by the late 1980s a very minor part of the collective national memory. Their function, like the Victorians, was that of subject rather than audience and as a consequence more licence was available to novelists who made use of them. Also, since the 1960s it has become the routine, rarely questioned mantra that the Great War was an instance of soulless imperialism, the pointless mass slaughter of an innocent generation – the immense popularity of the musical, staged and filmed as *Oh What a Lovely War*, and more recently *The Monocled Mutineer* and Ben Elton's *Blackadder Goes Forth* testify to this as the popular consensus. Novelists were therefore provided with an audience whose responses would be benignly predictable.

Barker had already made use of the literary reputations of Sassoon and Owen as prisms for our perception of the war and Thorpe in *Nineteen Twenty-One* takes this a stage further by setting his novel in the year preceding that which many regard as the apex of modernism – 1922 saw the publication of Joyce's *Ulysses*, Eliot's *The Waste Land*, Yeats's *Later Poems*, Woolf's *Jacob's Room* and D. H. Lawrence's *Aaron's Rod*. The narrator, Joseph Munrow, is a novelist manqué aiming 'to write a giant novel of our times' and he is also Thorpe's means of exploring the effect of the war upon the history of twentieth-century literature. Munrow escapes conscription, respectably, but is thereafter affected and fascinated by his battle-scarred contemporaries who haunt postwar Britain like ghosts of their former selves. An avowed realist, he wants to write the novel that will fully capture the experiences of his peers, and while he feels he has an advantage over the veterans – objectivity and relative sanity – he is confounded by writer's block, a problem he attempts to overcome with diligent, sometimes macabre research. On one occasion he visits the sites of the major battles of the Western Front, a location where in 1921 the bones of the unrecovered corpses still poked through the topsoil. The novel's *raison d'être* is to address the question of why the war, the most apocalyptic and incomprehensible in modern history, was largely ignored by practitioners of an equally unprecedented mode of writing, the modernists. The answer, according to Thorpe, is relatively straightforward. The modernists were largely noncombatants who used their avowed aesthetic as a guilt-dispelling strategy of avoidance; those involved were too traumatized to offer a comprehensive naturalistic account; and Munrow, caught between the two, enacts this thesis.

Another example of the Great War as the foundation for a counternarrative is Sebastian Barry's *A Long Long Way* (2005). It begins in 1915 and all of its major characters are Irish, predominantly the 18-year-old Willie Dunne who, too short to follow his father into the police service, responds to Kitchener's appeal and enlists – an act endorsed by the Irish nationalist leader John Redmond who took Lloyd George at his word that support in the war effort would be rewarded by home rule. The hideous experiences of the Irish troops are supplemented by the Easter Rising in 1916; having witnessed their comrades literally torn to pieces on the Western Front, they return to find their homeland in a state of colonial civil war and themselves regarded by many as traitors. Even though the political-national contexts are broadened the novel shares with its British counterparts a sense of how, 90 years on, the distant and unimaginable can only properly be understood with the assistance of the inventive resources of fiction.

World War II was, though unwelcome and horrible, far less morally ambiguous than its predecessor; a just and honourable campaign against a demonstrably evil aggressor. This might be the reason why so many professional writers who lived through and fought in the war have offered relatively slight treatment of it in their work: to make use of such experiences in what is, in the end, a recreational and diversionary medium, tarnishes their memory. Hence the contemporary novelist, detached by a generation or more from the event, faces a dilemma: how can they make literary claims upon territory that their immediate predecessors, who knew it intimately, have kept at a respectful distance?

Faulks in *Charlotte Gray* (1998) opts for a combination of the heroic and romantic. The eponymous heroine falls in love with a fighter pilot and when he fails to return from a mission she volunteers as an intelligence officer, is parachuted into occupied France and assists the Resistance in attempting to protect vulnerable children from transportation to a concentration camp.

Thorpe in *The Rules of Perspective* (2005) reprises his aesthetic conceit of *Nineteen Twenty-One*, but this time shifts from literature to the visual arts. Two main characters are involved, Corporal Neal Parry, an aspiring American commercial artist, now part of the post-D-Day push across Western Europe, and Herr Hoffer, acting director of a museum in Nazi Germany. Thorpe continually juxtaposes the pure horror of the war against the potential of art, by its nature, to improve upon its subject, and raises an obvious question. Even though the ethics of the conflict were unambiguous can its horrific particulars ever be the inspiration for art? The answer is itself a conundrum; art persists and must persist as a token of civilization but when the latter collapses it should take its particular aesthetic with it.

Sarah Waters' first three novels exposed the lurid, sometimes horrific, underpinnings of Victorian decorum and in *The Night Watch* (2006) she turns her attention to the London of World War II. The narrative moves between the wartime years of 1941 and 1944 and then to 1947 when the citizens of the capital were trying to balance their sense of relief against the dreary aftermath of the conflict. The novel is meticulously researched. Speech idioms and tactile particulars are rendered with convincing yet understated authenticity and provide a canvas for her principal themes of gender and sexuality. Kay, a mannish lesbian, finds her vocation as an ambulance driver, routinely performing feats of courage and acting as an emotional buttress for her less secure colleagues, male and female. Helen, also a lesbian, runs a marriage bureau with Viv and both help to rejuvenate and provide support for individuals psychologically damaged by the war. The novel is not simply an apologia for lesbianism against the costive prejudices of 1940s Britain; rather it seeks to show how war is indiscriminately unpleasant and can force to the surface the inherent selflessness of individuals, irrespective of their sexuality.

David Baddiel's *The Secret Purposes* (2004) shows that even World War II is not entirely immune from the presumptuousness that often accompanies creativity. It is an account of the wartime experiences of a Jewish refugee who arrives in England from continental Europe, faces a tribunal who judge him a potential enemy of the state and is despatched to the Isle of Man. Baddiel's point, lumberingly overstated, is that anti-Semitism was also a feature of British society. Polemic and political revisionism masked as fiction is not uncommon but the alignment by implication of bumbling, officious British civil servants, with those who executed the Final Solution indicates that the rich treasury of recent history is prone to misuse.

The resurgence of the historical novel since the 1970s provides an intriguing codicil to the tensions between realism and postmodernism in mainstream fiction. With few exceptions – principally Ackroyd – historical fiction has made unapologetic, manipulative use of the conventions of realism. All of the standard mechanisms of mimesis and authenticity have been redeployed and instead of encountering fictionalized versions of ourselves and our peers we are now offered the supplementary excitement of watching the past as though time travel had allowed us to witness its convincing particulars. The slightly prurient thrill of knowing so much about the private lives and thoughts of so many people, which was always part of the allure of the classic realist text, has now been extended to involve us in comparisons – moral, ethical and cultural – between our time zone and theirs.

Chapter 6

Crime and Spy Fiction

Since the 1970s the mainstays of British crime writing have been Reginald Hill, Colin Dexter, Ruth Rendell (aka Barbara Vine), R. D. Wingfield, Ian Rankin and P. D. James. Dexter's Morse, the detective inspector without a Christian name, operates as an intermediary between the enclosed micro-societies of Oxford colleges – he is himself a graduate of the university – and the apparent vulgarity of the world outside, often bearing witness to the endemic nastiness of both. Wingfield's Frost, degreeless and lacking Morse's appreciation for classical music and other aspects of high culture, compensates with an intuitive almost feral intellect. He is a mild version of Hill's Detective Superintendent Dalziel, a corpulent Yorkshire hedonist with an inclination toward brutality when conventional methods of detection fail him. Rendell's Inspector Wexford is a mid-cultural approximation of Morse and more comfortably suburban than Frost and Dalziel, and P. D. James's Commander Dalgliesh stands out as a figure who bestrides contemporaneity and the pre-1960s golden age of crime writing, the latter beginning with the distractedly brilliant Sherlock Holmes and in the 1940s involving the likes of Edmund Crispin's Oxford Professor of Literature Gervase Fen. Dalgliesh inhabits a Britain that is unmistakably recent (1970s–2000s, and like many of his peers he seems able almost miraculously to avoid the more significant signs of aging), yet he maintains an enigmatic aloofness from its more vulgar and base tendencies. He is a published poet, a dimension of his life that seems, intentionally or not, appropriate given his creator's equal skill in deploying literary craftsmanship as an antidote to the abominations of violence and death.

Frequently these major-domos of the CID will have a full-time junior assistant, whose function is to point up their recondite genius and flaws. Dalziel, the foul-mouthed misogynist, is perfectly partnered with Pascoe, the *Guardian*-reading, politically correct graduate, and Morse's Lewis brings an occasional dose of working-class common sense to his senior's more abstruse reasonings. Rendell puts a slight twist upon the formula by making Detective Sgt Burden Wexford's uncomfortably ambitious intellectual equal.

The reason why writing such as this is ranked as a subspecies of fiction per se lies in its adherence to and maintenance of a predictable formula. This allows of variations – sometimes despite the best efforts of the detective the suspect might remain at large or the identity of the true perpetrator uncertain – but some elements are by consensus inflexible. The detectives – and even their entrepreneurial cousins the private investigators – are always presented as morally superior to the lawbreakers. Certainly, the former will be well laden with character defects, largely as a salve to authenticity, but a clear line of demarcation always exists between what they are inclined to do, even in the most arduous circumstances, and offences committed by the people they investigate.

This is understandable given that the attractions of crime writing are underpinned by a fabric of hypocrisies and self-contradictions. Fiction, along with its relatives theatre and film, frequently gratifies an enduring but rarely admitted taste among a large number of its readers: the prurient thrill which comes from witnessing something terrible or macabre while remaining immune from it or its consequences. For many readers this will be accompanied by commensurate feelings of guilt, fuelled partly by a personal sense of unease at taking pleasure from the distress of others, albeit fictional, and also by a sense of social responsibility, a suspicion that an attraction to depictions of criminal misbehaviour might carry a trace of condoning or complicity. Hence, most crime writers and their readers appear to have entered into a tacit consensus on how the guilty attractions of reading about crime should be ameliorated by a countercurrent of dependable honesty and attendance to the absolutes of right and wrong.

As a consequence of this, mainstream crime fiction is tied to self-limiting conventions similar to those that inform the medieval morality play or the kind of Victorian novel which promulgated the ethical norms of the period. Characters and circumstances can be made believable only to the extent that they do not fail in their predetermined functions as indices to abstract codes of behaviour. Realism – in its broadest definition as the ability to explore and represent without comment any form of human circumstance, inclination or activity – is therefore severely constrained.

US crime fiction has shown itself more inclined to transgress this formula, often by shifting the narrative focus away from the mindset of the investigator and toward that of the perpetrator, a procedure which carries an attendant question: might you, reader, be capable of this? Mid-twentieth-century classics include James M. Cain's *The Postman Always Rings Twice* (1934) and *Double Indemnity* (1936), and Patricia Highsmith's *Strangers on a Train* (1950) and *The Talented Mr. Ripley* (1956). Soon afterwards US writers began to pose questions regarding the sacrosanct state of the police themselves. In John Ball's *In the Heat of the Night* (1965) endemic racism within Southern policing is exposed, and in virtually all of Elmore Leonard's novels from the 1970s onwards the criminal and the detective are equally dismissive of ethical codes of behaviour; the narrative is driven simply by whether the latter or the former will in the end triumph and neither is presented as by their nature the more admirable or amiable. In the same vein Joseph Wambaugh's groundbreaking *The New Centurions* (1971) and *The Choirboys* (1975) offer us California-based police departments made up of alcoholics, racists, drug addicts, perverts, even murderers, albeit via a filter of very dark comedy. Walter Mosley's black private investigator Easy Rawlins acts as a lens for the strata of exploitative violence, corruption and racism in US society from the 1940s to the 1960s. He is a decent man but no better than he has to be, distrusting the police and the legal system as a whole and often surviving via his ability to incite fear in others. Mosley's exercises in dispassionate naturalism find a more disturbing echo in Lawrence Black's Keller (*Hit List*, 2000). Keller occupies the centre of the narrative as a compelling beguiling presence, a man of dry wit and integrity. His profession? Self-employed hit man. James Ellroy in *American Tabloid* (1995), *White Jazz* (1992) and *The Cold Six Thousand* (2001) intercuts invention with meticulously researched scenarios from US politics and social history of the 1950s and 1960s. J. F. and Edward Kennedy appear alongside, sometimes meet, figures from the Mafia and characters – some fictional, some actual – who frequently cross the line between CIA-sponsored terrorism and pure criminality.

The British writer best known to have made rather modest claims upon the US form of unbridled crime fiction is Ian Rankin, whose series involving the Edinburgh-based Inspector John Rebus began with *Knots and Crosses* (1987). Rebus is prone to depressive bouts of introspection, often accompanied by infusions of alcohol, and he seems by temperament and background to fit in with the rough urban working classes who are responsible for much of Edinburgh's day-to-day fabric of criminality. At the same time, however, he never quite dishonours his profession, his litany of failed relationships is presented as a tragic consequence of his commitment to the job and he views, and has the reader view, with circumspect disdain the pomposities of the Edinburgh middle classes and nouveau riche. Some have treated Rebus's fictional environment as comparable with that created by Irvine Welsh but this is part of the false mythology of the Scottish literary renaissance (see pp. 165–8). In truth, Rebus is only a little more unorthodox than the likes of Dalziel and Frost. He makes something of his existential crises and coat-trails his working-class Scottishness, with its collision of roughness and vulnerability, but beyond that the formulae that inhibit the mainstream of British crime fiction remain undisturbed.

By far the most impressive British crime writer of the 1970s–1990s period is Bill James. Sadly and unconscionably he is also the least recognized, featuring neither in Martin Priestman's *Crime Fiction from Poe to the Present* (Northcote House/British Council, 1998) nor *The Cambridge Companion to Crime Fiction* (ed. Priestman, Cambridge University Press, 2003). James's novels, involving principally, though not exclusively, Detective Chief Superintendent Colin Harpur and Assistant Chief Constable Desmond Iles, ran from *You'd Better Believe It* (1985) to *Pay Days* (2001) and the moral and ethical truancies of his policemen bring to mind Wambaugh and Ellroy. Harpur is a serial adulterer who is particularly besotted with Denise, a local undergraduate student almost half his age. His wife, Megan, begins an affair with his ex-colleague, recently promoted to the Metropolitan Police and, in *Roses, Roses* (1993) is stabbed to death – probably by the henchman of a villain Harpur has had sent down, we never know – during her return from London. Iles, a man of lupine sophistication and dry wit spends some of his time berating the liberal imbecilities of his senior, Lane, while occasionally exploding into almost murderous spasms of rage against both colleagues and villains, particularly those among the former, Harpur included, who have slept with his wife.

Iles attempts, habitually, to seduce one of Harpur's teenage daughters and for downmarket lechery trawls the docks for as yet unfallen virgins who he can rescue from local pimps, but always ensuring that he has sex with them first. Also he murders a local gangster, who seems immune from prosecution, in a particularly sadistic, ritualistic manner. Add to this cast Jack Lamb, a wealthy dealer in stolen art protected by Harpur as his best informer plus 'Panicking' Ralph Ember, sex addict, killer and keeper of the bar where most of the local criminal desolates gather and you have a menu that is the most bizarre and refreshing alternative to conventional British crime writing since William Harrison Ainsworth's *Jack Sheppard. A Romance* (1839).

Alongside his fascinatingly grotesque cast James is a consummate stylist, bringing to the rather staid mechanisms of the crime novel a learned darkly comic bitterness redolent of Waugh or the Amises father and son. The only author who can rival James for unorthodoxy is Jake Arnott. *The Long Firm* (1999) was celebrated as the most original crime novel in living memory but in truth it is an adaptation of the techniques of James Ellroy to a British setting, specifically London in the mid-1960s. The narrative is shared by a young rent-boy, a hardened villain called Jack the Hat, a dissolute Tory peer, a fading starlet called Ruby Ryder, and a young sociology teacher, all of whom are drawn into the orbit of the mobster Harry Starks. The technique is impressive because although we never have transparent access to the mindset of Harry, the five narrators disclose a presence at once characteristic, pitiable and frighteningly ruthless. Like Ellroy, Arnott furnishes the text with enough period detail to secure authenticity without clogging the narrative, and more significantly he interweaves invented characters and events with some very real ones. The Krays, Tom Driberg, Peter Rachman, Evelyn Waugh, Liza Minelli and Johnnie Ray all play cameo roles which both correspond with biographical fact and often cross the line into the realm of the possible and credible. Ruby, Rachman's sometime lover, informs us that he prefers sex on top and facing away from her and Lord 'Teddy' Thursby notes in his diary that at the previous night's party he 'Nearly tripped over Tom Driberg, Honourable Member for Barking, on his knees, energetically sucking away' (*The Long Firm*, Sceptre 2003, p. 59).

Arnott's overall objective, one suspects, is to impart to crime fiction a degree of purpose and gravitas, to shift it beyond its popular status as an easy recreational mode to that which engages the reader at a deeper intellectual and temperamental level. His choice of the 1960s testifies to this purpose in that it is routinely regarded as the decade in which Britain finally unshackled itself from the codes of morality and behaviour and the class-based social structure that had been its formative elements for the previous century. Arnott addresses many of these issues, most specifically sexuality: he presents Harry Starks as open, energetically homosexual while in all other respects the complete antithesis of the stereotypical figures that were and still are associated with gayness. Significant political events such as the abolition of the death penalty and the legalization of homosexual acts are strewn into the chronology and it is evident that Arnott is, in part, offering an alternative account of the recent history of British society, obliging us to see behind official mythology to a world in which policemen and politicians are habitually corrupt and certainly not morally superior to professional criminals. It was clearly influenced by Ellroy's *American Tabloid* (1995) in which Peter Bondurant, Howard Hughes's confidant and fixer, Jimmy Hoffa's hit man and occasional CIA operative, and Kemper Boyd, favourite of FBI boss Hoover offer us a tour through the hidden, violent, often deranged world of American politics and law enforcement. Ellroy extended his state-of-the-deplorable-nation exercise into *The Cold Six Thousand* (2001), involving new characters and mature versions of the originals, as does Arnott in *He Kills Coppers* (2001). In this he introduces the adhesive tabloid journalist Tony Meehan who witnesses the abundant foulness beneath the tacky spectacle of England from the 1966 World Cup victory to the Thatcher years, and in *Truecrime* (2003) we reach the 1990s accompanied by some of the phlegmatic aging figures from *The Long Firm*, Harry and Ruby included.

Several other writers have tilted at precedent, but compared with James and Arnott their gestures seem innocuous. Sarah Dunant's Hannah Wolfe is the first British postfeminist private detective (*Birthmarks*, 1991; *Fatlands* 1993 and *Under My Skin*, 1995), Judith Cutler's D.S. Kate Power is her CID counterpart (*Power Games*, 2000), and Frances Fyfield moves us closer to the legal technicalities attendant upon crime with her dauntless barrister Helen West and intrepid solicitor Sarah Fortune. But in terms of the cosseting predictabilities of the genre these new women detectives are little more than Miss Marples with strident political outlooks and active sex lives.

Minette Walters frequently shifts the narrative away from any obvious alliance with the state of mind of the investigator or perpetrator and attempts a form of documentary realism. Her account of the murder of a black woman and the subsequent police investigation – which incorporates deliberate parallels with the Stephen Lawrence case – in *The Shape of Snakes* (2000) is particularly effective in this regard. Walters and Ruth Rendell, writing as Barbara Vine, also give attention to the psychology of crime; not the motivation of professional criminals, but the more perverse, obsessive causes of stalking, harassment or unpremeditated assault. The virtuoso of this latter hybrid of crime writing and socio-psychology is Nicci French (actually the pairing of Nicci Gerard and Sean French) who began with *The Memory Game* (1996) and has produced six similar novels up to and including *The Land of the Living* (2003). All of the above are effective literary artists in their own right but their achievements are somewhat pallid in comparison with the crime novelist who continually created an unsettling amalgam between the enigma of pure evil and its compulsive attractions, Patricia Highsmith.

Christopher Brookmyre with *Quite Ugly One Morning* (1996) debuted as the Scottish version of Carl Hiaasen. The latter's novels are slapstick derivatives of the trend pioneered by Elmore Leonard with armed robbery and murderous intuition routine features of US daily life. This does not come across as particularly aberrant when set in Florida but Brookmyre's location is provincial Scotland and in all of his books, up to and including *All Fun and Games Until Somebody Loses An Eye* (2005), one senses that the battle between exhilaration and farce will always favour the latter. Mark Billingham (*Sleepyhead*, 2001 and *The Burning Girl*, 2004), Frank Lean (*Above Suspicion*, 2001) and Ron Ellis (*Mean Streets*, 1999 and *Ears of the City*, 1998) all attempt to graft the nihilistic brutality of the US onto the urban environments of Britain, respectively North London, Manchester and Liverpool. The mismatches are conspicuous. Billingham's DI Tom Thorne, Lean's Inspector Dave Cunane and Ellis's retinue of policemen and private eyes strain toward various states of ruthless cynicism and debauchery, sufficient to match the ghastliness of their territories but in each instance one senses an awkward exaggeration of character and setting; both seem at once absurd and incongruous.

Established novelists at the high end of the cultural spectrum frequently experiment with crime writing but one has the impression that they intend not so much to revivify the subgenre as to make use of its hidebound conventions as a background to their superior talents; in short, they are slumming. Martin Amis with *Night Train* (1997) has fun with standardized formulae, causing his narrator to be an evasive, unreliable US policewoman casually indifferent to a preponderance of noirish horrors and unable, in a fashionably postmodern manner, to resolve the case and therefore finish her story. Graham Swift in *The Light of Day* (2003) exploits the scaffolding of detective fiction for more earnest speculations on the human condition (see pp. 179–80). Julian Barnes, disguised as Dan Kavanagh, during the first half of his career, published several amusing and occasionally thought-provoking novels involving the quixotic bisexual private eye Duffy (see *Fiddle City*, 1981 and *Putting the Boot In*, 1985) and one is caused to wonder if his early dalliance with the form played some part in the genesis of his celebrated Man Booker shortlisted piece *Arthur and George* (2005) (see above, pp. 95–6). Barnes raises questions about the very nature of detection, fabrication and the pursuit of truth, using as he does a hall-of-mirrors procedure whereby he fictionalizes the creator of the world's best-known detective while following a procedure and dealing with subjective emotional registers similar to those we associate with Doyle's creation, Holmes. The British attempts to evolve a hybrid of crime and postmodern fiction seem conspicuously forced and incongruous compared, say, with their most celebrated US counterpart, Paul Auster's New York Trilogy (*City of Glass*, 1985; *Ghosts* and *The Locked Room*, 1986). Auster does not so much deviate from as interrogate the lineage of Raymond Chandler and Dashiell Hammett to Tom Wolfe in which the routines of ordinary existence can suddenly become part of a deterministic nightmare outside the subject's and, as Auster indicates, the author's control. Crime writing, in the US has for most of the twentieth century been closely allied to its upmarket counterpart – realist and experimental – not because of some consensual indulgence on the part of the literary establishment but for the more straightforward reason that it reflects a fabric of experiences, mediated and actual, that most Americans take for granted. From the existence of organized crime – particularly the

Mafia – as an element of the social and economic infrastructure through the acceptance of armed policemen and FBI agents as vigilantes and nemeses to a judicial system that is fundamentalist in its retributive zeal, crime is much closer to the routine mindset of the average American than it is to their British counterpart. This does not mean that America is on average a more dangerous place to be than the UK but twentieth/early twenty-first-century existence is composed to a large degree of secondary images and representations conveyed by film and the news media, and in this respect US readers encounter crime writing more as an extension of this experience than a frightening excursion from it.

British writers who blur the distinction between good and evil or explore it fetishistically as a dimension of the creative spectrum are peculiarities, self-conscious deviants from a wholesome tradition. W. J. Burley's Cornwall-based 'Wycliffe' series, Peter Robinson's Yorkshire-based DCI Banks, John Harvey's Charlie Resnick of Nottingham and more recently John Lawton's Chief Superintendent Troy (*Blue Rondo*, 2005), Patrick Neate's Tommy Akhtar (*City of Tiny Lights*, 2005), Alexander McCall Smith's Isabel Dalhousie (*The Sunday Philosophy Club*, 2004) and Christopher Fowler's harmlessly quixotic Bryant and May of London's Peculiar Crimes Unit (*Seventy Seven Clocks*, 2005) are all permutations upon the basic design that gave us Morse, Frost, Dalziel, Rebus et al. Even Michael Dibdin's endearingly amoral and eccentric Aurelio Zen, a man who regards villains with as much indulgence as he does the inefficient corrupt Italian authorities to whom he answers (most recently in *Back to Bologna*, 2005), is becoming an avuncular almost self-parodic version of his former presence.

The contrasts between P. D. James's *The Murder Room* (2003) and Arnott's *Truecrime* (2003) are fascinating. In the former Dalgliesh seems little altered since his debut 41 years earlier and his extracurricular interest in a 31-year-old Cambridge English lecturer, begun in a previous novel, ends with them agreeing that 'they might get to know each other'. Death and killing are attended to with equally respectful decorum – they seem, like sex, matters to be treated with solemnity and caution. James's style is consistently correct and elegant and even her low-life criminals seem able to maintain proper command of syntax, despite their other delinquencies. Arnott, on the other hand, abandons a commanding stylistic register in favour of the clipped, fragmentary mode that reflects the speech patterns and life-styles of his characters. Morality and correctness exist but they seem constantly mutable, forever preyed upon by the unpredictabilities of a society with no agreed sense of order. As to the question of which more accurately reflects Britain at the close of the twentieth century, the consensus would probably favour Arnott but it should be remembered that crime fiction in all its manifestations involves a resolute perversion of actuality. All fiction is impressionistic; pure naturalistic accuracy is an ideal to be aspired to – by some – and never realized, but crime writing complicates matters by feeding upon the reader's least becoming inclinations. Until little more than a century and a half ago public executions were one of the most popular public spectacles in Britain. They were not, of course, referred to officially as entertainments and the contrast between their formal function as the sombre exhibition of the judicial process and their real bidding to a blend of prurience and vicarious sadism added further to a sense of guilty excitement. Crime writing plays upon similar registers by setting up a contrast between our fascination with death, violence and gross illegality and our regulatory attendance to an ideal, a world involving a spectrum from day-to-day normality in which crime is, we hope, an abnormality, to our reliance upon those agencies, usually the police, who protect us from it. So although P. D. James might often be perceived as unfashionably decorous in her treatment of the worst potentialities of humanity, her popularity – along with that of similarly traditional British crime writers – testifies to the fact that she does indeed engage with a level of reality experienced by most of her readers, in which crime is seen as a fact of life but not one to be fetishistically savoured or allowed to obscure the prevailing decencies of those not involved in its commission.

It would be neglectful to leave crime fiction without giving some attention to its close relative, the spy novel. Both appeal to many of our baser registers – predominantly a sense of thrill at witnessing disturbing, even life-threatening occurrences without having to endure their actual consequences – but the spy novel supplements this with an aura of tragic hermeticism. Sometimes as a life-long commitment, sometimes despite themselves and often as an act of betrayal characters inhabit two levels of existence: one which might plausibly resemble the reader's and the other a sequestered state known only to themselves and their coparticipants.

Graham Greene in pieces such as *The Confidential Agent* (1939) and *Our Man in Havana* (1958) conferred a half-hearted degree of respectability upon the spy as the unacknowledged, sometimes farcical, foot soldier of global political conflict while Ian Fleming took the genre to the other end of the literary spectrum with Bond as the cynosure of virtually every male fantasy.

Since the 1960s one novelist has dominated British spy writing and his importance and qualities as a writer per se have been obscured by the down-market, populist reputation of his chosen genre. John Le Carré's best known work is the trilogy of novels featuring the MI6 agent George Smiley, *Tinker, Tailor, Soldier, Spy* (1974), *The Honourable Schoolboy* (1977) and *Smiley's People* (1979). Smiley is an idealist wrapped in an enigma. Half the time he puts up with life as a reclusive scholarly figure, regularly cuckolded by his aristocrat wife and disobliged by ambitious, purblind colleagues. When yoked into action he embodies the best one would expect of the Western democratic conscience. He is a sceptic, distrusting of all abstract systems of ideology, but he has an instinctive, empowering recognition of the basic distinctions between right and wrong. The engine of the trilogy is the long-term conflict between Smiley and the quasi-monastic KGB figure Karla. The various strategies and responses engineered by each propel narratives that offer some of the most challenging questions in fiction regarding the nature and ethics of the Cold War – Le Carré offers the prose equivalent of epic poems in which the absolutes of existence are lain bare and scrutinized, and here we face a paradox. No other novelist can claim to have written so challengingly and with such authority about the nature of the post-WWII global enmity between Western democracy and the Warsaw Pact, but because Le Carré's work is designated as a non-mainstream subgenre, an entertainment, his achievement has gone largely unrecognized.

As the polarities of the Cold War gradually mutated into localized conflicts so Le Carré began to turn his attention to what had been at the peripheries of his 1960s and 1970s writing. In *The Secret Pilgrim* (1991) Smiley reflects upon how the West had maintained its conscience because of, not despite, the threatening presence of the post-Stalin monolith, and in *A Perfect Spy* (1986) we witness via the suicidal Magnus Pym the destructive psychological effects of working in the intelligence community. In *The Little Drummer Girl* (1983) an English actress is recruited by Israeli intelligence to infiltrate a Palestinian terrorist network and this theme of the somewhat listless individual suddenly obliged to confront moral and political issues as participant rather than an opinionated outsider became the predominant theme of most of his novels of the 1990s and 2000s: *The Russia House* (1989) shows us the disintegrating Soviet Union and *Single and Single* (1999) explores the effects of this upon the disputed territories of the Caucasus. In *Absolute Friends* (2003) we follow Ted Mundy from his childhood in postimperial Pakistan, through the riot-torn West Berlin of the late 1960s and Cold War espionage to the present day of obsessive counterterrorism. *The Constant Gardener* (2001) is Le Carré's exploration of the hypocrisies and hidden motives that underpin the industrialized world's patronage of poverty-stricken Africa. He once told an interviewer that 'the spy novel encapsulates...public wariness about political behaviour and about the set-up, the fix of society' (*Newsagent and Bookseller*, 30 November 1978, p. 22). In the modern world where political strategies and their consequences are filtered through a bewildering network of discourses – some costive and protective, others provocatively misleading – the spy, even the involuntary type, becomes a special kind of witness, able uniquely to experience the divergence of truth from public dissimulation.

Le Carré can make a particular claim upon uniqueness since none of his competitors comes close to his achievement of transforming the spy novel from a self-limiting subgenre to a chronicle which surpasses mainstream fiction in its capacity to deal with world issues. Len Deighton, first with Harry Palmer (*The Ipcress File*, 1962; *Funeral in Berlin*, 1964) and later Bernard Sampson ('Game, Set and Match' trilogy, 1983–5; 'Hook, Line and Sinker' trilogy, 1988–90), deglamorized intelligence work and extended the Greene tradition of grimy authenticity but in the end his novels reflect little more than a self-consuming, inward-looking state of mind. More recently Alan Judd has produced retrospective novels focusing upon the role of MI6 during the Cold War (see *Legacy*, 2001) yet despite his qualities as a writer and historian he only tackles issues that Le Carré had explored and left behind with Smiley.

Recent practitioners of popular spy fiction, in particular Frederick Forsyth and Gerald Seymour, have both improved upon Fleming and preserved, for their own sake, his mass-market appeal as the creator of vicarious thrills. Henry Porter in *Remembrance Day* (1999), *A Spy's*

Life (2001) and *Empire State* (2003) attempts with Robert Harland to amalgamate the repressed, quietly tortured Englishness of Smiley with a more glamorous international lifestyle and narrative. In the end the latter triumphs, and excitement is substituted for Le Carré's meticulous pathology of an era and a dilemma.

Part III

Sex

Philip Larkin famously averred that 'sexual intercourse began in 1963' and his reference to 'the Chatterley trial' pointed to the fact that before the 1960s sex and sexuality were things that novelists could only write about as if they didn't quite exist. Everyone knew that they did, of course, but for the best part of two centuries the pretence was maintained; much was implied and the rest was up to the reader.

Coincidentally or not, the era during which candour replaced enforced discretion also involved much more significant developments – intellectual, collective and often legislative – regarding the inbuilt assumptions and prejudices that accompanied the recognition of gender difference and sexual orientation.

The rules on what men and women were supposed to be and do had obtained for more than two millennia; they derived from Judeo-Christian dogma but had been enforced and maintained by men for the simple reason that they ensured the pre-eminence of maleness: mostly heterosexual maleness, if only by pretence.

Feminism, the women's movement, and gay rights have in a relatively short period contributed to a radical transformation in the way that most individuals think about gender and sexuality; society now would be almost unrecognizable to the average person of 1963. All this is beyond dispute but the intriguing question remains as to how it has been dealt with in fiction. The issue is immense given that attempting to write a novel that does not in some way involve gender difference and sexuality would be like trying to construct a sentence without a verb or a noun. As a consequence I have based my selections of books covered in this Part upon the following. There have been, particularly with regard to feminism, novels which self-evidently engage with ongoing debates on gender. The question which attends these works, but is rarely addressed, is whether their allegiance compromises their quality. It is, of course, possible to write novels carrying ideological baggage that can be admired as works of art by those alienated by or even indifferent to their political import, but such an achievement is immensely difficult, as figures such as Orwell have shown. I have, therefore, attempted to distinguish between writing that is self-limitingly polemical and that which blurs the distinction between literature's role as a reflective medium and its counterfunction as an instrument of provocation.

It would be absurd to regard male authors as oblivious to the developments that largely focus upon their counterparts across the gender divide, and as we shall see their engagements with what amounts to a diminution in status range from the pitiably correct through the laughable to – and these are much the minority – the resourcefully self-contained.

Post-1970s gay fiction is an intriguing phenomenon in that it at once proclaims its status and short-circuits our attempts to classify it as a subgenre. The classic case is Alan Hollinghurst's *The Line of Beauty* (2004), a magnificently evocative glance back to the mythology of Thatcherism and the 1980s. It ought perhaps to have been included in chapter 3 but I have placed it here because Hollinghurst uses gay sexuality as a narrative lever and a prism. A whole network of previously repressed impulses – greed, personal fulfilment, narcissism, hedonism and of course homosexuality – seemed to have been released by the 1980s. Hollinghurst's ability, albeit two decades later, to incorporate two equally tendentious but seemingly incompatible conditions and ideologies indicates either that the disintegration of homophobic prejudice was assisted by Thatcherism or that he is rewriting history in the manner routinely licensed by fiction.

Chapter 7

Women

Virginia Woolf's *A Room of One's Own* (1929) is a remarkable essay, predating the collective notion of feminism by almost four decades and pre-empting a number of the ideas that we have come to associate with the late twentieth-century women's movement. Woolf creates the hypothetical figure of Shakespeare's sister, as talented as her deified sibling but destined to have her literary aspirations stifled by a society and culture that instinctively regarded women as intellectually inferior to men. The 'room' of the title is largely figurative, an opportunity to work creatively within a discourse or space that is not dominated exclusively by the conventions of a male-orientated culture. But, as we shall see, it also carries a more literal, prescient resonance of women writers having the money to work independently. Poetry, she argues, is least receptive to female participation, the speaking presence of each text being traditionally a patriarchal figure of authority. The novel, however, is 'young enough to be soft in [women's] hands' and she praises Aphra Behn, Jane Austen and the Brontës as practitioners. In the final section Woolf discusses the concept of 'androgyny', a blending or harmony between qualities conventionally regarded as ensuring the separation of 'masculine' and 'feminine'.

Although Woolf did not herself indicate a causal link between her opinions on the status of women writers and her own creative choices many since have argued that modernism is a cooperative vehicle for her vaguely sketched notion of 'androgyny', types of writing that transcend the conventionally inscribed mannerisms of masculine and feminine. The modernist novel famously deposed the narrator from the role as overarching patriarchal presence and instituted instead a loose, shifting spectrum of discourses. In Woolf's writing stream of consciousness transforms narrative from an instrument of control into an impressionistic canvas.

Two of Woolf's more notable contemporaries, May Sinclair (with *Mary Oliver: A Life*, 1919 and *Life and Death of Harriet Frean*, 1922) and Dorothy Richardson (with the *Pilgrimage* sequence, 1915–67) employ radical, experimental techniques as a means of shifting the text away from those conventions of realism which appeared to ally writing with the socio-cultural fabric of maleness. Unfortunately, however, modernist fiction remained on the periphery of the social and cultural mainstream. Perversely, while its aesthetic set it beyond the male-dominated canon and procedures of classic realism it also disarmed it as a proactive medium.

During the 1950s and 1960s the British novel, predominantly in its realist manifestation, engaged with sexuality, sexual activity, desire and its consequences in a way largely unprecedented in the history of fiction. Significantly the authors of the vast majority of these works were men, the perspectives – albeit sometimes generously open-minded and liberal – pre-eminently masculine and the activating characters male. John Braine, David Storey, Kingsley Amis, John Wain, and Alan Sillitoe all contributed to a new spectrum of alliances in which character and narrator perceived women with what might best be termed predatory heterosexual empathy. Women characters were respected, sometimes even portrayed as more complex, prescient figures than their male counterparts, but alongside this would come a degree of wariness and puzzlement, a sense of desire (unless the women in question were undesirable) as the overpowering inclination. The best known almost archetypal presence in which all of this coalesced was Bill Naughton's eponymous *Alfie* (1966) with Michael Caine's memorable screen portrayal catching the mood of the novel and its 1963 radio play prototype perfectly: he speaks to camera and whatever we might feel about everyone else in the text/film we always have to deal first with his craftily apologetic perspective.

The women's movement and the collateral ideology of feminism became a public, collective phenomenon from the mid-1960s onwards and the first large-scale attempt to apply those modes of thinking to literature was Kate Millett's *Sexual Politics* (1969, Virago, 1977). Millett presented the novel written by men as a simulacrum of the repressive, manipulative social mechanisms which ensured that in society women were assigned inferior, submissive roles. Millett's was an interpretive polemic in that she did not indicate how this alleged cultural hegemony might be altered, either by women or men. Similarly Sandra Gilbert and Susan Gubar in *The Madwoman in the Attic* (Yale University Press, 1979) contended that women would, as authors of traditional novels, be obliged to maintain a respectful distance from the narrative voice and remain as anonymous artisans involved in a craft designed by and for men. During the same period, however, a number of writers began to make claims upon an incipient notion of women's fiction and, despite the implication by Millett and others that traditional fiction was geared toward patriarchal prejudices and assumptions, they did so as realists.

Lynn Reid Banks's *The L-Shaped Room* (1960), Nell Dunn's *Up the Junction* (1963) and *Poor Cow* (1967) and Margaret Drabble's *A Summer Bird-Cage* (1963) and *The Millstone* (1965) all present early 1960s British society via the perspectives and experiences of their young female protagonists. Dunn's are poorly educated, working-class figures obliged to endure the casual misogyny and sometimes violence of their male counterparts. The detail, at least for those not blind to the everyday lives of what were still the majority in London, was less shocking than the fact that the reader is obliged to share the female first-person narrator's sense of fear and despair rather than simply observe it from the outside. Banks and Drabble move their women up a class to, respectively, lower-middle and educated bourgeois. Banks's Jane Graham becomes pregnant and is drawn into a deterministic spiral of what appear to be choices but are in truth decisions made on her behalf by men in positions of authority. An intriguing contrast occurs during her exchanges with her namesake Jane the prostitute who occupies the basement of the same house in Fulham. The latter has, she claimed, used the one item that men desire but which she can either withhold or sell to maintain a degraded independence. The question of whether this is the only option available to women is left tantalizingly unanswered. Drabble's figures are more autobiographical, notably Sarah in *A Summer Bird Cage* who has ambitions toward academia and fiction writing and Rosamund in *The Millstone* who has begun an academic career. In both instances a two-dimensional cultural fabric is invoked – partly fiction and partly real – and it is the one used so effectively by the predominantly male writers of the 1950s. At one point Sarah states that she wants to write a novel like

Amis's *Lucky Jim*, with the academic establishment parodied and by implication the middle-class intellectual milieu ridiculed by someone inside it. It becomes clear, however, that even though she could work as an academic and publish fiction she would always, as a woman, feel uncomfortable in the latter as the observer, rather than the observed, and in the former treated with grudging tolerance as someone operating outside her conventional gender-designated role.

Up to the 1970s novels by women about women were robustly realist in tone and manner and given that Woolf had envisioned a remodelling of fiction to accommodate nonmale perspectives and experiences this raises several questions; principally, had women writers who maintained an allegiance to conventional form betrayed the cause initiated by Woolf and become female practitioners of a determinedly male discourse?

Doris Lessing's *The Golden Notebook* (1962) is the most celebrated and widely debated example of proto-feminist fiction produced between the 1940s and 1970s. It pays due allegiance to modernism by having the central character Anna Wulf subdivide perceptions of herself into four notebooks: the black book for her African life; the red for her (predominantly Communist) political thoughts and affiliations; yellow records her aborted attempt at fiction; and blue documents her experience of psychological breakdown; and the golden one, which concludes the novel, is Anna's attempt, in the throes of a nervous breakdown, to unify the disparate strands. It could be argued that the intention here is to replace the seamless narrative structure of realism with a fragmented spectrum in which various aspects of Wulf's identity are present but none predominates, and further proposed that the novel is an ambitious attempt to create a multi-narrative which fully incorporates a woman's sense of divided selfhood. Conversely it might be claimed that such a fictional canvas is just as reductive as its realist counterpart: to regard all women as less capable or inclined than men to regard their lives as a coherent unity is surely an example of gender stereotyping. Indeed Lessing herself appears to acknowledge this in her use of a narrative which frames the four notebooks, called *Free Women*, which is also about Wulf, her problems and aspirations, and is as coherent and orderly as a nineteenth-century journal.

The Golden Notebook is a pivotal work, but not in a predictable sense. Certainly it carries forward ideas from Woolf but it is also immensely prescient in its enactment of a dynamic between radicalism and naturalistic transparency. This would from the 1970s onwards manifest itself as a division between women who saw experiment as prefiguring a sense of duty to their gender and those who were unapologetic realists.

Of the former Angela Carter is the most celebrated pioneer. Her novels – the best-known being *The Magic Toyshop* (1967), *Nights at the Circus* (1985) and *Wise Children* (1991) – are in varying degrees hybrids, and the most conspicuous pairing is between the conventional novel and the fairy or folk tale. The latter are primitive antecedents of the novel, their narrative structures less observant of the nonliterary conventions of time and space and their characters generally possessed of magical powers. Also, figures in folk and fairy stories tend to exaggerate or symbolize standardized human roles and archetypes. Carter borrowed from this literary subgenre to purposively disrupt the prevailing representative conventions of the novel. The principal figure of *Night at the Circus* (1985), for example, is a circus trapeze artist called Fevvers whose act is based upon the attractive illusion that human beings can fly. Jack Walser, a journalist, becomes fascinated by Fevvers because he suspects that the illusion is fact, that she is superhuman, and Fevvers in those parts of the narrative she controls, claims, exclusively for the reader, that she is indeed part-bird. Consequently the reader is caught along with Fevvers and Walser in a triangle of narrative perspectives, all somewhat skewed and suspect. We are not sure if Fevvers is telling us the truth and nor is Walser clear about how his suspicions might be confirmed. To complicate matters further Walser's interest is, partly, sexual, so that by sharing his sense of fascination we, as readers, are divided in line with our gender. Carter interweaves realism and fantasy so that the standard expectations of how gender division is represented in fiction and how such representations are received are at once undermined and brought into sharper definition.

It is rewarding to compare Carter's work with that of her near contemporary Fay Weldon. In purely technical terms Weldon is a more traditional writer. She sometimes shifts between first- and third-person narrative as a means of accentuating the women's perspective but this method is hardly radical, given that Kingsley Amis achieved a similar effect in *Take A Girl Like You* (1960). The settings and most of the characters of the novels are plausibly contemporaneous. Her readers from the 1970s onwards would recognize in her fiction versions of the world in which they lived, the only difference, most specifically for men, would be an accompanying sense of relief that they had not stepped from the latter into the former. Weldon is that rare breed, a transparently aggressive writer with an unambiguous polemic. Millett (1969) argued that male novelists used their writing as part of an empathetic conspiracy between patriarchal representation and the false objectivity of literary art. Weldon uses her novels to exact revenge upon both.

Weldon is a prolific if somewhat repetitive writer and by virtue of the attention it has successfully canvassed *The Life and Loves of a She-Devil* (1983) can be treated as her magnum opus. Ruth Patchett is not a mythological or supernatural devil; she is frighteningly human. Her husband Bobbo begins an affair with Mary Fisher, author of romantic novels in which wealth, glamour and success abound. Ruth burns down the family home, hands over the children to Mary and Bobbo and thereafter the novel comprises a catalogue of Ruth's vengeful and self-promotional enterprises. One of these is the Vesta Rose Employment Agency set up to revitalize women who had previously played such roles as wife, mother and general underdog. Her partner in this is one Nurse Hopkins who Ruth had rescued from her self-denigrating work in an old people's home. In the same institution she also contrived to wean Pearl Fisher, Mary's mother, off tranquillizers and have her despatched to the home of Mary and Bobbo where she could torment her daughter. Ruth also undergoes plastic surgery to make her look exactly like Mary, taking on thereafter the roles of mirror-image nemesis and vengeful alter ego.

This is but a fragment of Ruth's odyssey, which by comparison makes Rabelais's fictions seem almost demure and circumspect. Indeed one suspects that it is Weldon's purpose throughout the novel to systematically target unashamedly patriarchal narrative devices or scenarios and install the women in the roles conventionally occupied by male protagonists. Weldon is undoubtedly an accomplished, provocative writer but her method in *Life and Loves of a She Devil* and indeed in other works involves self-evident drawbacks. Ruth is licensed to dispose of all obstacles that obstruct her route to revenge and success and along the way to operate as a proselytizing exemplar to other women who have not realized their full potential. Aside from the general question of whether literature per se is diminished in quality when used as a vehicle for doctrine Weldon's creations are extravagances, testing credulity and battling to avoid self-parody.

The problems raised by Weldon are twofold. If one is to empower and foreground women characters can the contemporary world be transplanted to the novel without radical alteration? If it can, then surely one must pause to reconsider the original motivating premises of literary feminism – that society and literary culture are patriarchal autocracies. As we shall see, elements of these two issues are addressed, albeit sometimes implicitly, in virtually all fiction from the 1980s onwards in which gender difference features as a central theme.

If one were to measure significance according to attendant levels of critical scrutiny – particularly of the specialized, academic variety – then Jeanette Winterson would without doubt be one of the most significant women writers of the past 20 years. The novel which brought her to public attention was *Oranges Are Not the Only Fruit* (1985), a fictionalized account of her own childhood and adolescence in Accrington, Lancashire. Author and central character are brought up by a family of strict Pentecostal Christians whose fundamentalist beliefs and ethic are at odds with Jeanette's wish for intellectual independence and more significantly her developing lesbian sexuality. Aside from a few quirkily appropriate echoings of biblical episodes the novel is largely a mixture of dry naturalism and sardonic observation. Subsequently, Winterson has, in a bewildering variety of ways, eschewed the protocols of realism and also – intentionally or not, it is impossible to say – revisited and reshaped the finite web of themes first addressed in *Oranges*. There are numerous, apparent, dissimilarities. *The Passion* (1987) is a quixotic blend of historical fantasy and magic realism, set during the Napoleonic period; *Sexing the Cherry* (1989) counterpoints the London of the Civil War and the Restoration against the activities of the idiosyncratic Jordan and more memorably the engrossing presence of the 'Dog Woman', part giant human, part canine and capable of defying the laws of gravity. *Written on the Body* (1992) returns us to the present and a love story shot through with the baleful effects of one party being afflicted by cancer. History crops up again in *The PowerBook* (2000), this time choreographed by a fissiparous narrator who seems to be an extension of cyberspace. Her recent novel *Lighthousekeeping* (2004) involves, as its title indicates, a lighthouse keeper and a young girl called Silver whose trips through time resemble half-recollected fairy stories. The variations and unpredictabilities within her work so far are striking, but equally persistent are threads which tie each novel to every other. Sometimes one will be given prominence and others subdued, and then this equation will be reversed, but the linkages are continuously present.

In *Oranges Are Not the Only Fruit* a complex mixture of desire and separateness propels the narrative. Jeanette's lesbianism is shaped by and shapes her personality and she becomes more than the rebellious teenager of traditional stories. Her willed isolation from the beliefs of her family and environment is the essential feature of her existence. In *The Passion* this same theme of a repressed, hidden identity and a figure whose very nature is at odds with the dictates of a circumstance is carried over into the story of Villanelle, whose love for the so-called Queen of Spades will lead her, literally, to lose her heart. Villanelle is loved, in turn, by Henri, a young orderly in Napoleon's army whose own gentle passive, affectionate temperament – in short his feminine characteristics – cause him at once to be treated as an outsider by his male peers and recognized by Villanelle as a fellow outcast. The motif of the outsider becomes more energized and vengeful in the Dog Woman of *Sexing the Cherry*, a figure who resists the patriarchal authority of Puritan England by virtue of being bigger and stronger than its representatives. *Written on the Body*, while in manner and tone very different from its two immediate predecessors, maintains and transmutes one of their key characteristics by making the narrator at once sensual and asexual. He/she is having an affair with the married Louise and we more than suspect that the relationship is between two women, but we can never be certain. The related concepts of secrecy and transgression are returned to but this time it is the reader rather than the subject or narrator who feels disconcerted. We know what is happening between these two people but given that the gender of the narrator/lover is determinedly ambiguous our conditioned response is skewed. *The PowerBook*'s narrator is female, probably, but instead of disguising her gender via straightforward techniques of phrasal and syntactical evasion Ali/Alix functions in cyberspace where virtually everything is possible but physical presence is not a condition of omnipotence. Silver, the narrator of *Lighthousekeeping* was born in 1959, the same year as her author. She lived with her mother in a house cut into a slope so steep that the chairs were nailed to the floor and, for their mutual safety, mother and daughter had to be roped together. When Silver was 10, her mother slipped over the cliff edge, heroically undid their rope and Silver proceeds into the rest of the narrative without ties, literal or figurative, to explore a world of stories and emotions, apparently freed from the usual confines of history or credulity. A reader with even a second-hand knowledge of *Oranges Are Not the Only Fruit* would recognize parallels, albeit modulated by symbolism and a sprinkle of magic realism. It is not that Winterson lacks the imagination or instinct to move beyond variations upon a narrative that is largely autobiographical and self-absorbed; the reason is more complex. In her book of essays *Art and Lies* (1995) Winterson seems preoccupied with three writers: Shakespeare, T. S. Eliot and Virginia Woolf. The first is of course the ultimate literary craftsman, capable of remaking the world from language; the second argued for and practised a new relationship between language and actuality; and the third combined the skills of the first two with a sense of destiny for herself and her gender. One suspects from the manner of the essays, at once imperious and familiar, that Winterson sees herself as the fourth member of this group. If this is the case then one is prompted to treat her fictional method not as involving recirculations and continuations of narrative but as an epic realization of Woolf's hypothetical *Room of One's Own*. Winterson's novels counterpoint their repetitions against an insistent drive toward dissimilarity and the latter manifests itself in linguistic versatility. She is, ultimately, writing about writing: exercising a control over language and its possibilities in order to guarantee for herself a special state of independence from a predominantly male, heterosexual literary culture.

Winterson's work causes us to readdress the question raised above regarding the relationship between realism, experiment and gender. Intriguingly one writer who is studiously ignored in Winterson's ex-cathedra writings on literature is Angela Carter. This omission is not unusual because it has long been a common tendency among writers who regard themselves as torchbearers for radicalism to feel threatened by the presence of others similarly disposed, and further to this it must be observed that such anxiety is heightened when there are so few potential contenders for the title of innovator-in-chief. The fact is that while Woolf's original pairing of innovation with women's writing has frequently been re-examined and expanded upon since the late 1960s there are very few who have attempted literary realizations of her prognosis – Carter and Winterson being the only ones of any significance.

Several women writers who began their careers in the mid to late 1970s made use of the novel as a vehicle for the fomenting feminist polemic, the best known being Zoë Fairbairns, Sarah Maitland and Michèle Roberts. Typical of their work is Fairbairns's *Stand We at Last* (1983) which gives an account of the lives and experiences of a succession of women from the mid-nineteenth century to the 1970s. Roberts in *A Piece of the Night* (1978) shifts through a shorter span of past and present as its heroine Julie Fanchot looks back to her time as a convent schoolgirl in the 1950s, Oxford, marriage and child-rearing in the 1960s and early 1970s and, by implication, compares all of this with her present existence, sharing a house in London with her daughter and lesbian lover. These books, including also Maitland's *Virgin Territory* (1984), are unconventional in the sense that they explore experiences and involve perspectives that are recognizably tied into the feminist agenda of uncovering women's lives and mindsets both retrospectively and in contemporary society. At the same time, however, they employ documentary realism as the most effective means of doing so – a strategy at odds with Woolf's modernist precedent.

Roberts has since the 1970s been one of the most prolific and widely celebrated of the writers who allied themselves with the first wave of feminist writing. Through the 1980s and 1990s most of her novels involved a historical perspective, part drawn from her own experiences from the 1950s onwards and part focusing upon more distant scenarios and mythologies. *The Visitation*'s (1983) chief protagonist is Helen Home, a girl who, not unlike Roberts, grows up during the 1950s and 1960s, supposedly a period more enlightened than, say, the prewar years but which is still, as Helen's experiences disclose, embedded with institutionalized and instinctive sexism. *Fair Exchange* (1999) fictionalizes the life and circumstances of Mary Wollstonecraft, and *The Looking Glass* (2000) takes us to France at the turn of the nineteenth century and discloses a social fabric in which desire, usually sexual, competes with convention and discretion and usually triumphs. Her best-known novel is probably *Daughters of the House* (1992). It begins with the return of the French nun Thérèse after 20 years to her family home now occupied by her English cousin Léonie. The initial antagonism gives way to recollections of the time they had spent there as teenagers, involving a blend of pseudo mystical/religious experiences and awakening sexuality. The novel is semi-autobiographical to the extent that both characters represent aspects of Roberts's formative experiences: French Catholic mother and English Protestant father; educated first in a north London convent before being released into adulthood in Oxford and London in the 1960s and 1970s. The Roman Catholic Church features in much of her work, partly because it involves institutionalized male predominance and more intriguingly as a counterpoint to the unbridled sexuality and unorthodox visionary experiences to which her women seem particularly prone. For example, *In the Red Kitchen* (1990) is partly an account of the celebrated nineteenth-century spirit medium Flora Milk, eventually betrayed by her own sister as a charlatan. The official, accepted account maintains the accusation of fraudulence but in her novel Roberts offers as much presence and authenticity to the spirits as she does to Flora and her sister. Hattie, a woman of the late 1980s, feels the proximity of Flora and meets her ghost in the cellar of a Victorian house which she and her lover are restoring – a conceit which subtly and implicitly raises two issues. First it puts one in mind of the broader feminist project of uncovering the lives of women from a past when most outside a privileged minority were condemned to anonymous secondary roles. Also, and more tentatively, it invites the reader to compare the period in which Flora existed with that of Hattie, a successful independent individual. And the second issue encompasses a straightforward question: to what extent has society granted women the levels of equality called for during the 1960s and 1970s?

Margaret Forster has combined fiction writing with an impressive record as social historian and biographer and her novels carry the imprint of her nonfictional research and writing. In *Shadow Baby* (1996), for example, she charts the parallel lives of two women, one born in the 1880s and the other in the 1950s. The contrasts between society at the turn of the nineteenth century and the second half of the twentieth register subtly and effectively, and by causing each character to share a particular experience – being abandoned at birth by their natural mother and in adulthood searching obsessively for this lost figure – Forster sets up an intriguing interplay between the mutations of history and immutable aspects of women's lives – in this case motherhood.

Forster's first novel *Georgy Girl* (1965) came to be regarded as a record of the alleged sexual revolution of the 1960s – principally because it was turned into a film with Lynn Redgrave and Charlotte

125

Rampling as the central characters – but in truth ungainly Georgy of the book is unsettled by her experiences of licensed hedonism in mid-1960s London. She values stability, not in the conservative sense of women playing designated, subordinate roles but as a guarantor of compassion and transparency. Forster's most recent novel *Is There Anything You Want?* (2005) has seven women of very different backgrounds and temperaments experience the nerve-wracking tension of waiting for results from a breast cancer clinic. It would be difficult to imagine a scenario more different from that of *Georgy Girl* but in both novels and in most of the 20 produced in the intervening three decades there is a common factor. The lives of, mostly ordinary, people are scrutinized and documented in a way that combines hard naturalism with empathy. Forster shows us the tragedies and injustices of existence and is particularly concerned by how women respond, often privately, to the confusing or unforeseen but she refuses to present gender difference as something for which there is an overarching theoretical prognosis.

Significantly Forster features in none of the academic studies of contemporary fiction published since the 1970s, including those which address themselves specifically to women's writing and the issue of gender. Given that her commitment to the broader agenda of feminism is unambiguous and self evident – her *Significant Sisters: The Grassroots of Active Feminism: 1839–1939* (1984) is a landmark study in the history of the women's movement – this omission seems puzzling, except that there is evidence to suggest that academia, as arbiter of what is read and discussed outside the media, harbours a prejudice against writers who do not match socio-political engagement with – à la Winterson – avante-garde execution and an inclination to unsettle the reader's expectations.

With this in mind we should turn our attention to the work of Anita Brookner. Her novels are frequently classified, often derogatively, as formulaic in that her central characters tend to be middle-class educated women who spend long periods of time in quietly elegant locations reflecting upon their modestly disappointing lives – existences which many people, despite themselves, would look upon as much with envy as sympathy. The best known of these is the Booker Prize-wining *Hotel du Lac* (1984), a poignant, slightly comedic account of a few months in the life of Edith Hope, spent at the eponymous Swiss hotel, during which she contemplates her particular fabric of relationships. The interpretive reflex, unchecked by most commentators, is to regard Brookner as a contemporary version of Jane Austen, with her women characters negotiating a similar comedy of manners updated to include sex. The enclosed, limited sphere of Austen's fictions tends to be treated as an unavoidable consequence of her gender and historical circumstances, and as therefore forgivable, but to find a version of the same in the work of a late twentieth-century woman novelist has been seen by many feminists as evidence of quiescence, even betrayal. Natasha Walter reviewing *Altered States* in the *Guardian* (14 June 1996) discerns in her work a compulsive, repetitive 'torpor' and Maureen Freely on Brookner's more recent novel *Leaving Home* finds that all her women characters seem to respond to disappointment with 'a meandering and unfocused lament,...the only promise her mouthpiece-heroine [of *Leaving Home*] makes is to dish out more of the same'. The most frequently repeated complaint against Brookner is that she recycles the same set of narrative formulae again and again. Freely says:

> There ought to be a limit to the number of times an author can deliver the same goods. *Leaving Home*...is Anita Brookner's 23rd novel. In fact it's her first novel redrafted for the 23rd time in just about as many years...Brookner remains the willing prisoner of a single endlessly repeating drama. (*Guardian*, 29 January 2005)

Aside from the fact that this is something of an exaggeration (*Lewis Percy*, 1989, for example, is about a man) one finds that the same charge could be laid against Jeanette Winterson. In her review of *The PowerBook* Jenny Turner asks, 'Is [Winterson] writing the same book over and over? Has she run out of new books to write?' (*London Review of Books*, 7 September 2000). Turner strikes a rare sceptical note among a general chorus of admiration for Winterson and the answer to her question is implicit in its rhetoric. Winterson may well be a repetitive writer but by continually reframing and disguising the same theme within an apparently inexhaustible catalogue of devices she satisfies what has become the expectation that formal experiment is the only guarantee of significance in women's writing.

Emma Tennant can, along with Carter and Winterson, be regarded as a writer whose work is shaped and informed by the more radical ideas of the feminist movement. In *The Bad Sister* (1978) the key female characters appear to inhabit two worlds, one comprising the standardized, credible routines of contemporary existence and the other made up of experiences which defy the conventions of time, space and credulity. The novel combines and animates ideas from feminist and Freudian theory. The latter's notion of a tension between conscious and unconscious states whose relationship is determined by a fabric of repressions and complexes is adapted to what one of the characters in *The Bad Sister* calls the 'double female self' and 'the inherent "splitness" of women' (*The Bad Sister*, Picador, 1979, pp. 101, 137). The tension between the two levels of narrative is the literary model of the actual problem, for women, of reconciling their long-repressed innate characteristics with social and behavioural formulae devised by men and still obtaining in late twentieth-century society.

In a number of her later novels Tennant rewrites key literary works from the past, the first and perhaps most bizarre being *Two Women of London: The Strange Case of Ms Jekyll and Mrs Hyde* (1989) whose subject and inspiration are evident in the title. While Stevenson's Jekyll finds a means of activating and releasing his murderous inner self in Hyde, Tennant brings Mrs Hyde into the late 1980s as a depressed slatternly mother of two who via a combination of drugs, including ecstasy, can become her fantasized self-image: Ms Eliza Jekyll, a well-educated, well-paid glamorous figure, the archetypal 'new woman' of the Thatcher decade. The murder, committed by Mrs Hyde, is motivated by a collective sense of dread among the women of the area following the activities of a serial rapist. Mrs Hyde suspects that the Hon. Jeremy Toller, a magistrate and businessman, is the perpetrator and kills him. It is disclosed eventually that she was mistaken in this but her error is treated not so much as a violent overreaction as one among many inevitable consequences of a woman's sense of displacement or 'splitness'. The narrative is made up of accounts by a variety of female witnesses, choreographed by an anonymous third-person narrator who is, one suspects, an extension of her creator. Ms/Mrs Jekyll/Hyde escapes to continental Europe and the novel ends with the narrator and the lawyer Jean Hastie cooperating to ensure that Mrs Hyde's children will be protected from more unsettling details of their mother's activities. Their reasons for this are charitable but not exclusively so in that it is more than implied that Hyde's act of murder is justifiable both in its own right and symbolically as recompense for several millennia of victimhood. Jean Hastie, we are told, has authored a scholarly monograph in which the book of Genesis is reinterpreted and Adam held responsible for his own act of disobedience and not, as established doctrine would contend, partially exonerated on the grounds of being led astray by his impulsive other half.

The novel is thought-provoking and commendably executed yet at the same time one suspects that didactic, and polemical import are slightly outdoing invention in claims upon the reader's attention. Indeed this self-created subgenre of revisionism (including *Faustine*, 1992, a reinterpretation of the Faust/Faustus myth; *Pemberley or Pride and Prejudice Continued* 1993; and *Emma in Love: Jane Austen's Emma Continued*, 1996) cannot help but be regarded as a creative manifestation of feminist theories of culture and literary history, which leads one back once more to the archetypal presence of Virginia Woolf.

Towards the end of *Art and Lies* Jeannette Winterson quotes a long passage from *A Room of One's Own* (*Art and Lies*, Cape, 1994, pp. 163–4) and focuses upon Woolf's image of the world in 'another century or so' when women 'have five hundred a year each of us and rooms of our own' and 'see human beings not always in their relation to each other but in relation to reality'. 'That' states Winterson 'is where I am in history' and her claim is unintentionally ambiguous. From the nature of her work we can surmise that in her view the legendary 'room' involves the figurative notion of a creative space particular to oneself and one's gender and that the new way of seeing human beings 'in relation to reality' is a correspondingly radical method of refashioning reality through language. This reading of Woolf is commensurate with Tennant's reclaiming of literary history, the premise of the latter being that the original writers were denied the 'room' to make the decisions that Tennant executes on their behalf.

It would not, however, be entirely improper to pose the question of whether Woolf is referring exclusively to an intellectual or existential condition in her famous hypothesis. One cannot simply dismiss the reference to 'five hundred a year' as a flippant aside. Woolf's privileged background enabled her to become a writer, and while she was certainly not sympathetic to anything resembling socialism her notion of a time when all talented women might realize their literary ambitions is tinged with the materialist image of independence as a corollary of having enough money to write books, and perhaps making enough from writing, to provide oneself with a literal 'room' in which to work.

The fact that Woolf's passage is ambiguous and open to conflicting interpretations is prescient given that a similar division would eventually be visited upon feminism and women's writing. The women's movement of the 1960s and 1970s made demands that were straightforward and pragmatic regarding matters such as equal pay, maternity leave, the legalization of abortion, free contraception and divorce law. Many of these were met in Britain by the 1974 Labour Government, particularly in its 1975 acts covering sex discrimination and equal pay, and by the end of the 1970s women were, at least in terms of the law, guaranteed a status in society equal to that of men. At the same time, however, the more radical element of feminism remained focused upon the psychological, physical and temperamental aspects of gender distinction that could not be accounted for in Acts of Parliament or legislated against. The American theorist Shere Hite, for example, argued that sexual intercourse was, for men, a triumphalist, violent act of rape voluntarily endured by women, an issue which would divide the 1978 Women's Liberation conference (see Sheila Rowbotham, *A Century of Women: A History of Women in Britain and the US*, Penguin, 1999, pp. 407, 431). The disagreements within feminism would be increased by the economic and social changes set in train by the Thatcher government of the 1980s. By the time that 'Thatcherism' had become a working ideology in the mid to late 1980s it embodied and, some might argue, reflected a dichotomy that also informed feminism. Few would contest that during this period a considerable number of educated and ambitious women – particularly those who had benefited from greater access to higher education – attained unprecedented positions of eminence, in both the private and public sectors. The problem, for some feminists, was that women appeared to have been allowed access to these new levels of independence and advancement via an aggressive masculinist code of ruthless profiteering.

The most famous literary treatment of this was Fay Weldon's *Big Women* (1997) which involves, in part, a thinly disguised account of the women's publishing house Virago. Virago began as an outlet for new women writers and set about republishing unjustly neglected women writers of the past, the latter project involving parallels with Tennant's rewritings of literary history. Eventually Virago became a fashionable and very profitable concern and following acrimonious exchanges between directors was sold for a vast amount to a long-established mainstream publisher, the type of acquisitive male-orientated organization that it had originally set itself against. Weldon's fictional version of Virago, Medusa, follows exactly the same route. The novel also concentrates upon the figure of Saffron, daughter of Zoe and Bull, cofounders of Medusa, who becomes during the 1990s a journalist and media executive. She is eventually instrumental in the sale of Medusa to 'ComArt', an intercontinental enterprise devoted entirely to making profit from the representation of self-serving fantasy in magazines and film. The symbolism is cumbersome, heavy-handed but nonetheless effective. The pragmatics of feminism, involving equal opportunity, have served their purpose and their ethical, theoretical counterparts have as a consequence been dismantled – women, given the opportunity, can be as aggressively manipulative and ruthless as men.

Those who might regard Saffron simply as an aberration, a salve to Weldon's disappointment with the apparent failure of feminism, should compare her with a similar, though less professionally successful, 'new woman' whose diary would be published as a novel a few months before *Big Women* and become one of the cultural signatures of the late 1990s and early 2000s. I refer of course to Bridget Jones. During its first two years in print Helen Fielding's *Bridget Jones's Diary* (1996) sold almost a million copies in the UK alone. The entries of this anxious, hopelessly ambitious and involuntarily amusing heroine touched a chord of empathy and recognition in women and when the book was published in the US in 1998 the *New York Times* offered a blunt explanation for its success: 'It captures neatly the way modern women teeter between "I am a woman" independence and a pathetic girlie desire to be all things to all men' (*New York Times*, 31 May 1998). Another reason for the novel's popularity was its form. We learn of Bridget's thoughts and activities predominantly via her diary entries but Fielding sets up a subtle tension in each of these between her public and private personae. The former involve what the *New York Times* refers to as her '"I am a woman" independence', beneficiary as she is of the achievements of the previous generation of feminists and honourable torchbearer for the same. The latter, however, shows us the real Bridget: continually nervous about her weight and appearance, convinced that her 'career' in the media will lead nowhere and concerned ultimately with finding a reliable, handsome and comfortably off man with whom she will have exuberant sex and play the role of dutiful housewife.

The novel has frequently been cited as initiator of a somewhat amorphous subgenre known as 'chick lit', a term that carries a subtext of tolerant reproval: entertaining, clever but not on a par with 'serious' writing. There is, however, cause to treat Fielding's invention as significant a comment upon feminism and women's issues as Weldon's Saffron.

The man with whom she finds contentment is Mark Darcy, whose name of course invokes the presence of Jane Austen and her similar account of wish-fulfilment, *Pride and Prejudice*. Fielding, who had worked in the media and publishing, would have been fully aware of Tennant's two sequels to this novel. *Pemberley* (1993) and *An Unequal Marriage* (1994) both disclose traits within Elizabeth Bennet and the original Mr Darcy that Austen would have been obliged by the conventions of the period to conceal, or so Tennant indicates. Fielding, contra Tennant, contends that some characteristics are an innate function of gender and immune from the vicissitudes of historical change. Books, she implies, can be rewritten in accordance with a new enlightened perspective, but for women like Bridget – and indeed Elizabeth – a relationship with the likes of Darcy is more important than aspirations to selfhood and independence. Perhaps to dispel any doubts that she is weaving into her entertainment an underhand, sceptical commentary upon literary feminism, in the sequel *Bridget Jones: The Edge of Reason* (1999) Fielding has Bridget interview the actor Colin Firth. Firth had famously played Darcy in the BBC adaptation of Austen's *Pride and Prejudice* (1995) and for this reason was later cast as Darcy in the film version of the first *Bridget Jones*. A more peculiar case of intergeneric intertextuality could hardly be envisaged and Fielding makes clever use of it. In Andrew Davies's screenplay Darcy is presented as an arrogantly sexy figure and Bridget asks Firth if he thinks Austen would have approved of this. Their discussion of historical revisionism rapidly spirals into a one-sided sexual fantasy with Bridget struggling to remain coherent as Firth recalls how Davies had insisted that Darcy should have 'an enormous sex drive'. 'At one point' he informs Bridget 'Andrew even wrote as a stage direction "Imagine that Darcy has an erection"'. Bridget appears thereafter to forget the ostensible topic of their exchange and noises replace words (*Bridget Jones: The Edge of Reason*, Picador, 2004, pp. 176–8).

There is little doubt that within the loftier spheres of literary culture – particularly academia – Tennant's liberation of Austen from the historical burden of patriarchy is taken more seriously than Fielding's contention that the late twentieth-century version of Elizabeth would benefit most from an abundance of hedonism, particularly sex. There is, however, cause to suspect that Fielding's invention, while popular and, some might argue, populist, is a shrewd diagnosis of a widespread sense of ambivalence among women 30 years after the culmination of feminist theorizing and activism.

A recent novel by Michèle Roberts, who built her reputation as a mainstream feminist, has puzzled critics. *Reader, I Married Him* (2005) announces through its title an intention to join what has become a form of seminar-by-fiction whose other participants include Winterson, Tennant and Fielding. Admission requires literary name-dropping, followed by subtle invitations to compare the given text with its predecessors, generally archetypal works by pre-1950s women writers. Roberts participates enthusiastically by creating in Aurora, her heroine, a living anthology of literary landmarks. Aurora has the habit of eliding her actual experiences with recollections of similar moments in the works of, among others, Austen, Charlotte Brontë, George Eliot, Elizabeth Gaskell and Dorothy L. Sayers, and by reinventing herself in this way she, or rather Roberts, raises questions about the relationship between women's notions of identity before and after feminism. Although the prospect of a profound debate on literature and gender is built into the book's fabric it is simultaneously dismantled by what happens in the narrative. We gradually become aware that Aurora, thrice married and widowed, is not so much entertaining the ghostly presences of her literary forebears as mocking them. The pilgrimage to Italy which occupies much of the novel is less cultural and religious than saturnalian. Aurora's old friend is now installed as abbess of a convent where every form of denial – particularly regarding drink, food and sex – is rigorously inverted and her curious fellow pilgrim Father Michael turns out to be a lot more interested in Aurora's orgiastic appetites than her spiritual well-being. As for her three late husbands, all of whom required her to conform to their self-obsessed and generally tedious lifestyles – and here the parallels with *Jane Eyre* and *Middlemarch* glint deceptively – reader, she murdered them.

Kate Saunders, in *The New Statesman*, is amused by the hall of mirrors effect of a novel 'packaged as chick lit' and indicating 'a respected author's bid for a larger share of the popular pound' while beneath the packaging lurks a more sinister spectacle: 'Think of John Lanchester and Thomas Harris in a threesome with Muriel Spark. There are no chicks here, thank God – only knowing old hens with talons of steel' (*New Statesman*, 24 January, 2005). Ajay Close in the *Sunday Herald* is more sceptical:

> ...capturing the spirit of the times can be a mixed blessing. Fine when you're cutting edge, rewriting cultural history (or 'herstory' as it was dubbed in the radical feminist 1970s), giving voice to the oppressed and turning a beady eye on the way we live now. But what happens when the zeitgeist moves on, when you've undermined patriarchal culture so successfully that you're thoroughly mainstream and, argu- ably, have more in common than the monolith you toppled than with the genderblind girlies of the 21st century? Then, if you're Michele Roberts, you write a chick lit novel. (*The Sunday Herald*, 9 January 2005)

Both reviews are, in truth, struggling with a novel that refuses to surrender to easy categorization, and the fact that their primary instinct is to fit contemporary women's fiction into such categories reflects an uneasy relationship between the cultural establishment and the writers themselves. Helen Falconer in a *Guardian* article sums up the problem:

> When women write cheerful, upbeat stuff about aspirational females out and about in the world, they are bluntly informed that it doesn't count as literary, it's just chick lit. Thus women authors have quite a hoop to jump through: how can they write about their own gender and give their characters exciting lives and happy endings without being swiftly relegated from literary to flittery? A tricky question, and one that many women solve by abandoning their Booker ambitions and taking the money. (*The Guardian*, 30 April 2005)

It is not even as straightforward as this. One of the less beneficial legacies of feminism is the network of expectations that accompany virtually every book whose author is self-evidently female. Irrespective of type – whether it be mainstream realist fiction, experimental writing or such subgenres as the thriller and detective/crime writing – many readers, particularly reviewers and critics, carry into their encounter of the text an acquired recipe of gender differentiation, a sense that post-1960s women writers and theorists have set standards and estab-lished precedents that newcomers must address. As a consequence all subsequent women writers tend to be judged by comparison with their groundbreaking gender-conscious forbears and contemporaries. To further complicate the issue, few if any would deny that what Close in the *Sunday Herald* refers to as the twenty-first-century 'zeitgeist' is very different both for men and women than the socio-cultural fabric that was challenged by and in some degree sustained feminist fiction in the 1970s and 1980s. Quite how and to what extent such changes have occurred cannot succinctly be described – opinions differ for instance on whether only middle-class or aggressively ambi-tious women have benefited from the purely economic and profes-sional aspects of gender equality – and this indeterminate progress is matched by an amorphous variegated fabric of opinions on what women writers should be doing and how well they do it.

Fielding, Weldon and Roberts offer a prism of perspectives upon women and society in the late 1990s and early 2000s. Each, in dif-ferent ways, is inclined to disrupt expectations regarding the nature and purpose of postfeminist fiction. Whether they do so as a purposive critique of the relevance of feminism today or to meet a perceived demand among women readers is a matter of opinion. What cannot be denied is that it is now far more difficult to distinguish between fiction that is avowedly feminist and that which is not and there is evidence to suggest that since the mid-1990s a large number of women writers have felt that engagements in fiction with the political and ideological subtext of gender difference is a redundant obligation, even an encumbrance, that the quality, individuality or peculiarity of their work is now of more significance than their adherence to a cause.

Susie Boyt's *Only Human* (2004) discloses the day-to-day life of Marjorie, whose husband died 17 years earlier before her marriage properly began. The glum irony of fate causes her to spend her time counselling those who should never have married at all – one likens his wife's dress to a rat's abortion. Her daughter, anorexic and alien-ated, has moved away; she still sleeps with her late husband's unwashed jumper. Frequently in public people ask for her autograph: she bears an uncanny resemblance to the star of a popular television hospital soap. This uneasy combination of black comedy and despair is deli-cately executed and Marjorie's purblind optimism regarding her clients' prospects and her own future is all the more enchanting because of its futility. The fact that Marjorie is a woman plays a significant part in the direction and fabric of the narrative but it is not given special or supplementary attention. It is difficult to imagine a novel with the comparable plot written 30 or even 20 years earlier which could have avoided giving particular emphasis to gender either involuntarily, as a contributory feature of her hopelessness, or more assertively as a means of compensating for her dismal existence. It is not that Boyt deliberately avoids issues raised by the literary feminists; rather she demonstrates that a shrewd discerning account of a woman's life in 2005 can be written without them.

On the face of it Marjorie has little in common with Jennifer, narrator of A. L. Kennedy's *So I Am Glad* (1995). Jennifer is 34, survivor of a pathological, forbidding conflict between her parents and now clinging to a thread of professional success as a radio newsreader. She seethes with 'unexpressed rage' and resents being treated as a pseudo-journalist, allowed only to read and never write the news – particularly given that the demise of a decade and a half of Tory government appears imminent. Throughout all this Kennedy plays games with the reader's expectations. Continually one is led to anticipate a moment of recognition on Jennifer's part, or a choreography of narrative threads on Kennedy's, that will point to gender as the cause for the former's thwarted ambitions or more general sense of alienation. But this never occurs. Instead her sex and indeed her sexuality are dealt with as crystallizations of her individuality and mindset. Her personal life involves a casual boyfriend, Steven, on whom she practises, albeit rather distractedly, impressively painful acts of sadism, and again one is caused to expect at least a hint of symbolism regarding revenge for her current status, shared of course with her sisters over several millennia. But, no, she is simply as temperamentally suited to sadism as her partner is to masochism. Eventually she meets a more alluring individual, the handsome, mature, enigmatic Martin who, amongst other things, glows in the dark, and claims, convincingly, to be Cyrano de Bergerac reborn – not Rostand's dramatized version but the real one. Does Jennifer believe him, and if so does this give proof at least to her susceptibility to a male-orientated fantasy? The question is raised, implicitly, and undermined quite brilliantly by a conclusion which obviates any curiosity as to whether he is either mad or a genuine reincarnation. Instead their relationship remains peculiar, indeterminate, perversely sincere, and all axioms regarding gender and temperament suddenly seem irrelevant.

Kennedy's more recent novel *Paradise* (2004), already considered, also seems designed to skew what have become standardized notions of the woman in fiction. The drunken monologue is a subgenre of fiction with a small respectable lineage which, with the exception of Djuna Barnes's *Nightwood* (1936), is possessively masculine. Jack London (*John Barleycorn*, 1913), Patrick Hamilton (*Twenty Thousand Streets Under the Sky*, 1935), Gordon Williams (*Big Morning Blues*, 1974) and Alasdair Gray (*Janine*, 1982) situate their central characters in circumstances with implicit yet prevailing rules and conventions. Specifically the male drunk, particularly when intoxicated in public, comprises several parts despair, heroic failure and licensed belligerence while his female counterpart is generally allowed little more than debauched vulnerability. Kennedy, through Hannah Luckraft, does not so much defy this tradition as ignore it. Hannah's job, background, and her, literally, unsteady relationship with Robert, a dentist who can match her bottle for bottle, is described by her with chilling accuracy. She blends unwitting omissions – such as being unable to remember where she was the night before or describe properly where she has just woken up – with moments of elegiac precision. 'You suit each other, you and God' she tells herself at one point, 'you're both alone'. Like Boyt's Marjorie, Hannah emerges as a convincing and absorbing fictional presence and for both one senses that this quality would be, if not diminished, then at least unnecessarily obscured had gender been presented as the determinative factor in who they are or what they do.

There is an interesting contrast between these and a near contemporaneous 'novel' by one of the veterans of feminism, Fay Weldon. I use inverted commas because *Mantrapped* (2004) is part invention, part autobiography, part reflections upon life and writing. While Weldon casts a jaundiced eye back to the hopes and, she avers, delusions of the post-1960s feminists her more significant message is unstated and involuntary: despite herself she can't stop writing about these issues and as a consequence they have become a burdensome accompaniment to everything else she might want to create or do. Weldon's narrative – autobiographical and fictional parts included – takes us through the previous four decades, and one is prompted to wonder what someone less preoccupied with the counternarrative of militant feminism would have done with a similar chronicle. Conveniently this hypothesis is made real by a writer who, coming from a generation subsequent to Weldon's, can make a more convincing claim upon impartiality. Sally Beauman's *The Landscape of Love* (2004) is one of those novels that reflects a fascination with what has now become the mythology of the 1960s and 1970s, which – particularly for those whose knowledge of those decades is vicarious – invites as much sceptical suspicion as nostalgia. It begins in 1967, the so-called summer of love, and involves three beautiful, amiably dysfunctional sisters and a hot-blooded trio of young men. The first part is narrated by Maisie, the strangest, most fanciful of the sisters. Maisie communes with nuns who haunt the semi-derelict abbey in which the sisters live – and one can't help wondering if her questionable grasp upon reality is designed by Beauman as a sardonic feint at the mantra recycled by veterans of the decade that life then was too exhilarating, blissful and dope-fuelled to merit clarity of recollection. Harsh reality takes over when the narrative is passed to Dan, one of the 1960s teenagers now down on his luck. It is the 1990s. Dan has feasted upon the 1980s boom and bust years and is now a despairing self-pitying figure, unable to decide whether the directionless optimism of the pre-Thatcher period or the ugly self-gratification of what came after is the more disappointing. Finally, Julia, another of the sisters, takes charge. She has become a Nigella Lawson-style celebrity and Beauman causes her to disclose, unwittingly, how layers of honesty, emotional commitment, charity and wit can enwrap hollowness and hypocrisy.

The novel tilts towards breathless melodrama with its elaborate maze of suicide, terminal illness, illegitimacy, even murder, but there is a more noteworthy subtext. The main characters, particularly the three narrators, are children of the 1960s and the one thing that they seem to have in common is long-term preoccupation with notions of selfhood instilled during their formative years. Sexuality and gender difference feature in the novel but mostly as grist to the protagonists' hungry states of self-absorption.

It would be both unfair and misguided to treat the early twenty-first-century relationship between feminism and fiction as moribund but evidence suggests that it is now as much a vocation or preoccupation as an engaging opportunity, its status buttressed partly by the well-established academic attachment to the broader sphere of gender studies.

When realist fiction addresses contemporaneity it takes on implicit, self-imposed rules and conventions. If its created social fabric and its characters are unrecognizable to contemporary readers the novel ceases to be realistic, and even fiction which creates a tension between naturalism and self-evident fantasy must first cause the former to correspond believably with the real world for the contrast to be effective. It is significant, therefore, that many female novelists do not now feel the imperative to use fiction as an instrument of protest against prevailing circumstances. Conversely they more often undertake a post-feminist version of negative capability, an ability to entertain and sustain conflicting views. The women characters are sometimes powerful, sometimes vulnerable, as frequently victims as provocateurs, yet their condition is never treated as symptomatic of inhibitive social mores and their motives involve much more than a self-conscious agenda of sisterhood.

Justine Picardie's *Wish I May* (2004) covers a year in the life of Kate, a freelance magazine journalist and single mother. Her involvement with her charming cousin Julian and later her relationship with the more uncomplicated builder Adam are emotionally demanding but not half so much as her haunted concern with the mysterious, unexplained death of her mother, which leads her into a compelling fascination with magic and physics.

Sarah Sands in *Playing the Game* (2004) tells the tale of Patti Ward, celebrity television news journalist, who becomes pathologically obsessed with the presence of the younger, multi-racial and unnervingly transparent, health correspondent Alexandra Khan. Patti sees her as a threat and it is at this point that Sands turns a familiar routine of expectations against itself. Standard, past representation of successful women in the media have treated factors such as age, loss of status, sexual jealousy, anxieties about appearance as a reliable recipe for an engaging almost believable narrative, but Patti's savagery transcends sexual stereotyping. It is frightening in its own right and the novel itself emerges as an equally merciless satire on everything from the banalities of modern newspaper production to the cheerfully defeatist Bridget Jones brand of farce.

Imagine the following plot. A prosecution lawyer ruins his own career by sleeping with an attractive witness for the defence. Meanwhile his son is in obsessive pursuit of a neurotic, beautiful actress who turns his adulation into a means of crushing him intellectually and emotionally. One would expect that two options are available to any author who would turn this abstract into a novel: that the men are foregrounded as guileless victims of their baser instincts or the women given prominence either as dangerous sirens or vengeful, newly empowered agents for their gender. Talitha Stevenson in *Exposure* (2005) confounds expectations by causing each option to militate against the other. Any attempt to attach notions of victimhood or predatory inclination to gender is cleverly disrupted and room is left for Stevenson to dissect her inventions with elegant dispassionate attention to detail. Similarly Nicci Gerard's *Solace* (2005) has the narrator Irene tell us with almost masochistic precision of how her husband deceived her, how her marriage fell apart and how in the end her previous sense of who and what she was perished. This could easily be mistaken for the woman-orientated 'therapy novel' in which the meticulous narrative reconstruction of a crisis assists the victim – and perhaps even a similarly affected reader – to rebuild her sense of identity. But with great subtlety Gerard causes us to suspect that Irene, while telling the truth about events, is an unreliable witness to her own feelings. Again, stereotypical notions of gender and victimhood are undermined and space is found for an untrammelled tale of disintegration and its aftermath.

Since the mid-1990s women novelists have become more inclined to treat the feminist movement with a mixture of circumspection, disinterestedness and, if only by implication, deference. The room of Woolf's essay is perceived differently according to an author's inclinations and preoccupations, but few would dispute that it is now available and not the cause for continued militancy – at least within the sphere of writing. But while feminism has mutated and manifested itself in women's writing so variously since the 1960s what has been happening at the other side of the gender divide?

Chapter 8

Men

In the opening pages of William Boyd's *Brazzaville Beach* (Sinclair-Stevenson, 1990), the narrator, one Hope Clearwater, having already disclosed her gender in the prologue, begins her story by reflecting upon two acquaintances, both male (p. 3). Hauser is not present, but she comments on his 'cynical gossip, all silky insinuation and covert bitchery'. Clovis, however, is sitting close by. He is, apparently, a curious figure, prone to shifts between 'raffish arrogance' and 'total and single-minded self-absorption' and given to 'instinctively and unconsciously cupp[ing] his genitals whenever he was alarmed or nervous'. Hope then describes how an ant seems to have trapped itself under her shirt and how 'Clovis impassively watched me remove my shirt and then my bra'. Clovis's indifference to what some men would treat as a sexually provocative gesture is eventually explained when we are told of how soon afterwards he clambers into a nearby mulemba tree, swings with 'powerful easy movements' through the branches and is 'lost to sight, heading north east towards the hills of the escarpment' (p. 4). Clovis is an ape. Boyd provokes in the reader a composite network of assumptions on maleness and follows up with an implicit glance toward the way that some women deal with these same issues. In Hope's case the blurring of the distinction between a subhuman and the general condition of maleness is in part a reflection of her enlightened postfeminist singularity and in equal degree her sense of affinity, as a human, with the apes which she and her colleagues are studying in Africa.

Boyd is of roughly the same generation as Martin Amis, Ian McEwan and Julian Barnes. He began his career as a fiction writer in the early

1980s and while his manner and technique are eloquently traditional, a refined continuation of 1950s contra-modernism, he also shows an inclination to have absorbed many of the principles of feminism. With odd exceptions such as Hope most of his chief characters are male, and while he does not attempt to apologize for or disguise the less than endearing aspects of their gender there is a distinct sense that he is fully aware that a large proportion of his readers are women. His male figures are no more sympathetically discerning regarding their female counterparts than were characters in novels from the 1950s and 1960s, but Boyd noticeably avoids a trait common among his predecessors and noted by feminist critics. He does not permit a complicit relationship between the character, the text and by implication the author but instead offers an impartial portrait of maleness, inclusive of its baser and less agreeable inclinations. *The New Confessions* (1987), charting the experience of John James Todd through some of the twentieth century's more percipient moments, is exemplary in this respect.

One can discern a related tendency, though differently realized, in the work of McEwan, Jonathan Coe, Justin Cartwright and Barnes. It is not that their male, or indeed their female, characters are modelled according to ideological archetype or idealistic projection – each author in his own way executes a form of brutal honesty – but there is a discernable attempt to isolate the male figures in the text from any implied sense of authorial endorsement. We encounter the most extreme manifestation of this in McEwan's first two publications, the short stories of *First Love, Last Rites* (1975) and *In Between the Sheets* (1978). These include accounts by an adolescent narrator of how he raped his younger sister, an adult who describes in meticulous detail his molestation and murder of a neighbour's nine-year-old daughter, and a man who is unsettled by having to inflict quite so much pain upon his masochistic girlfriend but equally fearful that she will treat his failure to do so as a sign of weakness. What we are encountering, in truth, is a gross exaggeration of the worst aspects of male sexuality. No comment ever accompanies these tales but one suspects that the more enlightened male reader is being urged to endure something resembling horrified recognition. The only story in which the mood lightens, albeit sardonically, involves two nurses who take revenge upon a pornographer by promising him a perverse treat, strap him to a bed and cut off his penis. The story, called 'Pornography' might well have carried the subheading 'Mea Culpa'.

Coe's *The Rotters' Club* (2001) and *The Closed Circle* (2004) offer a more circumspect version of hapless maleness. Certainly the women of the novels are hardly flawless but Coe executes a neat codicil by making sure that their shrewder representatives share with the reader the spectacle of masculinity deflated by its own absurdities, pretensions and overarching ambitions. Barnes is equally egalitarian in *Talking It Over* (1991) and *Love etc.* (2000). Having each character speak directly to an anonymous reader sets them outside the protective conventions of narrative or dialogic exchange. Transparency becomes something that will eventually track them down, and the men suffer more noticeably than the women.

Aside from the general tendency among post-1970s male novelists to engage self-consciously with gender differentiation there is a particular brand of fiction by men that has proved both popular and contentious – contentious because commentators are divided on whether it is a commendable examination of maleness or the perpetuation, thinly disguised, of its prefeminist manifestations: 'lad lit'. Its most commented-upon representatives are Nick Hornby, Tim Lott, Tony Parsons and Simon Armitage. Typically the main character or characters will be men who attained a degree of adulthood – one is reluctant to say 'reached maturity' – around the end of the 1980s and thereafter find themselves in a social milieu that is, as far as their sex drive is concerned, at once seductive and perplexing. Their female counterparts seem able to match them in terms of confidence, intelligence, social bravado and hedonistic endurance and many authors and characters treat this as a credible licence for the behaviour and stylistic traits which have come to characterize the subgenre. Hornby's *Fever Pitch* (1992) is a memoir-monologue in which he combines self-evident wit and intelligence with a coat-trailing involvement in subculture, in this case football. The book can be regarded as a rehearsal for his first fictional creation, Rob Fleming of *High Fidelity* (1995). Rob's fixation with rock music is partly his means of retreat from more demanding engagements with the real world and partly an index to them. Rob's relationship with Laura begins with his compilation for her of a tape of the 'best' contemporary music and his eventual understanding of why their relationship has ended is marked by his collateral recognition that he should have thought more about the music she liked. When caused by their break-up to reflect upon the broader nature of existence, his replacement for Nietzschian pondering is a compilation 'top five' of his most memorable romantic failures, and his compensatory affair with an American folk-rock singer has as much to do with her calling as her personality.

Will in *About a Boy* (1998) seems a continuation of Rob in all but name. At 36 he has never held a job and lives comfortably from the royalties generated by the annual surge in nostalgic-masochistic purchases of the novelty song 'Santa's Super Sleigh', penned by his late father. Will, handsome, sexy and lazily lecherous joins a local branch of SPAT (Single Parents – Alone Together). He invents an ex-wife and two-year-old son and sets about persuading the otherwise exclusively female members of the group that he is, like them, sensitive and emotionally scarred, with a view to seducing the more attractive ones. His deceits are uncovered by Marcus, the 12-year-old son of a fellow SPAT member, with whom Will forms a bond. The friendship between Will and Marcus, incorporating Will's charitable dealing with the latter's dysfunctional feminist-hippy mother, indicates that Hornby was steering his particular brand of lad lit toward more demanding issues. There are, for example, intriguing questions regarding the topic of male maturity raised by Will's and Marcus's moments of mutual recognition. At the same time the novel shares with its predecessors a possibly deliberate strategy of evasion. We are never certain of whether the principal characters are being held at a distance as slightly odd, pitiable products of gender and circumstance or whether Hornby is shamelessly inciting a degree of amused fellow feeling among predominantly male readers.

This same sense of calculated ambivalence resurfaces in Tim Lott's *White City Blue* (Viking, 1999), which opens with the estate agent narrator showing an attractive female client around a flat in West Kensington. In the process he persistently puts up signposts for the reader. His 'Beemer' is parked outside; the 1990s, like his twenties, have come to an end; he needs bigger and more regular commissions on his sales. This guarantees a degree of recognition for anyone who is even obtusely aware of the late 1990s property boom and the more general atmosphere of money-from-nowhere that went with it. Then, seamlessly, he shifts attention to his client, assessing the likely cost of her designer clothes as he would the price of a property and summing up the combined attractions of her hair, face, figure and legs like a surveyor who knows the market very well. Her watch is Raymond Weil and in her bag is a copy of 'something by Virginia Woolf'. 'I could also tell from the fact that it was dog-eared in three places in the first ten pages that she was reading it out of a sense of duty rather than enjoyment, which was fine by me' (p. 6). Cleverly and ruthlessly Lott is toying with two levels of response. On the one hand one might imagine the passage being enjoyed by a reader, not exclusively male, who doesn't even have to suspend disbelief, while there would be others who might see the unhindered intermeshing of wealth, materialism, sexuality and identity as a sardonic pointer to the kind of novel made famous by Jackie Collins – what Collins had dangled before us as unrealizable fantasy is now apparently commonplace in the lives of young city folk who know how to make money. The tantalizing appearance of Woolf points up this potential division. We are never certain of whether Lott intends us, or indeed his narrator, to recognize this as a darkly ironic comment on the destiny of feminists or treat it simply as part of an impressive range of fashion accessories.

It is impossible to determine finally if Lott intends the book as a scathing comment upon a society skewed by its own materialism and narcissism or as an indulgent panacea to readers who take such a condition for granted. In truth, he probably intended both, given that this would broaden his prospective readership.

At the other end of the lad lit spectrum, but no less disingenuous, are novels that exchange clumsy or blatant masculinity for a version that almost drowns itself in sensitivity. Ben Elton's *Inconceivable* (1999, later filmed as *Maybe Baby*) is a dire example of this, followed more recently by Simon Armitage's *The White Stuff* (2004) and Tony Parsons' *The Family Way* (2004). The young males in these books try to achieve self-effacing empathy with their women partners, not just in dry ideological terms but at a more wondrous biological level. Children are a common theme. Armitage's Felix tries to deal sympathetically with his partner Abbie's desperation for a child: he wants one too but she is nearing 40 and the clock is ticking. There is a woeful episode in which she leaves Felix in the car and sets off for coffee from the service area. She returns with six jars of baby food, two bibs and a Noddy cassette, arranges these on the dashboard and completes her desolating performance by suspending a pair of booties from the rear-view mirror. The scene was no doubt intended as an illustration of how a male writer and his fictional representative can have sympathetic knowledge of the distress experienced by a woman in Abbie's situation – how else would the former be able to evoke it so memorably and the latter respond, as he does, with such tactful maturity? Despite his intentions, however, Armitage distils empathy into embarrassment and Abbie becomes almost a caricature of the unbalanced female.

In *The Family Way* Parsons, apparently following the same agenda, overreaches himself even further by writing a novel about motherhood from the perspective of three sisters. The reader is bombarded with poignantly charged scenarios. One sister is a successful career woman whose partner has obediently had a vasectomy; another is a junior doctor who becomes, unhappily, pregnant after a one-night stand; the third, desperate for a baby, is condemned by endometriosis to infertility. Parsons wears his research proudly, loading the exchanges between the sisters with insider knowledge on miscarriages, fertility treatments, adoption agencies, maternity procedures and abortion, all laden with an abundance of sincerity and fellow feeling that makes the male characters of the novel seem emotionally retarded. The men, despite their hopeless concessions to ideological correctness, are united in their submission to a primal sex drive. Although Parsons is by no means as accomplished a writer as McEwan, Boyd and Barnes, one can detect a continuity within their work: maleness is treated with almost apologetic unease while the more variegated notion of womanhood is accorded a confounding, almost mysterious status.

One should not, however, regard this as a trend common to all post-1970s male novelists. There are a considerable number of exceptions, the most notable being Martin Amis. John Self, the narrator of *Money* (1984) provoked a litany of censures from feminist critics, most famously Laura A. Doan's contention that he treats actual women and their pornographic representations as interchangeable, denying both 'personhood, placing her in the ultimate state of disempowerment and disembodiment' (in Nicolas Treddell (ed.), *The Fiction of Martin Amis*, Palgrave Macmillan, 2000, p. 77). Doan's point is valid, but she and most of her confederates seem unable to distinguish clearly between Self and his creator. One is never quite certain of whether it is Amis or Self as his apparent avatar who is being charged with rabid sexism and this is due to Amis's deliberate and – irrespective of one's opinion on its motives – ingenious manipulation of the reader's expectations. As we have already seen 'Martin Amis' appears in the book and on several occasions taxes a bored distracted Self with such questions as 'Is there a moral philosophy of fiction? When I create a

character and put him through certain ordeals, what am I up to –
morally? Am I accountable?' (*Money*, Penguin, 1985, p. 260) and 'The
distance between author and narrator corresponds to the degree to
which the author finds the narrator wicked, deluded, pitiful or ridiculous' (p. 246). The mischief becomes apparent when we compare the
rather withdrawn gnomic figure of Amis with his interlocutor Self,
who has for the duration of the novel taken over from the former as
energetic stylist. By allowing his brilliant garrulous alter ego to disclose tastes and temperamental predispositions that few men would
publicly own up to Amis offers the reader a prism of interpretive mismatches. He undermines the postfeminist tradition in which male
novelists keep examples of the less agreeable aspects of their gender
at arm's length, and in *The Information* (1995) his sense of irritation
at this realignment of writing according to nonliterary ordinances
becomes further apparent. At a meeting attended by the two competing novelists Richard Tull and Gwyn Barry, two newspaper columnists
and the Shadow Arts Minister Gwyn offers his writerly manifesto

> 'I find I never think in terms of men. In terms of women. I find I
> always think in terms of....*people*.'
> There was an immediate burble of appreciation: Gwyn, it
> seemed had douched the entire company in common sense and plain
> humanity. (p. 30)

All apart from Richard, who offers an inventive hypothesis:

> It must make you feel nice and young to say that being a man means
> nothing and being a woman means nothing and what matters is being
> a...person. How about being a *spider*, Gwyn? Let's imagine you're a
> *spider*. You're a spider and you've just had your first serious date. You're
> limping away from that now, and you're looking over your shoulder,
> and there's your girlfriend, eating one of your legs like it was a chicken
> drumstick. What would you say? I know. You'd say: I find I never think
> in terms of male spiders. Or in terms of female spiders. I find I always
> think in terms of...*spiders*. (pp. 30–31)

As the novel proceeds Gwyn's felicitous concern for equality of representation becomes part of a game played between them with Gwyn
as languid tormentor and Richard as hapless victim, whose only pal-
liatives are his own acid comments. When Gwyn informs him that

'Guess what. We had an intruder last night', Richard, almost instinctively, replies,

> 'Really? Did she take anything?'
> 'We're not really sure.'
> 'How did she get in? Was she armed, do you know?'
> Gwyn closed his eyes and inclined his head, acknowledging the satire. He had a habit, in his prose, of following a neuter antecedent with a feminine pronoun. From *Amelior*: 'While pruning roses, any gardener knows that if she...' Or, from the days when he still wrote book reviews: 'No reader could finish this haunting scene without feeling the hairs on the back of her...' Richard clucked away to himself, but these days he often opted for an impersonal construction, or simply used the plural, seeking safety in numbers.
> 'Through the front door.'
> 'She didn't turn violent, did she?'
> 'Come on, don't be a tit. It's very upsetting actually.' (pp. 238–9)

There is no record of William Boyd's response to this passage, if indeed he ever saw it, but it was clearly intended to register beyond the confines of Amis's novel. Amis was certainly not conducting an anti-feminist campaign. What infuriated him was the use of literature as a vehicle for an ideological or political agenda. In an essay called 'On Masculinity and Related Questions' (reprinted in Amis's *The War Against Cliché: Essays and Reviews, 1971–2000*, Cape, 2001) we find what is effectively a rehearsal for the scene involving Richard, Gwyn, the journalists and the minister, but here Amis is more transparent regarding his own opinions. 'Feminists' he explains, claim a 'moral equivalence for sexual and racial prejudice'. He agrees that there are affinities and that these are 'paradoxically, encouraging' in that 'we all feel such impulses'. While our parents felt them more strongly than us, 'Our children, we hope, will feel them less strongly than we feel them' (p. 9). His principal point is that this process of evolution cannot be accelerated by literary intervention, the reshaping of the world according to a polemic or an idealized prognosis. The subject of the essay is Robert Bly's *Iron John. A Book About Men*, an anti-feminist diatribe which veers involuntarily toward self-parody. Amis mercilessly helps it on its way and in doing so makes his own case that literature should not immunize itself from the 'impulses' of the real world, a case that would be illustrated by the assembly of male grotesques who populate *Yellow Dog* (Cape, 2003). Xan Meo, after his knock on the head, de-evolves, sheds the outer layer of his postfeminist self and we, the readers, are left with an unsettling presence. After an energetic performance as a foul-mouthed, unpredictable, sex-obsessed lout he writes his wife a letter reflecting on why he had, amongst other things, taken to brutalizing her and lusting after their four-year-old daughter. 'Men were in power for five million years. Now (where we live) they share it with women. That past has a weight, though we behave as if it doesn't. We behave as if the transition has been seamlessly achieved. Of course there's no going back. I went back. As through a trapdoor I dropped into the past' (pp. 306–7). The rest of the novel takes us with him through this trapdoor into the company of Clint Smoker, impotent tabloid spokesman for equally cretinous male readers, whose column deals often with cases of sexual assault: 'And who does the judge think he's kidding? He's got the gall to tell us there was "no provocation" when the bird was wearing a school uniform.' On the face of things Clint is more repulsive than the pitiable King Henry IX who drifts between affectionate trysts with his comatose wife and queen, occasional sex with his Chinese mistress and – his preferred option – moments alone with his TV set, but it is a close contest. Both, along with the habitués, customers and entrepreneurs of the California pornography industry – also meticulously scrutinized – raise the question of why Amis has elected to pack the novel with caricatures of unreformed maleness. He does so to prompt comparison with the new regiment of inventions – mostly the creations of men – who from the 1980s have variously apologized for their maleness, reaped appropriate punishments for their unfortunate state or tiptoed cautiously around the precise notion of what being a man might actually involve. True, Amis's figures are far more unpleasant, but in making them so he shows that in both cases fiction can involve a purposive distortion of actuality; if it's politically correct and in tune with the prevailing intellectual consensus, however, we tend not to notice.

A rather more muted, plausible version of Xan's torment, is the most profound characteristic of Henry Nagel, the subject of Howard Jacobson's *The Making of Henry* (2004). Henry is 60, forcibly retired from the University of the Pennine Way, and is recently, puzzlingly, the inheritor of a luxurious West London flat which he suspects holds the clue to his late father's other life of mendacity and probable adultery. These plot-lines, though fascinating enough, are but scaffolding for the novel's enduring theme, Henry's obsession with women: 'Nothing in his life has interested Henry more than this. Woman. Never mind the phenomenology or metaphysics of woman. Just the aesthetic of her. Just the *prospect*' (p. 71). Henry is capable of falling in love with women and he exhibits an interest and respect for women who are, as individuals, interesting. But every encounter, however informal, carries an unbidden subtext – a fascination with the way that sex makes virtually everything else peripheral. Henry is neither proud nor ashamed of this. He simply regards it as part of the complex, mostly burdensome, nature of existence, at least as a man. Indeed all of Jacobson's novels, from his debut *Coming From Behind* (1983) onwards, are, aside from their ostensible subject, drawn into an orbit around a persistently addictive enigma, the difference between men and women. *Who's Sorry Now* (2002) offers us Marvin Kreitman, a successful middle-aged businessman who is too tender to be called a rake; he loves his wife and two daughters and is also openheartedly besotted with five secret lovers. He is not happy, but he can envisage no other state. Once a week he lunches with his friend Charlie, a monogamist who shares with his wife his Christian name, joint authorship of a series of children's books and what he describes bitterly as 'nice sex'. The exchanges between Marvin and Charlie lead them to wonder what changes might be wrought to their respective and apparently immutable conditions if they swapped roles. They do so and their wives and lovers unwittingly cooperate. Jacobson, brilliantly, makes this unlikely sex-comedic scenario credible and thought-provoking. What he refuses to do is suborn or neutralize the potency of sexual difference by framing it within a disguised thesis on gender relations and power structures. His characters, men and women, are each granted an urgent individuality by his having them refuse to conform to expectations on how sex makes people behave and think.

Chapter 9

Gay Fiction

Howard Jacobson in *Who's Sorry Now* includes a figure called Nyman as a subversive master of ceremonies or Lord of Misrule. He arrives as a lycra-suited courier and remains on the edge of the action to create various levels of unease among the other characters, particularly the men. He does this principally because he is a homosexual and although Marvin and Charlie are by no means homophobic they are nonetheless confused. They know, or think they know, enough about their own sexual inclinations and how women respond to them to be able to deal with collateral effects, but homosexuality – from its instinctive drives to its correlative notions of selfhood – is pure hypothesis.

Nyman's paradoxical status as both disruptive and enigmatically self-contained might well be a sardonic comment by Jacobson upon the ways in which homosexuality has registered in fiction since the 1980s. One of the first British novels to proclaim itself – in terms of its mood and central characters – as unambiguously gay was Alan Hollinghurst's *The Swimming Pool Library* (Chatto and Windus, 1988). The action occurs during 1983 and the main character and narrator is one William Beckwith, educated at Winchester and Oxford and of minor aristocratic stock. Beckwith charts his sexual career with the disdainful aloofness of a connoisseur, his partners ranging from working-class rent-boys, through the deliciously attractive, and black, Arthur to the more tastefully platonic relationship with James, his friend since their Oxford days. Aside from offering with unprecedented clarity a chronicle of homosexual life in the early 1980s the novel is implicitly aware of its role as an historical document. Beckwith regards 1983 as the year when gay hedonism reached its apex and describes himself as 'riding high on sex and self-esteem...it was my time, my *belle epoque*'. A year later AIDS would cast a seemingly vengeful shadow over the season of abandon and hard-won freedom. The perspective is further lengthened when Beckwith meets the ageing Lord Nantwich, or more specifically finds him collapsed in a public toilet and rescues him from the less charitable attentions of others drawn likewise to the location. Beckwith and Nantwich become friends and the latter tells him stories of the earlier more furtive era of gay life. These eventually involve Beckwith's grandfather who as Director of Public Prosecutions in the mid-1950s had initiated the ruthless implementation of laws forbidding homosexual activity. Nantwich himself was arrested and imprisoned in 1954 for soliciting, and when asked by Nantwich to become his biographer Beckwith, after troubled reflection, declines. His reason for doing so is never explicitly disclosed but at the same time the decision becomes the thematic epicentre of the novel. Beckwith is aware of the opportunity and responsibilities that would come with the biography. It would, in part, be a history of repression and homophobia up to and indeed following the 1967 Act which legalized homosexuality. Beckwith would, moreover, feel obliged to denounce the power-structure represented by his grandfather and from which he and his peers have now been liberated. Yet when he ponders the differences between his generation and Nantwich's he finds curious similarities. Homosexuals no longer fear prosecution but he recognizes a shared sense of excitement at being able to cross the border from a world shared with heterosexuals to one that is more exclusive, involving its own codes of recognition and rituals of behaviour. Images of dissimulation and doubling reverberate through the novel. The swimming pool library of the title refers to the special privileges granted to Beckwith who as a prefect at Winchester could preside over clandestine sessions of seduction and sex in the swimming pool changing rooms. In adult life the Corinthian Club is the preserve of gays in the same way that the London gentleman's clubs have long been the confidential meeting places for those who dominate the political, legal and cultural establishment.

The notion of homosexuality as involving an almost addictive sense of separateness and collective alienation is the predominant feature of all of Hollinghurst's subsequent novels. *The Folding Star* (1994) concerns Edward Manners, a disaffected English art historian living in Belgium and pursuing two obsessions. One is Luc, his teenaged private pupil who both flirts with and frustrates him, and the other is the *fin de siècle* Symbolist artist Edgard Orst whose tortured paintings bespeak his hopeless pursuit of an English actress whom he regards as his muse. A variety of psychological and sexual parallels between the two are mooted and explored. Can art be detached from instinctive sexual attraction or does one enrich the other? More specifically is Manners's own desire for Luc in some way purified of its, for him, louche sexuality by his elevation of his pupil to the same status as Orst's beautiful muse? Luc eventually goes missing and Manners's pursuit of him, mostly via local gay bars, becomes an odyssey of self-recognition. The men he meets and who have also encountered Luc are similarly besotted and Manners gradually accepts that his attempt to identify himself with a heterosexual artist was guilt-ridden, romantically bathetic and misguided. He was denying a particular refinement of sexuality, a compulsion that is particular to gays.

The Spell (1998) takes us back to England with Alex, a middle-aged, middle-class civil servant deciding to become less discrete about his homosexuality and setting off on a journey of self-discovery involving gay youth culture, convivial one-night stands and drugs. The latter are introduced to him by Danny, son of the bisexual architect Robin, whose partner is Justin, Alex's previous long-term lover. The complications are by degrees fascinating and distracting and one is left with the impression that Hollinghurst is not simply reflecting the communal inclusivity of gayness but also making a claim upon gay fiction as a collateral subgenre in its own right. Every act and moment of interaction seems touched, in all his novels, by an alliance between lust and evanescence, and few if any of his characters seem able to transcend their own version of this state. Certainly, Howard Jacobson's principal male characters experience a comparable sense of all activity, formal or extemporary, as conjunctive with sexual desire, but he does not infer that this predicament is shared by all male heterosexuals.

Hollinghurst's acclaimed Booker-winning *The Line of Beauty* (2004) returns us to the 1980s, and a number of the plot-lines of *The Swimming Pool Library* are self-consciously reprised. Nick Guest is 20, recently down from Oxford and coming out. He joins the London gay scene, loses his virginity on a blind date with a black working-class man named Leo and subsequently moves up several classes to an affair with Wani, the spoiled, narcissistic, coke-snorting son of a Lebanese multi-millionaire. This novel differs from Hollinghurst's first because he has had almost 20 years to reflect on the 1980s, not just as a significant period for gay consciousness but in terms of the broader context of what happened in Britain as a whole: Thatcherism. A counternarrative accompanies Nick's coming to terms with his previously repressed sexuality as he plays witness to the activities of the Fedden family in whose grand Notting Hill house he stays for the duration of the novel. Hollinghurst provides an abundance of clues and anyone who had read or even seen the film version of Waugh's *Brideshead Revisited* will recognize deliberate parallels. The Feddens are the Marchmains, complete with a neurotic daughter, Catherine, and son Tony, Nick's unpredictable companion/confidante. The difference is that while the Marchmains represented the decline of all that Waugh valued – chiefly the certainties of Catholic doctrine, old money and natural aristocracy – the Feddens are the new nobility, brutal hedonists in awe of the woman who appeared to have brought about this renaissance of exorbitant wealth; there is even a mildly amusing scene in which Mrs Thatcher herself deigns to visit the Fedden household. The question of why Hollinghurst is coat-trailing Waugh's fable and his own earlier fiction is answered in the closing part of the novel. The stock market crash of 1987 and the escalating AIDS crisis affect Nick in different ways. He watches the catastrophe that besets a family whose tenuous claim upon genuine commitment and emotion are apparently founded upon their ability to pay for both and in quick succession he learns that the two men who effectively introduced him to himself, Leo and Wani, both have AIDS. Hollinghurst is reframing the vexed issue of his first novel regarding gay identity as split between individuality and communal affinity. Now he broadens the parameters but his conclusions are less ambiguous. The sardonic, satirical tone of the first parts is exchanged in the conclusion for a more earnest unfettered report of an unfolding tragedy, and for Nick the wailing that accompanies his host's financial disaster is laughably absurd compared with his own sense of having been selected and pursued by a disease with a malicious agenda of its own.

In Adam Mars-Jones's collections of short stories *The Darker Proof: Stories from a Crisis* (with Edmund White, 1987) and *Monopolies of Loss* (1992) AIDS is the predominant theme. The condition and its effects are dealt with in a way that abolishes any clear distinction between black comedy and merciless naturalism. In 'An Executor', for example, Charles dies from AIDS and his partner has to deal with his family's desire to keep the cause of his death secret. Alongside this he faces the practical problem of disposing of Charles's vast store of leather bondage and fetish equipment and one is left with the impression that this blend of tragedy and desolate farce is an exclusively gay experience. Mars-Jones's single novel *The Waters of Thirst* (1993) engages with AIDS without addressing it directly. The narrator William has been in a long-term monogamous relationship with Terry since the 1980s and, having apparently avoided HIV, contracts a potentially terminal form of kidney disease. The grim irony of this is not lost upon William, who as a gourmet and wine connoisseur is now obliged to live without salt and alcohol. Eventually, enforced denial becomes a pseudo-masochistic form of self-denial as he fantasizes over pictures and videos of a gay porn star. The unspoken subtext is that for gays who protected themselves against AIDS there remains a sense of having unnaturally tamed a primal instinct and that some malevolent ally of the disease is visiting its deadly irony upon William. The novel concludes in a hallucinogenic miasma following William's liver transplant operation. It is implied that he is now afflicted with AIDS itself by virtue of a postoperative morphine injection and we are left with an image of the fates themselves as vengefully homophobic.

Dominic Head argues that British gay fiction has created its own 'socially withdrawn' niche and displays a tendency to 'replicate the limits that it anatomises' (*Modern British Fiction, 1950–2000*, Cambridge University Press, 2002, p. 117). This hint that gay writing may have become narcissistic is dealt with less tactfully by a self-proclaimed contributor to the subgenre, Philip Hensher. His novel *Kitchen Venom* (1996) is the gay counterpart to Michèle Roberts's *Reader, I Married Him*. Neither goes so far as to fully betray its acknowledged parentage – respectively fictional engagements with gay identity and feminism – but each comes close to self-caricature. John is a senior House of Commons clerk who faces a dilemma. Will he set up home with Giacomo, the Italian rent-boy with whom he has fallen in love, or should he keep his sexual affiliation a secret and maintain his comfortable closeted life as widower with two daughters? The choice itself eventually becomes untenable in that dissimulation is what makes both aspects of his life worthwhile, so to avoid exchanging the thrill of deceit for the lesser attractions of transparency he murders Giacomo. If this were not sufficient surrender of credulity to the grotesque then the identity of the narrator supplies a special touch of deviancy, for she is Margaret Thatcher. The bittersweet relationship between gay lifestyle and the social and political mood of the 1980s has become a recurring motif in gay fiction. Hensher adds a twist to this by having Thatcher tell the story shortly after her own downfall, 1992, and having her dwell upon a tenet which unites her with John – secrecy. Secrets, it seems, are vital elements in a Machiavellian philosophy of existence – and are in their own right sensual and gratifying, a maxim which Hensher seems implicitly to endorse. Hensher exchanges the balance between celebration and lamentation established by Hollinghurst and Mars-Jones for a more unpredictable vision of a skewed hedonism. He stops short of parody but Will Self is not so circumspect.

Dorian: An Imitation (2002, Penguin 2003) updates Wilde's Faustian classic to the early 1980s. Self's Dorian comes down from Oxford in 1981 and the novel charts his career of murder and abomination up to 1997. The dates are significant, coinciding as they do with the marriage of Diana Spencer and Prince Charles and the former's death. Lady Diana appears in the novel not so much as a character as an almost disembodied icon created by the media and venerated by the masses. Dorian meets her on several occasions but more significantly Self also creates a split-screen account of their separate lives. As Diana walks up the aisle of St Paul's, Dorian is spending the afternoon in a well-appointed Knightsbridge flat, sharing needles with friends who eventually celebrate the event with what is described as a 'conga line of buggery'. When Diana receives her ring (and the double entendre is not accidental) a virulent early manifestation of HIV passes along the conga line.

Dorian sometimes murders his victims in a conventional manner and on other occasions deliberately infects them with AIDS. (Diana during her televised 'hands on' ministrations to AIDS patients visits one of the latter.) Dorian carries the disease but remains arrogantly immune from its effects and one cannot but wonder at the target of this merciless blend of satire and literary sadism. For those familiar with the fictional milieu created by Hollinghurst, Mars-Jones and Hensher points of recognition begin to multiply. The wealthy, hedonistic cast of Dorian's friends and victims mirrors the social montage of *The Swimming Pool Library*. Dorian, like Beckwith, enjoys slumming but in this case chooses to pleasure a Soho rent-boy with an infected overdose of heroin. Beckwith's Lord Nantwich is reproduced by Self with an update of Wilde's Sir Henry Wotton, ageing, vitriolic, affected and humourlessly camp. Nantwich experiences two levels of detachment from the ordinariness of life, the first granted by his aristocratic status, the second by his sexual orientation. But while he only hints that their combination grants him a special claim upon superiority Wotton is far less restrained, referring, for example, to Diana variously as 'Thickie Spencer', 'The Royal Broodmare', 'The Royal Fag Hag' and 'Her Royal Regurgitation, the Princess of Clothes'. One wonders also if Self is turning a baleful rebarbative eye toward Mars-Jones's short stories in which the experiences of AIDS sufferers, their friends, partners and relatives are depicted with an endearing meticulous honesty. When Wotton falls terminally ill he describes himself as feeling 'gothic with disease – as if Cologne Cathedral were being shoved up my fundament'.

The novel received mixed reviews but even those who indulged Self's apparent determination to shock were unsure of his broader purpose. Others, the majority, saw it as a gratuitous exercise in provocation. Jonathan Heawood in the *Observer* (29 September 2002) detects a 'whiff of homophobia in the depictions of the Eighties gay scene', and in *The Times* (16 October 2002) Ruth Scurr avers that 'unless you are a bigoted, homophobic, misogynist, racist aristocrat, [this] novel will make you sick.' One might find Self's technique offensive but it is evident that his objective is to both exaggerate and consequently challenge a mythology of exclusivity that he sees as a defining characteristic of gay culture, particularly in fiction.

Part IV

Nation, Race and Place

The questions of difference which attend the issues of gender and sexual orientation are charitably straightforward when compared with those raised by the beguiling trio of race, location and nationality. Some problems are immediately apparent. Racial differences, for example, would for most of us, despite ourselves, be a correlative of skin colour. For the vast majority of white people resident in Britain in, say, the 1950s difference of colour meant separateness and, for many, assumptions of superiority. The latter, racism, still exists but it has for most Britons, white and nonwhite alike, been overtaken by the knowledge and acceptance of an enlarged social fabric born initially out of the disintegration of the Empire. Within this fabric, however, there are innumerable strata and divisions of alignment and affiliation. Consider a random sample of six people, each of whom has at least three grandparents who arrived in Britain from the West Indies half a century ago and another half dozen who can trace a similar family history back to the Indian subcontinent. Of the 12 it is likely, indeed almost certain, that each would, if asked, provide a different version of inclusiveness with regard to the country in which they exist and the personal history attendant upon this. Aside from its colonial heritage, what of Britain itself? Some would claim, convincingly, that the very notion of Britishness is an administrative convenience. Others would further affirm that the cultural and national differences elided by the concept should be recognized and provisioned with political identity: Wales and Scotland now have parliamentary assemblies which grant their respective regions partial independence from Westminster. And then we come to Ireland. The Government of Ireland Act of

1922 provided the Northern six counties and the Southern 26 with separate parliaments based respectively in Belfast and Dublin. In 1922 following divisive civil war the South became the Irish Free State and in 1937 detached itself further from the UK by redrafting its Constitution to include a political and territorial claim upon the Northern Six Counties, and renamed itself as Eire or the Republic of Ireland. The political history of Ireland, up to and including the so-called Troubles, subsequent ceasefires and elected assemblies, is simple and transparent compared with the spectrum of opinions and claims upon national and cultural identity which underpin it.

Last of all we have the tendentious concept of England and Englishness. Jeremy Paxman claimed mischievously that the English have never properly defined themselves 'because they haven't needed to' (*The English. A Portrait of a People*, Michael Joseph, 1998, p. 23). The reason for this, he implied, was that post-1066 England had always been the predatory, ascendant nation and was therefore content simply to exist rather than, as its immediate neighbours were obliged to do, self-consciously proclaim its identity in order to maintain it. There are, of course, images of 'Englishness' encoded in cultural discourse – cricket, class-conscious imbecility, Gilbert and Sullivan, cream teas, modest forbearance, smug xenophobia, thatched cottages et al. – but these are so numerous, synthetically populist, regional and frequently antithetical as to virtually undermine any sense of a single immutable unit. Indeed it might be argued that the only secure notion of England and Englishness becomes evident from those perspectives upon identity and statehood which treat the United Kingdom and Britain as a repressive unnatural entity with England as its motivating force.

It would seem then that within these islands the permutations upon identity, separateness, conflict and division are almost without limit. But to consider how these are addressed in fiction it would be best, for reasons that should become apparent, to begin with Scotland.

Chapter 10

Scotland

Cairns Craig has written that 'in terms of the novel no period in Scottish culture has, perhaps, been as rich as the period between the 1960s and the 1990s' (*The Modern Scottish Novel: Narrative and the National Imagination*, Edinburgh University Press, 1999, p. 36). During the 1960s and 1970s realism was the predominant mode with novelists such as George Friel, Alan Sharp, Carl MacDougall and William McIlvanney offering contemporaneous chronicles but by the 1980s some novelists had begun to re-examine the interdependencies of national identity and writing, and few would dispute that the initiator of this new trend was Alasdair Gray.

Lanark: A Life in Four Books (1981) fulfils all of the standard criteria for experimental postmodern writing. It has two settings: contemporary Glasgow is realized with grim attention to detail while the dystopian realm of Unthank is self-evident fantasy. The eponymous principal character drifts between the two and the standard formulae of narrative design are further complicated by experiments with typography, with at one point two strands of the text unfolding simultaneously via twin columns on the page. It would do a grave injustice to the wilful perversity of the book to call it an allegory. Instead Gray invites the reader to follow him through various states of invention and inference, constantly leaving clues and hints toward some sort of overarching intention. At one point Lanark discovers beneath Unthank an institute where scientists and technicians have set about exploiting the poor in the most seamlessly pragmatic ways possible: they use them literally as fuel and food. Swift's *A Modest Proposal* is brought to mind but Gray goes further by challenging the very discourse that makes, or used to make, conventional allegory possible. During his various excursions Lanark opens a door marked, appropriately enough, 'Epilogue' and there finds his author Nastler. An exchange between the two follows in which Nastler explains that Lanark's project – principally to expose the injustices that underpin the institutions and mindsets he encounters – is fatally flawed. It cannot succeed because it is too unorthodox, robustly unwilling to conform to the conventions of accessibility, coherence and realism which effectively dominate fiction. We are left in little doubt that these suppressive exploitative forces of the novel are predominantly British but it is the subtext involving Nastler which has established it as a landmark in the recent history of Scottish fiction. Unlike other postmodern, reflexive conceits such as Fowles's appearance in *The French Lieutenant's Woman*, Nastler, the controlling presence of *Lanark* (and indeed Lanark), is clearly not Gray. He embodies an implied, though unnamed, literary autocracy which tolerates decentralized, unfixed narrative experiments only as peripheral amusements. The real work of literature, involving statements about the world in which we live, should be left to rationalists whose fictional prose accords with the same criteria of order and transparency that govern its nonliterary counterparts. When Lanark hears the story of Duncan Thaw it is narrated by an absent 'oracle' who does not respond to Lanark's questions on who exactly he is and if he is telling the truth. Instead the 'male pompous elderly voice' (*Lanark*, Picador, 1994, p. 105) continues with the narrative as if Lanark does not exist, and the whole exercise seems designed to show that the detached anonymity of third-person narrative carries with it the inference of heartless authoritarianism. If the novel can be said to involve something so conventional as a message it is that a conspiracy exists between those who control society and perpetrate its injustices and those who play a similar role in determining the efficacy and appropriateness of linguistic registers, the governance of culture.

Gray's second novel *1982 Janine* (Cape, 1984) involves Jock McLeish whose world is made up partly of self-generated fantasy and the persistent dilemma of being trapped between anger and attrition. Many of his fantasies are brutally sexual and he treats these as symptomatic of a general condition in which the state, specifically 'Britain', is 'organised like a bad adolescent fantasy' (p. 138). His outbursts against mechanistic state control are brief and random because he feels trapped also within a discourse that is not of his own making. 'Thinking', he states 'is a pain because it joins everything together' (p. 66).

At least two of Gray's novels, *The Fall of Kelvin Walker* (1985) and *McGrotty and Ludmilla* (1990) are written in an orthodox, realist manner. Both describe the lives of young Scots in London and much attention is given to how such figures feel at once out of place and suddenly better aware of the political ethos and culture that, from a distance, exercises control upon their home country. If one were to raise the question of why Gray chooses to suspend the postmodern technique that seems so vital to his inbuilt message on British colonialism the answer lies partly in the setting: only those novels set outside Scotland defer to the conventions of realism, that predatory, alien mechanism that is best left south of the border.

Gray's more provocative fiction is important because for the first time it allies formal experiment with a specific political agenda. Since the beginning of modernism literary radicalism has been associated with a revolutionary ethos that is predominantly intellectual and aesthetic. There are, necessarily, political inferences but these have tended to be circumstantial and unpredictable. Within the broad spectrum of modernism and postmodernism the political affiliations of authors have ranged from neo-fascism (Pound) through smug conservatism (Eliot), snobbish indifference (Woolf) to Marxism (Berger). Moreover, for each there has been no clear causal relationship between their technique and their political outlook. Gray, however, established a creative paradigm in which every divergence from and challenge to the methodological archetypes of fiction carried a concurrent assault upon British territorial and cultural colonialism and its particular manifestation in Thatcherite Conservatism.

A point addressed in Gray's early fiction and taken up by a number of other Scottish novelists is the friction between language as a personal register of identity and the monolithic impersonal structure of the novel. What began in *Lanark* with the struggle between the unpredictable, idiosyncratic Thaw and his detached indifferent oracle would mutate into the thematic signature of James Kelman.

Kelman's best-known novel *How Late It Was, How Late* (1994) involves the indignant, belligerent Sammy Samuels, a hard-drinking Glaswegian connoisseur of expletives. The narrative is an assembly of episodes with no apparent sense of continuity, which is no doubt intended as an apt reflection of his life, but the most significant feature of the novel is its stubborn refusal to distinguish between first- and third-person narrative. Much of it is composed of Sammy's mono-logues, in which syntax and spelling reproduce his particular collo-quial speech patterns and these sometimes blend into a hybrid third-person mode. Both contain almost equal degrees of bitterness and sustain a similar demotic style and frame of reference but the latter exerts the same cool omniscient detachment as the conventional third-person voice. The overall effect is to place the grim injustices visited upon Sammy in bleak perspective without according him a collateral state of victimhood within the texture of the novel. In short Sammy and his narrator are in alliance against the world they depict.

There is, for example, a passage of dialogue between Sammy and the doctor who has been appointed by the health service to assess his disability benefit. The exchange takes on an air of black comedy as the doctor advises him with 'respect of the visual stimuli presented to you you appeared unable to respond' and Sammy responds more concisely with 'So ye're no saying I'm blind?' In a different context this would be a straightforward clash between social registers and implied backgrounds but because the dialogue is effectively contained within the discourse made up of Sammy and his narrator the doctor appears as a pompous mildly absurd outsider. The conclusion of the exchange is tinged as much with textual triumph as class conflict:

'I find your language offensive.'

'Do ye? Ah well fuck ye then. Fuck ye!' (p. 225)

The technique is effective and Kelman's use of the novel as a vehicle for the working-class Scottish culture, or as Geoff Gilbert puts it 'creative endeavour in a time of punishment' ('Can Fiction Swear? James Kelman and the Booker Prize', in *An Introduction to Contemporary Fiction*, ed. Rod Mengham, Polity, 1999, p. 231), has been widely celebrated, but is it entirely original? Kingsley Amis is hardly a figure one would even remotely associate with the post-1970s Scottish literary renaissance but it is possible to find in his first novel *Lucky Jim* (1954) the formal prototype for *How Late it Was, How Late*. Certainly the linguistic register of the former is lower-middle-class English rather than working-class Scots, but in each there is the same cunning alliance between the protagonist and his wily narrator, in effect two versions of the same presence, who cooperate to undermine the prevailing conventions of cultural order and decency. Levels of abuse and collateral offence mutate with history – Amis, had he used the word 'fuck' in 1954 would never even have got into print – but the responses from establishment stalwarts such as, in Amis's case W. Somerset Maugham, and in Kelman's Rabbi Julia Neuberger and Simon Jenkins were remarkably similar. (See above, p. 8 and Gilbert, p. 231).

Kelman might have upset the refined sensibilities of the British literary establishment but compared with Irvine Welsh his descent into the miseries of urban estrangement is cheerily Dickensian. Welsh's *Trainspotting* (1993) has been praised for dragging the moribund discourse of fiction writing closer than ever before toward the multigeneric carnival of popular culture, which by the 1990s seemed set upon combining narcissistic amorality with a determination to offend as many people as possible. The novel's closest relative in film is probably Tarantino's *Reservoir Dogs*. In the latter the characters are professional villains while for Welsh's Renton, Begbie and Sick Boy the casual criminality of drug dealing, addiction, theft and violence is bound into the fabric of day-to-day life. But Welsh and Tarantino have much in common. Both pretend, very effectively, to be producing nihilistic, unstructured pieces with no sense of moral or intellectual coherence while at the same time each manipulates mercilessly the reader's/viewer's desire for some notion of continuity, even comfort.

Stylistically, Welsh joins the Gray–Kelman school of patois-narrative. In *Trainspotting* the first-person mode shifts between different characters and in virtually all instances the urban Edinburgh dialect of reported speech migrates into the narrative. The small spectrum of perspectives seems hardly necessary when each of the characters appears equally culpable and hopeless in a common miasma of poverty, crime, violence and self-destruction, but Welsh manages to sew into the first-person passages what amount to speculations on the cause of their condition. Scotland, Scottishness and an array of questions attending both became a persistent refrain. He disabuses us of the myth that the Irish are 'the trash ay Europe'. No, 'That's shite. It's the Scots. The Irish hud the bottle tae win thir country back, or at least maist ay it' (p. 190). This appears to be a drink-sodden rant, but gradually such apparently unfocused, discontinuous laments begin to acquire not only a precarious shape, but a cautious rationale. 'Ah've never felt British' he tells us 'because ah'm not. Its ugly and artificial.

Ah've never really felt Scottish either, though. Scotland the brave, ma erse; Scotland the shitein cunt'. We should not mistake this for a compound of nihilism and self-loathing because there is, apparently, something that unites the Scots: 'We'd throttle the life oot ay each other fir the privilege ay rimmin some English aristocrat's piles' (p. 228). *Trainspotting* is usually presented as having abstained from recognizable engagements with morality, ethics and national identity but beneath its anarchic sheen there is an impressive stratum of calculation. We should note, for example, that it is not England and Englishness per se that is the target of this polemic but 'English aristocrats', a well-worn and threadbare target but one guaranteed to draw an alliance of loathing from young politically self-conscious readers, English or otherwise. Renton recalls becoming angry when in London he heard the Scots described as 'porridge wogs'. He goes on to add that 'Now ah realise that the only thing offensive about that statement was its racism against black people. Otherwise its spot-on' (p. 190). So, despite being capable of violence, theft and in such a state of desperation as able to nonchalantly retrieve his heroin suppositories from an unflushed toilet bowl, Renton maintains a commendable level of political correctness. The most famous passage is where he turns his scorn toward the seemingly psychotic Begbie, who is 'intae baseball-batting every fucker that's different; pakis, poofs, n what huv ye'. He does not forward an explanation for Begbie's hatred of difference, at least in standard psychological or ideological terms, but he implies a great deal:

> nae good blamin it oan the English fir colonising us. Ah don't hate the English. They're just wankers. We are colonised by wankers. We can't even pick a decent, vibrant healthy culture to be colonised by. No. We're ruled by effete arseholes. What does that make us? The lowest of the fuckin low, the scum of the earth [...] Ah don't hate the English. They just git oan wi the shite thuv goat. Ah hate the Scots. (p. 78)

This seemingly shapeless tirade actually frames a thesis subtle enough to have been designed by a political spin-doctor.

Begbie is not so much a homophobic racist as an embodied symptom of an all-encompassing condition of repressive colonialism: he rechannels his own sense of victimhood into particular acts of violent intolerance. Englishness is depicted, subtly, not as the grand animating force of colonialism – that would aggrandize imperialism – but as its feckless accomplice.

The regular denigration of Scottishness as a hopeless, emasculated self-caricature of its own mythology is reinforced by the contrast between the world of Renton, Begbie et al. and the Edinburgh of a few streets away where the quaintly preserved ancient city hosts its famous Festival. We do not need to be told that while the latter is composed of layers of invention the former is transparently grisly. But before assuming that Welsh's desperados, and indeed the author himself, bespeak Scotland's virtual extinction we should ask why the book was so popular, particularly among young Scottish readers. Anarchy is one of those bifurcated words which for its advocates carries myriad registers of longed-for unorthodoxy and rebellion while for others it evokes chaotic degradation. Welsh achieves a similar effect by enacting in each of his characters a set of contrasts; repulsiveness is balanced against pitiable desperation and more effectively victimhood is pitched against moments of angry eloquence. The effectiveness of his strategy became manifest when the Scottish National Party reprinted Renton's desperate soliloquy in a 1996 recruitment form in preparation for the 1997 general election (excluding references to 'cunts', 'pakis' and 'poofs'). The passage was not explained because it didn't need to be. By 1998 Renton had become a folk anti-hero both in the book and more recently in its film version (played with jagged charm by Ewan McGregor); become just the kind of embittered presence who would serve the SNP well as a link between the Scottish literary renaissance and the realpolitik of securing votes: Scotland, he averred, had reached a social, cultural and political nadir and the only way up was via decolonization.

Welsh returned to his cast of Brueghelesque degenerates almost 10 years later in *Porno* (2002). In the intervening period Renton had settled in Amsterdam living comfortably from the suitcase full of loot he carried out of *Trainspotting*. Sick Boy had spent much of his time in London attempting to lose his heroin habit and Begbie has recently completed a prison sentence for manslaughter. Gradually, each of them is drawn back to the scene of their original misdeeds with the focus sharpening upon Sick Boy, who takes over his aunt's pub and seeks to supplement his income with his endeavours in the amateur pornography business. In fact all that has changed from the original is that the miscreants seem to have each acquired a sense of ambition and entrepreneurial flair and, appropriately enough, they exchange their previous self-destructive drug-dealing enterprises for something more dependable – pornography. Welsh does not put up political and historical signposts but it is difficult to envisage any reader who doesn't carry into the book an awareness that since 1993 some things in Scotland have changed, principally the establishment in 1999 of its first, semi-independent, parliament for three centuries. Welsh implies that while some things, at least on the surface, have altered for the better, as many are swept under the carpet of nationalistic self-gratification. Noticeably England features hardly at all in the ravings of his cast. Instead they are busying themselves with a degenerate off-spin of post-Thatcherite entrepreneurialism and a commentary on this is supplied by an English film student called Nikki Fuller-Smith who flirts with Sick Boy and offers a Foucauldian analysis of his activities. She explains that consumption is by its very nature a depersonalizing force, and that pornography is an honest manifestation of capitalism per se. She does so in the jargon-ridden manner of the bourgeois English intellectual and, of course, Sick Boy does not understand a word she says. His language is different, his own, and he is more interested in her body than her pretentious exegeses of sexuality. Again, Welsh is inviting the reader, particularly the educated middle-class reader, to do some literary slumming, and once more he uses the characters' linguistic registers almost as a cult signal, a means by which the reader might take part, vicariously, in a world where unspeakable and shamefully exciting things go on. The fact that these registers also carry the radical baggage of non-Anglocentric badness, a Celtic particularity stripped of comfortable myth or nostalgia, is symptomatic of a persistent tendency within post-1970s Scottish literary culture, both in its creative and literary critical manifestations. A commendable exception is Janet Paisley's *Not For Glory* (2001) in which she eschews a blatant political agenda. It is a hybrid work with interlinked short stories set in and around a village near Falkirk and as each character moves from centre to background we become aware of an evocative tension between their individuality and their shared linguistic provision. Unlike Welsh, Paisley does not inform the latter with a brutalist cache.

Alan Warner's first novel *Morvern Callar* (1995) was generally thought to signal the arrival of another version of Welsh. The setting is slightly different – the dire cityscape of Edinburgh-Leith is exchanged for the hopeless monotony of a coastal town – but the eponymous heroine seems possessed, or rather unpossessed, of the same numbed emotions as Welsh's characters. After finding her boyfriend dead on the kitchen floor, he having slit his own throat, she sends the type-script of his recently completed novel under her name to a mainstream publisher in London and they forward a generous advance. With this, plus the contents of the poor chap's bank account, she sets off through various parts of the Mediterranean on an odyssey of booze, dope, music and sex. A curious aspect of the novel is the dichotomy between the callous indifference with which she treats her boyfriend's death and the asides that disclose a genuine sense of compassion for those who seem condemned, like her, to spend their existences in a town where futility is *de rigueur*. There is, however, cause to suspect that the effect is more purposeful than negligent because as the novel proceeds Morvern evolves into a surprisingly complex character. She seems able to apply a form of emotional anaesthetic to those dimen-sions of her life that are unalterable and, she implies, whatever post-humous distinction might have followed from her boyfriend's name on the title page of his work it wouldn't bring him back to life.

In the sequel, *These Demented Lands* (1997), Morvern's bacchana-lian excursion becomes more earnest as she appears to be chasing a point of origin, some sense of a shared heritage, specifically in the Hebridean Islands where her foster mother is buried. Significantly the novel is far more fragmented and discontinuous than its predecessor, and this indication that Warner is using his fiction as a means of exposing the false mythology of Scotland as a single comprehensible entity is confirmed in *The Sopranos* (1998). The sopranos are Orla, Manda, Kylah, Chell (for Rachel) and Fionnula, teenaged members of the choir of Our Lady of Perpetual Succour School for Girls. They're based in the same town as Morvern but for much of the novel are at large in the big city while they wait to represent their school at a national singing competition. Once released from the dominion of Sister Condron (referred to, inevitably, as Sister Condom) they set off on what amounts to a pilgrimage of indulgence, paying homage at the shrines of McDonald's and the innumerable pubs and clubs while in exhausting pursuit of the sacraments of drink, drugs, clothes and, most exalted of all, sex. Many readers would surely recognize skewed parallels with what had become one of the classics of pre-1970s Scottish fiction, Muriel Spark's *The Prime of Miss Jean Brodie* (1961).

Miss Brodie's chosen elite of 16-year-olds seem almost like prototypes for Warner's anarchic band, primed by their charismatic teacher to escape the confines of 1930s Edinburgh and satisfy their repressed sexual and intellectual inclinations. The fact that Miss Brodie's own programme of liberation is founded upon her commitment to fascism fuels the novel's considerable moral ambiguity and complexity, with critics unable to decide on whether Spark is prompting us to feel pity or contempt for Brodie or, similarly, for her pupil and nemesis Sandy who betrays her and ends the novel as a nun. So despite the fact that anti-establishment individualism is the animating force of the novel the reader is left with the impression that this is, in any manifestation, ultimately futile. Warner, however, sides with the girls. He begins the novel with a brilliantly evocative paean to teenage irresponsibility:

> they've youth; they'll walk it out like a favourite pair trainers. It's a poem this youth and why should they know it, as the five of them move up the empty corridors? We should get shoved aside cause they have it now, in glow of skin and liquid clarity of deep eye on coming June nights and cause it will go...(p. 2)

The passage raises an intriguing question. Does the very act of writing about the freedom of youth impose upon it the constraints that come with authorial intervention? Warner accepts the challenge and attempts to set his characters free, at least from the circumscriptions of judgement that might come with a more conventional novel, most pointedly one such as Spark's. One suspects also that there is something about the location of Spark's submissive dirge to fatalism that resonates through Warner's implicit rebellion against it because when we recall the moment that releases Morvern from her seeming life-sentence of hopelessness it too carries a Scottish literary register. There is a well-known passage in Archie Hind's *The Dear Green Place* (1966) in which Mat Craig, unpublished novelist, reflects upon his lack of success.

> All the background against which a novelist might set his scene, the aberrant attempts of human beings and societies to respond to circumstances, all that was bizarre, grotesque and extravagant in human life, all that whole background of violence, activity, intellectual and imaginative ardour, political daring. All that was somehow missing in Scottish life...(p. 87)

The tragic drama of this is that Craig is not really thinking about Scotland at all but basing his hypothesis upon the predominant characteristics of the urban English novel. It is the kind of novel that Morvern's boyfriend has written and, with magnificent irony, the fact that she has had nothing to do with it is what enables her to embody and energize the one she is in.

The determined attempts by Gray, Kelman, Warner and Welsh to free Scottish fiction from the suffocating maw of its English counterparts and antecedents have been both successful and to a lesser degree counterproductive. Consider for example the work of Michel Faber, an author born in Holland, brought up in Australia and based in Scotland since 1992. His first book was a collection of short stories called *Some Rain Must Fall* (1998), each of which seems an honorific to the postmodern grotesque. We listen to a recently murdered woman as she pursues her killer to his marital bed, and encounter God as a rather sad preadolescent who finds the world in a dustbin, suspends it from his bedroom ceiling and assuages the boredom of childhood by listening to the pleas that issue from it. The settings for these pieces are sometimes implicitly Scottish though rarely proactively and one must assume that the judges for the Saltire Society Scottish First Book of the Year Award deployed their criteria for Scottishness indulgently, perhaps assuming that aberrancy and implied location were sufficient to place Faber in the same cultural bloc as Gray, Kelman et al. It won the award.

Under the Skin (2000), his first full-length novel, reflects a robust determination to resist classification. Isserley, its main figure, spends her time driving a battered Toyota pickup truck around lovely glens of Scotland hoping to encounter well-muscled male hitchhikers, one of whom describes her as 'half Baywatch babe, half little old lady'. Just as we begin to suspect that Isserley is a postfeminist sexual predator we discover that her desires are more elemental: she is a cannibal. She is, moreover, absolved of psychopathy by her background, being literally an alien, a person from another planet fuelling up on earthly resources. Faber's work is a fine example of the 1990s flowerings of grotesquery considered above (see pp. 51–61). *The Guardian* (1 April 2000) celebrated its stylish peculiarity and in doing so positioned its author within a secure cultural and literary context. He would 'add spice to the Scottish literary renaissance' and might prove to be 'Dr Jekyll to Irvine Welsh's Mr Hyde, or some sleeker incarnation of

Alasdair Gray'. Certainly the Highlands offer Isserley a suitable location for her predations, with plenty of isolated places to entrap and lure her victims, but its Scottish setting is almost incidental to the bizarre core of the narrative. It might have drawn a comparable sense of grisly seclusion from the Welsh mountains or the English fens. The *Guardian* review concludes that 'Room will now have to be made for Faber alongside Alasdair Gray, James Kelman, Irvine Welsh and A. L. Kennedy'. Certainly the first three of Faber's associates engage provocatively in their fiction with the condition of Scotland and the perceptions and nature of Scottishness, but Kennedy? In novels such as *So I Am Glad* (1995) and *Paradise* (2004) the principal protagonists are undoubtedly Scottish but it could be argued that by placing Kennedy's fiction within a particular, albeit recent, tradition of writing where nationality is as much the animus as the framework of the text our appreciation of her value as a novelist per se is skewed by preconditions that we attach to her work before we read it.

A similar issue attends Ali Smith who, along with Kennedy and Faber, has won the Saltire Society Scottish First Book of the Year Award. Scotland is a peripheral feature of her early stories, and completely absent from *Hotel World* (2001) and *The Accidental* (2004), but she too is frequently referred to as part of a new wave within the Scottish literary renaissance. In a review of *The Accidental* in the *Irish Times* Eileen Battersby wrote that 'if initially Smith demonstrates that she is yet another clever, confident Scottish writer with more than nationality in common with A. L. Kennedy she also defers to the subversion that renders Alasdair Gray such an original' (21 May 2005). Given that the novel in question is concerned exclusively with very English people and set in East Anglia – a fact which becomes evident in the rest of the review – this ring-fencing of her innovative tendencies as a function of nationality seems at best a distortion of perspective. In fact Smith herself acknowledged this in a *Guardian* interview where she expresses her unease with being seen as indicative of a collective condition rather than as an independent artist. 'I was published because I was fashionable. Because I was gay, and because I was Scottish' (22 May 2005).

The increasing sense of separateness which has emerged in post-1970s Scottish fiction carries with it an incipient paradox: it faces the possibility of becoming as peremptory and inclusive as the Anglocentric cultural discourses from which it has sought to detach itself. This image of it as a version of what it sought to undermine has been fashioned, in part, by literary criticism. Liam McIlvanney contends that 'because of the Scottish novel's status as a kind of substitute or virtual polity, Scottish novelists have been acutely conscious of the politics of *form*' ('The Politics of Narrative in the Postwar Scottish Novel', in *On Modern British Fiction,* ed. Zachary Leader, Oxford University Press, 2002, p. 186). He goes on to list the formal characteristics which 'have been matters of profound symbolic and ultimately political significance', and these include: 'the disposition of the narrative, the relationship of character to author and narrator, the autonomy or otherwise of the protagonist, the linguistic profile of the text'. To designate the radical, innovative use of any of these technical subcategories as a subversive characteristically Scottish gesture seems misguided, given that almost identical counterparts could be located within non-Scottish fiction. Without acknowledging this problem McIlvanney seeks to resolve it by offering an even sharper definition of 'the politics of form'. 'For many postwar Scottish writers, the novel has been a suspect device, a form whose narrative traditions, linguistic conventions, and "ontological assumptions" have worked to marginalize the kind of working-class experience which has most pressingly engaged these writers' attention' (p. 207). Implicitly, but unambiguously, he appears to concede that the new brand of Scottish fiction is only able to establish its identity in terms of class, the most obvious example being the use of working-class Scottish patois as the core structural element of the text. This raises the question of whether a novel focused upon middle-class Scottish life which involves reported speech and a third-person narrative that, but for a few regional particulars, were largely indistinguishable in print from those of a novel set in London, would qualify as Scottish fiction? According to Carl MacDougall, in *Painting the Forth Bridge: A Search for Scottish Identity* (Aurum Press, 2001) it would not. He argues that the spoken first-person mode in which dialect subordinates rather than counterbalances other textual features is the only intrinsically Scottish feature of contemporary fiction. Kelman in a 1989 interview put it more bluntly. 'British novelists are blind to the fact that the "third party voice" they use to tell their stories is totally biased and elitist, economically secure, eats good food and plenty of it, is upper middle class paternalist' (Kirsty McNeill, 'Interview with James Kelman', *Chapman,* 57, 1989, p. 5). It is, apparently, the novelist's duty to avoid guilt by literary association: 'Getting rid of that standard third party narrative is getting rid of a whole value system.' Perhaps this is why Candia McWilliam, born in Edinburgh and twice short-listed for McVitie's Prize for Scottish Writer of the Year, is rarely, if ever, placed within the subgenre so robustly embodied by the likes of Kelman. Her novels and short stories while frequently set in Scotland and engaging with the Scottish notion of identity are written in a manner that reflects her years as a journalist for *Vogue*. Lush self-consciously literary metaphors and images tend to crowd narratives already well stocked with the minutiae of consumerism. Their quality is indisputable but, at least according to Kelman's criteria, they simultaneously betray what they invoke.

Cairns Craig shifts the emphasis from speech to writing and contends that typography has become the site for political and cultural conflict. In his thesis the 1707 Act of Union marked the death of a predominantly spoken Scottish linguistic culture and thereafter written, printed texts became the means by which Scots identity, at least in its linguistic form, was subordinated to its southern colonizer. He identifies in recent Scottish fiction an inclination to undermine the conventional notion of the printed text as a record of the methodical, sequential progress of language. This began in Gray's *Lanark* where the 'Index of Plagiarisms' of the epilogue involves two separate columns of print which operate as simultaneously competing counter-narratives. Kelman in his early fiction abandoned inverted commas as visual registers of the relationship between reported speech and the rest of the text – a practice instituted by Joyce and frequently emulated thereafter – and in *A Disaffection* (Secker and Warburg, 1989) he began to experiment with the visual format of the text as a supplement to the conventional relationship between syntax and print. For example, one aspect of the nonliterary world which cannot easily be accommodated by the standard devices of fiction is the moment when a thought process and its linguistic counterpart closes down either as a result of boredom, indifference or confusion, and then, following an interval of indeterminate duration, the subject resumes his or her discourse, while not necessarily returning to the original topic. Kelman uses the shape and spaces of the text to represent such moments:

> Nowadays it is a day he could stay in bed and nobody would notice. A day when, if he felt like it,

And what did that Russian poet say about doing things as opposed to having them done to you? (p. 88)

In the cold light of day, when sexual gratification has Receded into the distant horizon, when he is once more of the disposition
   In fact, she is not even what can objectively be described as 'good looking'. (p. 89)

Kelman refined and used the technique more persistently in *How Late it Was How Late* and in Craig's view it involves an overtly political gesture: 'typography becomes the symbol of its own culturally repressed condition: to overthrow the rule of type is synonymous with overthrowing the type of rule under which the culture has struggled for self expression' (p. 181). His argument is persuasive, but it might be noted that Kelman, and indeed Gray, have actually borrowed from the literary culture that, according to Craig, they are attempting to undermine. During the eighteenth century critics argued continually over Milton's blank verse method, which frequently involved the use of the line break – enjambment – to create a bifurcation of linear meaning. For many this seemed to involve an attack upon the secure continuities of speech by the silent monolith of print, and in the twentieth century the use of typographic shape in free verse as an adjunct to syntax has become commonplace within mainstream poetic writing. Irvine Welsh, almost with a respectful nod toward Gray, conducts gratuitous experiments with layout and visual format in *Filth* (1998) and Janice Galloway in *The Trick is to Keep Breathing* (1989) uses the spatial disposition of chunks of text as a means of continually disrupting the usual relationship between the reader's visual register and narrative continuity. These devices are radical certainly, but they are not without precedent, with examples ranging from B. S. Johnson's employment of the book and the page as physical counter-points to their narrative content to e. e. cummings's manipulation of space and typeface in his visual poetry.

   The hypothesis raised by Kelman is mildly bizarre. He implies that books which disclose their author's identity as middle class and Anglo-centric carry repugnant political freight, which raises the question of what type of novels such people can or should be able to write: presumably only works that are not about themselves or their lives? Craig, on the other hand, is happy to connive with writers who have

175

ransacked the fabric of mainstream literary culture – including by implication its Anglocentric determinants – and claim the spoils as intrinsically Scottish innovations.

The most conspicuous, pervasive feature of the Scottish renaissance – and I include within this both the fiction and the ex-cathedra discourses that attend it – is a tendency to present Scotland and Scottishness in terms of their dynamic relationship with the Anglocentric/ British behemoth that some would argue has variously inhibited, obscured and dominated Scottish culture for three centuries. Leaving aside the political acuity, or otherwise, that underpins this, what becomes most apparent is an unwitting paradox. The new Scottish novel seems dependent for its animus upon a continual almost fetishist concern with its relationship with somewhere else. From Gray's embattled notion of conventional techniques of representation as redolent of Anglicization to Welsh's use of the vernacular as a weapon we encounter a perverse confection of loathing and dependency: if it weren't for the suffocating presence of Britain, post-1970s Scottish writing would not be possessed by such anger and excitement. This is apparent even in Kelman's recent novel, *You Have to Be Careful in the Land of the Free* (2004), which is based in the United States. More specifically it is based in and around the monologue of Jeremiah Brown, Scotsman, seated at a bar in Colorado and reflecting upon his experiences in the US just prior to his journey home. Brown's thoughts are rendered in a way that counterpoints his working-class Scots vernacular against a fussy, self-consciously literary English mode. One must assume that this is, in part, a jibe at the long tradition, from Waugh through Kingsley Amis to William Boyd, of the English littérateur abroad in America who leaves the reader in no doubt as to his position in the cultural ascendancy. In Kelman's novel the strained Englishness seems completely out of place while Brown's rough Scot's register is amiably compatible with his recollections of the 'Uhmerka' of tough menial jobs, irresponsible poker games and beautiful jazz singers. Although the US might be the ostensible subject of Brown's musings his inferred antagonist lies much closer to home, and with this in mind we should turn our attention to the nature and composition of these phenomena that the Scots so love to hate: England and Englishness.

Chapter 11

England, Englishness and Class

It is a perverse irony that the notion of England against which the Scots, and indeed many others, feel secure in their antipathy is a chimera. It is an incontrovertible truth that the political epicentre of what was once the British Empire and is now the loose fabric of Britain is England, or more accurately, London, and that England is similarly the focus for British economic activity. Beyond that, however, any attempt to locate a social, cultural or a collateral literary unity within England is the equivalent of chasing shadows. Fiction testifies to this because in the majority of novels set principally in England and comprising mainly English characters the issues of nationality or region are of negligible significance. Novels which even in an obtuse way address some element of Englishness are significant because of their rarity, and even within this eclectic subgenre there are no tangible similarities between texts or implicit notions of comradeship between authors.

Among these exceptions perhaps the most notable, at least for their singularity, are the novels of Graham Swift. *Waterland* (1983), probably his most celebrated, is not so much set in the East Anglian Fens as a perverse and ultimately inconclusive meditation on how this region suffused all aspects of the life of Tom Crick. The fact that he tells his story from the here and now in Greenwich causes his habit of tying recollection into vividly portrayed local detail to be all the more striking; it is as though the minutiae of place are the preservatives of an otherwise dissipating sense of significance. There is the famous scene where after the abortion in Martha Clay's cottage he describes how he disposes of the dead foetus by pouring it from a bucket into the River Ouse: 'A red spittle, floating, frothing, slowing sinking. Borne on the slow Ouse currents. Borne downstream. Borne all the way (but for the Ouse eels...) to the Wash' (*Waterland*, Picador, 1984, p. 274). The grisly, unsettling nature of the experience is made almost to appear concordant with the landscape. The agitated repetition of the double-edged 'borne' reminds us of what the foetus dispatched from the bucket might have become and the sense of the Ouse as a river with an idiosyncratic nature of its own, its 'slow...currents', its carnivorous eels, brings the passage eerily close to a sense of someone, or thing, being laid to rest in a grotesquely appropriate manner. Tom, and by implication Swift, cautiously avoid any simplistic notion of location as somehow begetting the nature of its inhabitants. Instead, the pervasive sense of place becomes the subject for meditative puzzlement and in this respect England is at once meticulously documented and depoliticized. The Fens are brought startlingly, often disturbingly, to life in the prose but we learn nothing of whether or not there is anything characteristically English about them.

Last Orders (1996) is a funeral odyssey which involves three of Jack Dodd's oldest friends and his adopted son Vince driving from the East End of London to Margate, there to deposit his ashes in the sea. For some of the journey they speak to each other but for most we listen to their particular interior monologues, randomly assembled histories of four Englishmen's lives, with occasional interruptions from Mandy, Vince's wife, from Jack's widow and, unnervingly, from Jack himself. Often their fragmented narratives collide or intersect but Swift manages to preserve a particular degree of separateness by allocating to them verbal idiosyncrasies and habits that are as particular as a fingerprint or a facial profile. His achievement in this is considerable given that all share the grammatical trademarks and vocabulary of the East End working classes. The novel is composed of 75 short chapters, each allocated to one of the seven monologists and bearing their name. Every fourth or fifth chapter a slight shift in perspective occurs and the heading is taken from the place reached by the party on its journey to Margate. The novel juxtaposes two timescales, one which follows the literal narrative from Bermondsey through Kent, and the other involving a framework circumscribed by the memories of the narrators. Both are orchestrated by a pervasive sense of place, involving the parts of London, and elsewhere, that anchor the recollections and the particular points on Jack's final journey that prompt memories of previous excursions along the same route to Margate. Aside from the emotional and reflective registers that rise and subside in the monologues, each is a capsule of the social history of South East London of the previous half century. But, like *Waterland*, there are no ideological underpinnings. This particular region of England is presented in vivid miniatures yet the only subtext is that these are inseparable from the multiplicity of impressions and susceptibilities of the storytellers. The routine socio-cultural clichés of Cockneyism are flagged up only to be dismantled in a novel where subjectivity is far more powerful than any shared notion of region or nation.

Many of Swift's key male characters are intractable watchers, concerned ostensibly with the big questions that attend their usually unhappy existences but in practice finding it difficult to tear themselves away from the compulsive and usually meaningless particulars of their location. It is appropriate then that one of his most recent should be a private detective. In *The Light of Day* (2003) George Webb's agency is run from an office above a tanning studio on Wimbledon Broadway. George is an ex-policeman, thrown out of the force for coercing a witness, veteran of a failed marriage and the occasional, distracted lover of his assistant, Rita, which sounds like the standard recipe for the rather mundane British cousin of the US thriller noir. It is supposed to because once these signals register other, more peculiar things began to happen. George's client is Sarah Nash, language teacher and translator, who employs him to spy on her husband, a gynaecologist, whom she suspects is having an affair with Kristina, the Croatian refugee they have allowed to stay in their home. This, at least, is how George recollects things, only to rapidly bring us to the present, two years on, with him visiting Sarah in prison and occasionally taking the time to lay flowers on her husband's grave. We can guess at, but never be quite sure of, the nexus of motives and events that separate these two points in time and the search for a solution is further complicated by the image of Sarah's late husband as a walking ghost and the unexpected presence of the Empress Eugenie (on whom Sarah is researching a book), widow of Napoleon III who following their exile from France outlived him for half a century in their grand house in nearby Chislehurst – now a golf club. If there is anything resembling consistency in all this it involves the intrusion of the extraordinary, even the fantastic, into the routines of suburban London. Indeed George, as narrator, appears unusually concerned with telling us exactly where particular events occur; off he takes us along Wimbledon Broadway to St Mary's Road, past Parkside and the hospital to Putney Vale Crematorium, along with excursions to Heathrow and Chislehurst. His account is as much like an A-Z map as a narrative, and one must assume that he is so obsessed with logging these places because they are so charmlessly ordinary. They seem to exist at the other end of the existential spectrum from the likes of a long-dead mysterious empress, a girl with knowledge of unspeakable atrocities and the single act of murder which exists at the centre of the story. Yet George is witness to the simultaneous presence of both and he seems fascinated – without saying so – by how the former can remain so comfortably unperturbed by the latter. This, perhaps, is as close as Swift comes to assigning a characteristic to England, or at least the suburb of SW19, as a place which exists at one inscrutably tedious remove from everything and everywhere else.

Adam Thorpe's widely acclaimed *Ulverton* (1992) is generally seen as an attempt to locate and represent the intangible qualities of Englishness but in this endeavour its method is self-limiting. For one thing the focus is exclusively upon a rural community which has remained largely immune from the effects of urbanization and the industrial revolution. It is moreover a historical novel comprising 12 interlinked stories which offer accounts of life in the eponymous village from just after the Civil War to the present day. This might have prompted an author with Marxian affiliation to present a cause-and-effect model of historical change, an explanation of the present in terms of the inexorable economic and political forces of the past. Thorpe however is more concerned with representation and style as authentic indices of period. 'Leeward 1743', for example, is in the epistolary mode, while 'Stitches 1887' offers us a peasant's interior monologue, and the final section, dated 1988, is in the form of a film script. This technique is intriguing but its true concern is the mutable spectrographic nature of language and the fact that Thorpe has chosen an English village and a period of English history as its subject is almost incidental.

A novel which addressed itself comprehensively to its title-subject is Julian Barnes's *England, England* (1998). The supposedly definitive features of English life and culture have been distilled into a theme park on the Isle of Wight, run by the entrepreneur Sir Jack Pitman. The standard retinue of architectural monuments – Big Ben, Buckingham Palace et al. – plus figures from myth including King Arthur and Robin Hood and legendary presences such as Dr Johnson, played by actors, all perform their ordained, predictable and emasculated functions. It is this final ordination, that the essential aspects of Englishness must be reduced to inoffensive performance, that animates the book because the role players gradually begin to exchange representation for dangerous actuality. Robin Hood's merry men branch out into real poaching and theft and Dr Johnson sheds his tourist-friendly persona to become an angry depressive, no longer willing to indulge the intellectual vapidity of his paying guests. Anyone attempting to locate purposive or unambiguous allegory in all of this will, however, find themselves continually sidestepped. There is a typically peculiar passage in which the King and Queen Denise – not actors but the real ones now obliged to supplement their diminished grandeur by performing in the theme park – are flying in their private plane from the mainland to the Isle of Wight. It is clear that they regard their duties with sanguine contempt: 'There'd been a script meeting at the Palace that morning and he'd practised his lines with Denise as they were waiting for take off. She'd nearly peed herself. She was a real best mate, Denise. But what was the point in paying good money if the audience didn't get it?' (*England, England*, Cape, 1998, p. 160). Barnes's peppering of this third-person account with touches of loutish demotic is an accurate reflection of the Royal Family's manner – somewhere between a parody of how they imagine that their subjects speak and an honest embittered acceptance of their belittled status.

Custom decrees that the flight is accompanied by two symbols of England's heroic past, a Spitfire and a Hurricane, the fighter aircraft which effectively defeated the Luftwaffe in the Battle of Britain. As outriders to the royal aircraft they are clearly intended to remind us of such institutions as the Household Cavalry, whose role as protectors of the monarch has been no more than ceremonial for two centuries and whose antique armoury and colourful attire last saw combat in the Napoleonic Wars. Barnes brings atrophied nostalgia to life by having the royal flight pestered by a small aircraft trailing a banner that reads 'SANDY DEXTER AND THE DAILY PAPER GREET HIS MAJ' (p. 161); these are representations of an, invented, media entrepreneur and his tabloid, by degrees fawning dedicatees of the Royal Family and in constant pursuit of any scandal that might attend it.

The theme park is less a choreographed model of England as an assembly of working cultural motifs whose relationship to each other is assumed to be predictable. As the passage goes on to disclose, however, impulsiveness can intervene. The King is irritated and indicates his displeasure to Wing Commander 'Johnnie' Johnson in the Spitfire who, seized by the emotions of his Battle of Britain 'rehearsal', shoots down the offending aircraft.

> There was a long pause. Finally the King having thought the matter over, came on the intercom. 'Congratulations, Wing Commander. I'd say, bandits discouraged'...
>
> 'Piece of cake, Sir', replied 'Johnnie' Johnson, remembering his line from the Battle's end.
>
> 'But I'd say that, on the whole, Mum's the word', added the King.
>
> 'Mum's the word, Sir'. (pp. 162–3)

The King and 'Johnnie' are perplexed because the roles they have been programmed to play carry a residue of genuine emotion and commitment and for a moment the tabloid press becomes for them as threatening to civilized values as the Nazism of half a century earlier. Barnes is here playing an ingenious game with the reader who will have witnessed the manner in which the popular press can manipulate perceptions of individuals, sometimes procuring for them a cult of celebrity and just as frequently destroying their public image – while seemingly remaining immune from any responsibility in this. Many readers will at some point have wondered how victims of tabloid scrutiny would, if they could, take revenge and 'Johnnie', equipped with machine guns, enacts a fair number of hypotheses.

Although *England, England* seems initially to be a parodic account of hollow nostalgia, a caricature of the illusions and falsities that constitute most people's notions of Englishness, it matures into a more fluid, surprising reflection upon the nature of collective identity. Examples of individuals such as 'Johnnie' and the King overriding the corporate plan while in some way abiding by its more emotive clichés segue eventually into the penultimate chapter where Martha Cochrane, employee of Pitman and puzzled witness to the narrative, finds herself in the Church of St Aldwyn conversing with what seems to be either a projection of herself or God.

Into her mind came an image, one shared by earlier occupants of these pews. Not Guilliamus Trentinus, of course, or Anne Potter, but perhaps known to Ensign Robert Timothy Pettigrew, and Christina Margaret Benson, and James Thorogood and William Petty. A woman swept and hanging, a woman half out of this world, terrified and awestruck, yet in the end safely delivered. A sense of falling, falling, falling, which we have every day of our lives, and then an awareness that the fall was being made gentler, was being arrested, by an unseen current whose existence no-one suspected. A short, eternal moment that was absurd, improbable, unbelievable, true. Eggs cracked from the slight concussion of landing, but nothing more. The richness of all subsequent life after that moment. (p. 238)

Barnes, via Martha, stops the farcical procession of emptiness, confusion and despair and indicates that moments of certainty, all the more powerful for their brevity, are possible. Her pseudo-mystical experience is a passive, reflective version of the struggles that beset the likes of 'Johnnie' Johnson and his namesake the doctor: attempts to act according to who they are within a world composed almost exclusively of questionable myths. The closing chapter, 'Arcadia', involves a village fete. It is some time in the future, Martha is in her contented dotage and although most of the characters are still playing roles they now seem more comfortable in doing so, as if they have found a tolerable median between story and fact. Jez Harris, for example, is the village farrier bedecked in a countryman's outfit 'which had hints of both Morris dancer and bondage devotee' (p. 242). Jez was once an American lawyer but he has not so much reinvented himself as chosen a way of life far better suited to his temperament.

Barnes's novel involves a double bluff. He seems at first to select easy targets for caricature and satirical execution: predominantly England as an assembly of brand names and performances all capable of drawing cash from the credulous tourist. But by the conclusion his characters have found among this chiaroscuro of impressions an England that is at once imperfect but compelling. In a period dominated by postcolonial guilt or sceptical indifference to nationality this novel, peculiarly, offers a kindly, quirkily patriotic view of Englishness.

Aside from the few novels where England predominates as a suffused fascinating presence there are hundreds more where it sits, often begrudgingly, alongside everything else, novels which, being set in England, are obliged despite themselves to acknowledge some of what

183

this involves. Class, with its consequences and peculiarities, is a phenomenon that inheres through all parts of the United Kingdom and Ireland but few would dispute that its germane, divisive elements originated, and persist, in England. It was during the 1950s that the novel first began to register a shift in the previously well-established complicity between literature and the middle-class mindset. Even with novelists such as Dickens and Arnold Bennett, who could ground their writing in the experiences of the working classes, a degree of distance was maintained between the self-evidently sophisticated nature of the writing and its uncultured subjects: the former might have treated the latter with sympathy but in doing so it reinforced an apparently unbridgeable social division. Kingsley Amis, John Wain and even Philip Larkin in his first novel *Jill* created characters – generally lower middle class to working class – who carried their disrespect for social convention into the fabric of the text and Alan Sillitoe, John Braine and David Storey would take this a stage further. No novel in English had ever before involved an opening comparable with Sillitoe's *Saturday Night and Sunday Morning* (1958) where Arthur Seaton, its central character, vomits his night's intake of beer and gin over a group of customers in his local working men's club and later offers the reader his personal manifesto; 'fighting every day until I die...Fighting with mothers and wives, landlords and gaffers, coppers, army, government...There's bound to be trouble in store for me every day of my life, because trouble it's always been and always will be'. It was not that the likes of Seaton would suddenly displace their more restrained, cultivated counterparts at the centre of British novels – indeed his true likeness would only reappear two decades later during the Scottish renaissance – but his arrival did prompt later novelists to regard middle-class Englishness not as coterminous with good writing but something that good writing might scrutinize without affiliation.

Martin Amis, for example, has evolved an idiosyncratic brand of classless fiction, most brutally evident in the presence of John Self, while his more polished creations such as Richard and Gwyn of *The Information* seem almost like displaced persons, struggling desperately to find room for themselves in a world that is laughingly indifferent to their poise and erudition. In Coe's *The Closed Circle* being middle class is represented as a genetic condition, a tenacious virus that has survived the 1960s and 1970s and Thatcherism, and re-emerged as a sad template for misdirected ambition. Joanna Briscoe's *Sleep With Me* (2005) begins with the moment that Richard and Lelia, a beautiful London couple, conceive their first child. Thereafter we witness the progress of the pregnancy alongside a meticulously layered presentation of the kind of people they are and the collective milieu in which they, exclusively, socialize. He is a broadsheet literary editor and their friends, if not all artists and academics themselves, are at least cultured types – an almost identical grouping to that which surrounds Doug Anderson in Coe's novel. Briscoe introduces to this the mysterious Sylvie, a plain, ordinary, unpretentious woman who has moved to the area, Bloomsbury, and who crops up in the company of Richard, Lelia and their friends in a manner that seems more than accidental. She becomes part of their social network and will in due course come to dominate and eventually almost destroy their lives. She befriends the women, offers a calculatedly modest sexual allure to the men and divides them against each other. Her motive is never fully disclosed, at least in terms of her psychological make up, and we are left with the suspicion that her function is that of strategic nemesis. She has a curious way of locating these aspects of hypocrisy, pretension and dissimulation that seem peculiar to middle-class life and one of the most unusual features of the novel is that while we know we should feel a degree of pity or empathy for her victims, we don't.

A scenario that is at once different while demanding comparison emerges in Candida Clark's *A House of Light* (2005). Katherine Clement is a photojournalist and freelance photographer who arrives back from an assignment in Africa just in time to find her flat in flames – an accident or a malicious act, possibly perpetrated by her embittered ex-boyfriend? The thriller-style opening becomes an ingenious counterpoint to what seems to be the agreeably predictable dimension of her life. Her father is a well-off, genial Englishman soon to be married to a predictably besotted American with children in tow. The run-up to the wedding, and reception – to be held in Clement Senior's charming leaky manor house – is laden with cleverly understated clichés on the quirkiness of England and the collateral attractions and/or puzzlements that these offer to Americans. At the same time, however, both are seen from Katherine's perspective, a woman who has witnessed both the grim realities of life beyond Britain and some feral nastiness within it. Again the once solid stratum of middle-class England becomes something observed from a distance, rather like the

Edwardians scrutinized from our end of the century – fascinatingly real and irredeemably disconnected.

It is interesting to compare a novel from A. N. Wilson's early writing career, *Wise Virgin* (1982), with his more recent *A Jealous Ghost* (2005). The former is set in the period of its publication but unless the reader were attuned to the inclinations, speech patterns and idiosyncrasies of male, bookish medievalists and their virginal academic helpmeets they could be forgiven for thinking that the clock has been turned back to approximately 1910. *A Jealous Ghost* centres upon Sallie, a young American postgraduate student, researching a thesis on Henry James's *The Turn of the Screw*, bored by London and taking a job as nanny to two children in a gloomy country house in Kent. The mother is mysteriously absent, perhaps dead, and the father, politely evasive, fascinates her both sexually and as that much-vaunted presence, the enigmatic English gentleman. The novel is not by intent an ally of Briscoe's and Clark's but it achieves, inadvertently the same effect. We know from Wilson's polymath presence as historian, biographer, literary editor and *Daily Telegraph* columnist that he holds a notion of Old Tory Englishness close to all of his opinions and impressions, yet in the novel it is as though he can't quite bring himself to admit to the tenuous nature of its present condition. Sallie is tantalized by an image of England that, until she encounters the real thing, is purely literary and as a compensation for her disappointment she elevates the house, Staverton, and the jealous ghost of the title to a state of impervious mystery: the upper middle classes have become pathologically mythologized.

Throughout Justin Cartwright's *The Promise of Happiness* (2004) the personnel offer a spectrum of puzzled, unsettled responses to what life, mostly in England, can offer them in the early twenty-first century, but diversity is matched by a pervasive, defensive feeling of unity. The sense of family is far more powerful for each of them than any other affiliation and Cartwright is conducting an ingenious experiment by juxtaposing a harshly realistic portrait of contemporary existence – where mendacity, nihilism, drugs, adultery, general despair are de rigueur – with a model of bourgeois Englishness that seems both comforting, nostalgic and grotesquely out of place. The contrast permeates all aspects of the novel and one is again left with the vision of the middle classes as an anachronism caught somewhere between fantasy and tragedy.

This is not to say that the middle classes have ceased to exist in English fiction. They do, but they occupy a niche which is notable for its endurance and comfortable insularity. Elizabeth Jane Howard, Margaret Drabble and Joanna Trollope differ commendably in the particulars of their craft but for all three middle-class England has since the 1960s persisted incorrigibly as a state of mind, a behavioural and intellectual mannerism which possesses all of their central characters. Regarding location alone Trollope's novels appear to treat England as exclusive to London, the Cotswolds, the Welsh Borders and the South West. All manner of plot scenarios occur – marriage breakdown, terminal illness, serial adultery, sibling rivalry, and the distressing effects of age, are persistent factors of the books – but they are initiated and endured by characters with a compensatory degree of inbred refinement and the fact that they take place against a background of gorgeous landscapes and incomparable villages has a quietly palliative effect. A sexual relationship between a girl who moves in with her best friend's recently bereaved father (*Next of Kin*, 1996) and a long-term extramarital affair conducted while all four parties remain close friends (*The Best of Friends*, 1995) might seem ideal material for new-gothic, Ian McEwanesque treatment but in the hands of Trollope all is executed and endured with an air of unhurried calm. Howard and Drabble instil, respectively, an extra dimension of psychological gravity and socio-political disquiet but for any reader not fully attuned to and comfortable with the mores, inflections and emotional registers of middle-class Englishness an encounter with their novels is comparable to the experience of a certain type of dinner party, a mixture of fascination and mild disbelief.

There is a curious if involuntary affinity between those who write on behalf of the middle classes and those who regard them as a rarefied species to be treated with caution and unease. Both indicate that bourgeois Englishness is no longer the predominant mood of the English novel and that it exists alongside many other strata of fiction.

The narrative skeleton of Julia Darling's *The Taxi Driver's Daughter* (2003) bears a reasonably close resemblance to that of Drabble's *The Witch of Exmoor* (1996) – the impact upon a family of a single act performed by a matriarch – but beyond that they seem to belong to different species of realist fiction. In Darling's novel Louise steals a single shoe from a Newcastle-upon-Tyne department store. Her motive is unclear – a moment of distracted impulse, an existential gesture, a joke? – but the legal system is indifferent to the peculiarity of the offence and the magistrate sends her to jail for three months. The novel is ruthlessly naturalistic in its documentation of the dehumanizing affects of prison upon this ordinary undemonstrative woman and the collateral consequences for her husband and two teenage daughters. Drabble's Frieda, a figure famed for writings on the role of women in postwar England, voluntarily exiles herself from the bosom of her family by selling her agreeable home-counties residence and moving to a ramshackle former hotel in the eponymous moor. Her offspring comprise Daniel and his sisters Rosemary and 'Gogo'. All are professionally successful, live in London or the surrounding, commutable, countryside and spend much of their summers in the likes of Tuscany. All, like their left-leaning feminist mother, have a social conscience and vote Labour. Indeed Gogo's husband, David, is to run for MP in a safeish Labour seat in Yorkshire. The novel was written, presciently, a year before New Labour's election victory in 1997, and the fact that David is second-generation Guyanese testifies to Drabble's acuteness in picking out Blair's multicultural selection policy as part of the anti-Tory mood of the mid-1990s. The novel takes its energy from the children's gradual feeling of disquiet at the possibility that Frieda has rewritten her will, and it seems clear that Drabble is offering us a moral fable: beneath the façade of responsibility and egalitarianism presented by New Labour and its middle-class followers is an equally powerful Thatcherite legacy of greed. Whatever one's opinions on the novel's political import it cannot help but be noted that Drabble's diagnoses of mendacity and dramatization of familial concern versus Machiavellian cunning occur in the rarefied zone of guaranteed aspirations and financial security. Compared with this Louise and her family don't simply embody a separate class, their condition compels Darling to create a very different fabric of representation. They cannot spend their time speculating on the moral and political probity of England. For them hypothesis has been exchanged for immutable, brutal fact. Darling is particularly impressive in her presentation of North East England as a region that dwells self-indulgently in a past where working-class solidarity – from the Jarrow marches onward – at least provided some cushion against the malevolence of capitalism and the state. The myth continues but when called upon by Louise's family it seems to have been replaced by selfish indifference.

While Darling's novel is set in a particular region of England it successfully undermines the sequestered archetypes who traditionally inhabit region-based novels. Carol Birch's multigenerational Manchester saga *Turn Again Home* (2003), and John Murray's *Jazz etc* (2003), a portrait of Cumbria and its people similarly juxtapose idiosyncrasy and singularity against popular typology: Murray's earnest confection of magic realism and inclement weather is particularly effective in this respect.

Niall Griffiths's *Wreckage* (2005) is excellent in its judicious matching of a subject with a challengingly appropriate treatment. It is set, largely, in present-day Liverpool. Darren and Alastair are lowlife apprentice criminals who become involved in a sequence of sinister errands, botched robberies and a case of grievous bodily harm over which they are eventually unable to exert any control. The mood of directionless, unapologetic bad behaviour recalls *Trainspotting*, but thereafter the similarities fade. Griffiths certainly has an ear for Scouse elocutionary habits and the dialogue is dynamic and convincing, but he juxtaposes this with a third-person mode that is neither localized nor anonymously middle English. Instead he employs a daringly portentous, sometimes apocalyptic voice as a means of counterpoising the activities of Darren, Alastair and their associates with those of their spectral forebears, people drawn into the macrocosm of types and inheritances that has characterized Liverpool's history since its beginnings as a muddy hinterland. Such a formula might too easily have become the vehicle for political or sociological diagnosis – a radical, unwashed version of Drabble's musings on the English middle classes. But Griffiths exchanges analysis for fascination. At no point does he infer that Alastair and Darren are victims of historical circumstance, 2005 manifestations of several centuries of exploitation and its criminal consequences. He makes no excuses for them, but at the same time we perceive them within the broader context of a city whose identity has been sustained by conflict – particularly regarding its Celtic incomers – and although Liverpool can by no person's estimation be regarded as a quintessentially English location Griffiths gives us cause to suspect that Englishness per se is a fissiparous condition, something that might pretend to cohesion but which in truth has always been and will continue to be in a state of mutation.

A similar thread is traced by Sam North in *The Unnumbered* (2004). The personnel of the novel are, literally, the dispossessed, some by choice and others involuntarily. It centres upon the relationship between Mila, a 15-year-old Romanian gypsy and illegal immigrant and Nio, 23, officially British but by inclination Greek, albeit second generation. Mila exists in a caravan on the edge of a car park adjacent to London's North Circular Road, an area constantly animated by movement and transit but in which no-one actually lives. Nio has chosen to reside in a shed in St Pancras Cemetery, his taste for the macabre extending to a prurient interest in the habits of patients of the Barnet psychiatric hospital, where he tends the grounds. Other creatures of this horribly believable wasteland include Lucas Tooth who preys sexually upon sad and lonely women, and not simply for financial gain. The novel edges toward the purely grotesque but stops short in allowing its peculiar characters, by degrees engaging, pitiable and repulsive, to wander into more familiar territories and contexts. They live false lives with forged P45s and driving licences and hold multiple jobs under aliases. They exist on the margins of what most of the novel's readers would treat as the actuality of England and London but oblige these same readers to look beyond this to a fabric of existence that is both shocking and credible.

Chapter 12

The Question of Elsewhere

Up to the middle of the twentieth century multi-culturalism in the British Isles had, predominantly, involved political conflicts and movements of population between the three Celtic nations and England and the arrival from Continental Europe of relatively small numbers of the oppressed and dispossessed, notably Huguenots and Jews. In the late 1940s, however, a new wave of emigration, mainly to England, brought with it unprecedented questions of integration and assimilation because the incomers were unlike any of their predecessors. The majority were either people of African descent from the West Indies or from the indigenous populations of what had in the days of Empire been the Indian subcontinent and was, post-Independence, made up of India and Pakistan. Smaller numbers came from what had previously been African or South East Asian colonies, and although these groups of individuals might have had little else in common they were unwittingly united by the fact that for most British people they were self-evidently different. They spoke differently and their physiognomy and skin colour were resolutely non-European. Some whites greeted the influx with a mixture of fascination and uncertainty. It was not as though these people were aliens; they had after all come from what had once been Britain's extension into the rest of the globe, the Empire. A considerable number of others treated them as inferior beings, persons who should stay within their own sequestered communities or – given that the rationale for their mass arrival was the postwar labour shortage – encouraged to leave as soon as they had served their purpose.

The British Nationality Act of 1948 granted rights of UK entrance and residence to virtually all citizens of the Empire/Commonwealth and the Act was motivated purely by economic factors. Britain's economy was still labour-intensive and the derisory wages which failed to entice home-based workers to the most basic jobs were an attractive prospect for their skilled and unskilled counterparts in India, Pakistan and the West Indies. Several months after the Act was passed the passenger ship *Empire Windrush* docked in London carrying several hundred immigrants from the Caribbean, a moment that is treated as iconic by many commentators and historians: the old Empire was coming home. The problem, however, lay in the fact that a considerable number of white Britons were, to put it bluntly, racist. The history of the various manifestations of conflict and integration since 1948 is too complex to easily summarize but the following should be borne in mind. The first publicly documented 'race riots' on British soil took place in Notting Hill in 1958 as a result of a largely, though not exclusively, West Indian community having continually undergone abuse and discrimination during the previous decade. During this period it was legal for anyone to deny entrance to cafes, restaurants or pubs or refuse employment or the sale or rental of property to someone whose colour of skin they disliked. The Race Relations Act of 1976 eventually criminalized certain manifestations of racism but the Act's function as a register of civilized, enlightened attitudes to racial harmony tells only part of a more complex story. The 1948 legislation was gradually dismantled, first by the 1962 Commonwealth Immigration Act which tightened restrictions for entry; in basic terms if there was not a pressing demand for a particular specialised profession for which the applicant was qualified entry would be denied. The Immigration Act (1971) allowed domicile only to those born in Britain or of British parentage, and the 1981 British Nationality Act abolished the former allowance – a condition seen by many as implicitly racist since it suggested that nationality was determined by genetic inheritance. Few social historians would argue that there was a direct link between the 1981 Act and the Brixton riots of the same year but the fact that the latter principally involved second and third generation Caribbeans indicates that more than thirty years after the *Empire Windrush* arrived integration was still as much a hypothesis as an actuality.

Until the 1980s Commonwealth immigration existed as a slight, marginal topic in the broader panorama of British fiction. The first novel to document the sense of awe and optimism that possessed most of the *Empire Windrush* generation was George Lamming's *The Emigrants* (1954). The novel, written only four years after its author's arrival from the Caribbean, is at once endearing and pitiably open-minded about what the famed 'homeland' might offer for the new migrants, but by 1956 Sam Selvon, a friend of Lamming, was beginning to register a feeling of uncertainty and isolation. As its title indicates, Selvon's *The Lonely Londoners* (1956) tells of how London-based West Indians had begun to fasten upon tokens of the places they had left behind – music, cooking, dress and linguistic patois particularly – as a collective reaction to a growing awareness of inhospitableness bordering upon contempt. Selvon's novels, specifically *Moses Ascending* (1975) and *Moses Migrating* (1983), provide a beguiling account of how the circumstances faced by Moses and his peers in the mid 1950s altered over the next three decades, generally for the worse. Selvon handles his characters' experiences of alienation and outright racism with a blend of resignation and humour as sharp as it is dark. In *Moses Migrating*, for example, Moses writes to Enoch Powell seeking financial aid for his forthcoming trip to Trinidad, which he drolly implies could be mutually beneficial.

Caryl Phillips was born in St Kitts, came over with his parents when he was one year old and began writing in Britain a generation after the appearance of Lamming's and Selvon's early novels. His first novel, *The Final Passage* (1985), might be seen as fictional revisionism since it tells the story of Michael and Leila who arrive from the Caribbean in the mid-1950s, and Phillips makes ample use of three subsequent decades of historical and ideological reflection. It is useful to examine his fiction alongside *The European Tribe* (1987), a collection of his essays, because the characters in the former frequently become avatars for the theses on Western politics and colonialism propounded in the latter. In *The European Tribe* he avers that racism in England is an intractable phenomenon, that even though enlightened liberalism has grown more vocal and influential little in truth has changed since the 1950s, particularly where racism finds it bedrock in the lower middle and working classes (see *The European Tribe*, Farrar, Strauss and Giroux, 1987, pp. 121–3). Leila in *The Final Passage* is of mixed English and Caribbean heritage and as such she enables Phillips to conduct an exploration of racial difference and alienation rather than to merely register their more obvious effects. Her husband, Michael, endures racism with bitter resignation and concentrates on making enough money from labouring jobs to realize his hope of one day returning to the Caribbean, but Leila is confronted by a problem that cannot be sidelined by pragmatism. For her racism comes with an attenuated blend of identification and betrayal. She is, and looks, half English. The English people she knew in the West Indies had maintained a polite, almost apologetic, distance form her – they were to a large extent the middle-class remnants of an Empire in decline – but the English, predominantly the working classes, of London, are more brutally honest, particularly regarding their visceral perceptions of her as mixed-race. There is an intriguing example of this when during her first day as a bus conductress the male passengers greet her with a mixture of sexual innuendo and racist remarks: she is enough like them to be deemed sexually attractive but at the same time sufficiently different to deserve abuse (*The Final Passage*, Faber, 1985, p. 184). Leila evinces sympathy and as a character she is credible enough yet at the same time one suspects that Phillips has created her partly as an ideological conceit. There are, for example, parallels between her function as someone caught between the polarities of Afro-Caribbean and English, colonized and colonizer and Phillips's presentation in *The European Tribe* of the British postcolonial condition as beset by schizophrenia, a strange conflation of loss, guilt and resentment. In one essay he scrutinizes Gibraltar as a microcosm of postimperial paranoia, as a place where 'Britishness' has become an unwitting, straight-faced parody of an ideal that might have existed a century earlier (p. 27), and one can't help but note parallels between his polemic here and his construction of the relationship between Leila and her environment.

In *A State of Independence* (1986) Bertram Francis becomes a version of Michael, mid-1980s. He returns to the Caribbean to find that he is now so Anglicized that he feels a stranger in his homeland, and that perversely the island has, two decades post-Independence, become a twisted representation of Thatcherite Britain, dedicated to the principles of rapacious consumerism and apparently intent upon annexing itself to its closest neighbour, that monster of capitalism, the United States.

There are numerous examples of literature being appropriated as a political forum, generally a vehicle for the mindset of its writer, and Phillips's fiction must surely belong in this category. Thus a question is raised as to whether his ideological principles cause him to deliberately distort or allegorize material which carries a clear historical import and this as a consequence casts doubt upon his novel's aesthetic and representational qualities. It is an important question because Phillips's techniques and mood are seamlessly naturalistic, and as such he demands comparison with a novelist who deals with race and post-colonialism in a compulsively unconventional manner, Salman Rushdie.

Rushdie's two best-known novels are *Midnight's Children* (1981) and *The Satanic Verses* (1988). The first won him the Booker Prize and was celebrated throughout the literary world as a landmark in late twentieth-century fiction, principally because it employs an exuberantly experimental method in its engagement with a sequence of controversial historical events, specifically India's transformation from British colony to independent state. *The Satanic Verses* deals with the postcolonial condition in an even more proactive, avant-garde manner but its fame was guaranteed less by what it did with history than by the history that enveloped it and its author, involving amongst other events minor riots and book-burnings by British-based Muslims and a death sentence on Rushdie from the government of Iran.

Midnight's Children (1981) is frequently compared with Sterne's *Tristram Shandy* in that its narrator Saleem Sinai is, like Shandy, quixotically unreliable. Both attempt to tell the story of their lives and each offers instead an apparently limitless sequence of digressions. There, however, differences begin to emerge because while Shandy extemporizes on everything and nothing in particular, Saleem's addiction to improvisation is tied to the equally uncertain nature and progress of the land of his birth, India. Events such as Indira Gandhi's prosecution for alleged electoral fraud and the Indo-Pakistan War of 1971 inform the text but only as they would in the discourse of an unstoppably loquacious figure for whom in the past they meant a good deal. In the present they vie for attention with recollections of his first attempts to ride a bicycle and childhood games of cricket. Rushdie's technique is founded upon his own somewhat eclectic theories of language and literature which themselves nod toward the archaic observations of J. F. Lyotard. Lyotard could be regarded as the ultimate post-structuralist/postmodernist, if it were not for the insistence of such thinkers that there is no such thing as an 'ultimate'. Rushdie is an enthusiastic disciple of Lyotard's central thesis that late twentieth-century existence is composed entirely and exclusively of competing discourses and modes of representation. Reality is no longer something possessed or experienced but rather an endlessly transient spectrum of effects. Rushdie's version of Lyotard's prognosis carries an endearingly optimistic touch. He ponders and accepts Lyotard's contention that the 'rejection of totalized explanations is the modern condition [...] the elevation of the quest for the Grail over the Grail itself, the acceptance that all that is solid *has* melted into air, that morality and reality are not givens but imperfect human constructs [...] This is what Lyotard called, in 1979, *La Condition Postmoderne*'. In Rushdie's view, however, this state demands not some philosophical counterbalance or reversion to the securities of faith. No, '...this is where the novel, the form created to discuss the fragmentation of truth, comes in...[this] is the point from which fiction begins [...] the challenge of literature is to start from this point, and still find a way of fulfilling our unaltered spiritual requirements' (*Imaginary Homelands*, Penguin/Granta, 1992, p. 422).

The idea that fiction, which by its nature is a fabric of effects and untruths, can in some way restore a sense of well-being to a collective state of mind comprising effects and untruths is beguiling to say the least, and one is intrigued not only by Rushdie's faith in this remedy but also by his reluctance to say anything about how and to what end fiction will fulfil its new role as redeemer. But given that his essay is in part a creative manifesto one might assume that his own fiction shows us its redemptorist thesis in action.

The Satanic Verses must, according to criteria offered by Lyotard or anyone else, qualify as the archetypal postmodern text because it is near impossible to describe its structure or purpose. In continually resisting paraphrase or exegesis it exposes as futile the inclination to make sense of anything. Two associates, Gibreel and Saladin, both of Indian origin, exist apparently simultaneously in several different historical periods and locations: contemporary Britain and Pakistan, Buenos Aires, Bombay, the England of the Cromwellian Commonwealth and seventh-century Arabia to name but a few. A degree of coherence could be wrested from this textual chaos by the persistent reminder of their jobs in Britain. Both work in the media, respectively in film and radio, and although Rushdie does not press the point one might assume that these roles are intended as appropriate for figures for whom space and time are limitlessly available and continually alterable phenomena. However, in case we might become too complacent or confident regarding their presence in Britain as the buttress for a reliable narrative, Rushdie has them arrive by an unusual, though symbolically resonant route; they plummet into London from an airliner blown up by terrorists.

The Satanic Verses, not least because of its political consequences – few if any novels can be said to have killed people; dozens died in riots in India, Pakistan and Turkey and one translator was murdered – has guaranteed for itself an enormous amount of public scrutiny and while its commentators frequently differ on matters such as its contribution to postmodernism or its blasphemous content they are in sound agreement on one point: no-one seems willing or able to indicate its rationale or purpose. Literature, being the aesthetic subspecies of language, can of course exist happily without an incorporate objective but its absence from Rushdie's novel carries an irony at once grotesque and instructive.

The structure of the novel corresponds closely with Rushdie's musings on the postmodern condition as fragmented, unreliable and uncertain; but the novel is also insinuatingly diagnostic. It indicates at various points how and why we can no longer find a reassuring mainstay for our doubts about practically everything. Section V for example offers a harrowing portrait of urban London in the late 1980s, a place where greed and exploitative nihilism have replaced anything that might resemble compassion or integrity. This rampant disdain for principle is embodied in a figure referred to as 'Mrs Torture' (pronounce it rapidly and connect with 'Margaret'). Saladin is sombre witness to all this while at the same time he is visited in dreams by a spectral presence called Mahound, a derogatory version of the name of the prophet Mohammed. Mahound is a troubled figure, uncertain of his own faith and distracted, lubriciously, by three female goddesses, Al-Lat, Al Uzza and Manat.

Critics have, with learned solemnity, treated the work as a late twentieth-century version of Joyce's *Ulysses*, a dynamic leviathan that both bemoans and magnificently represents the state of humanity – a dream of a lost faith mired in heartless consumerism. This postmodern interpretive festival was, however, accompanied by a formidably literalist sequence of readings and consequences. It was banned in India, South Africa, Bangladesh, Sudan, Sri Lanka and Pakistan and on 14 February 1989 the Ayatollah Khomeini of Iran issued a fatwa sentencing Rushdie to death under Islamic law. Rushdie became a state-protected fugitive, accompanied by members of Special Branch and moved between MI5-approved safe houses for the subsequent 10 years. Given Rushdie's oft-expressed contempt for Mrs Thatcher and her regime, connoisseurs of black comedy would, if this itself were a piece of fiction, be suitably impressed, and there is more. Rushdie, reflecting upon his particular experience of having spent his early years in India and then his teens and adulthood in Rugby School, Cambridge University and the London advertising industry, fastens upon the notion of disjunction as the animating principle of his writing, particularly his attempts to capture his sense of double affiliation to two nations, continents, cultures and traditions: '...we will not be capable of reclaiming precisely the thing that was lost; that we will, in short create fictions, not actual cities or villages, but invisible ones, imaginary homelands, Indias of the mind' (*Imaginary Homelands*, p. 10). This could be seen as a rationale for Rushdie's creation of Saladin as an intermediary between the world of Mrs Torture and the absent homeland that floats on the edge of his memory. One might even venture to perceive Mahound, the humbled, slightly debauched version of Mohammed, as symptomatic of this intermingling of two cultures with the venerated singularity of Islam infected by the prevailing decadence of Saladin's life in London. That, at least, would be an option available to sophisticated, Western theorists (see for example, Homi Bhabha's *The Location of Culture*, 1994, in which can be found many parallels with Rushdie's *Imaginary Homelands*) who treat the disintegration of a coherent narrative or the hybridized fictional character as a fitting literary engagement with the postcolonial experience. One is slightly puzzled therefore by why a vast number of ordinary individuals, specifically Muslims, who shared with Rushdie the experience of a divided cultural inheritance, interpreted the novel as a blatant insult to Islamic belief. It would seem that, for them at least, the distinction between the culture of their homeland and that of their colonizer was anything but blurred or hybridized. It was manifest and unambiguous and Rushdie, because he had allowed the one to infect the other, was guilty of treachery.

I raise this point not to encourage sympathy with those who wanted to silence and punish Rushdie; quite the opposite. If Rushdie was guilty of anything then it was a, perhaps unwitting, preponderance of postmodern indulgence. By refusing to concede that there was and is a radical difference between post-Enlightenment Europe and the theocratic cultures of the Arabic and Asian world, and more signifi-cantly that this demands choice rather than liberal equivocation, he effectively abetted the dreadful fate that befell him in 1988–9. The bitterest irony of the protracted saga attends Rushdie's proclamation in his article in *The Times* of 28 December 1990 that he would now unequivocally 'embrace Islam'. He added that he now had a better 'understanding' of the faith, that he would reconsider his representa-tions of it – implying a rewriting of offending passages – and that he had ordered the paperback edition of the novel to be suspended. Rushdie's moment of born-again recantation was brief and spurious (following the Islamic authorities' failure to reciprocate he withdrew it) but it involved an important subtext because what he had also done was to forswear the aesthetic and intellectual preconditions that had underpinned his writing so far. His enthusiastic advocacy of an imagi-native, postmodern realm incorporating, rather than delineating, the mindsets and legacies of Europe and Asia had been briefly exchanged for an espousal of the latter at the expense of the former, an act which was moreover mendacious and hypocritical.

Though condemned for a decade to absence from unprotected public life Rushdie was not silenced and has gone on to produce work which at least in manner maintains his affiliation to a particularly Euro-Asian species of magic realism. But from *Haroun and the Sea of Stories* (1990) to *Shalimar the Clown* (2005) one suspects that the self-consciously outrageous tilts at credulity and coherence are more protective than demonstrative. In an essay written three years after the fatwa was declared he told of how he had spent a thousand days in a 'balloon':

> Trapped inside a metaphor, I've often felt the need to redescribe it, to change the terms. This isn't so much a balloon, I've wanted to say, as a bubble within which I'm simultaneously exposed and sealed off. The bubble floats above and through the world, depriving me of reality, reducing me to an abstraction. (*Imaginary Homelands*, pp. 430–1)

Rushdie's situation was unenviable to say the least but one can't help but noting in this passage an outstanding, pitiably unwitting, case of self-directed burlesque. He has become the victim and more signifi-cantly a version of his own creative manifesto: that grey area between 'reality' and 'abstraction', the figure as 'metaphor', promised in his fiction, is now his own day-to-day regime. Perhaps as a means of regaining some contact with reality he began in his fiction to chart a more anaesthetized, emasculated track away from it. Certainly he has continued to mix, blend and distort myths from Western and Eastern cultures but he has done so with fear-struck hyperbole.

Shalimar the Clown interweaves the stories of Shalimar Noman and Max Ophuls. The harmony of mid-twentieth-century Kashmir that had permitted Shalimar, a Muslim, to marry his childhood sweetheart Boonyi Kaul disintegrates into violent fundamentalist conflict. Max Ophuls, survivor of the Nazi Holocaust, enters the narrative as US ambassador to India, has an affair with Boonyi and returns to the US with their daughter India. In due course Max becomes involved, on behalf of the US, with the interim conflicts of the subcontinent, ostensibly as an anti-terrorist tsar but in truth as agent for overweaning capitalism. As a 'novel of ideas' *Shalimar the Clown* involves the kind of cumbersome, simplistic symbolism one might expect of a precocious teenage enthusiast of multi-culturalism. One has the impression that Rushdie is offering an inclusive egalitarian picture of victimhood, with Hindus, Muslims and Jews all thrown into the same dystopian casserole of sectarianism, mass murder and diaspora. Blame, he implies, must be shared among humanity, and whatever the credibility or otherwise of this model it chimes unnervingly with a post-*Satanic Verses* desire to make his fiction so prismatic as to be immune from a particular, or rather a particularly hostile, interpretation. Further to this the novel is so drenched in linguistic play and swipes at credulity as to reduce magic realism to a state of battered redundancy. Names and identities mutate with the careless abandon of a parlour game and characters of every hue seem capable of superhuman acts: a Ukrainian potato witch communicates with cobras, a dead mullah is found to be composed of old machine parts and a jail-breaker walks on air over the prison wall. No myth or cultural legacy is immune from another – Greek and Hindu are shown to be twins, for example. Max's London-based landlady of Indian origin and the upper-middle-class Home Counties woman he attempts to seduce speak like characters from the *Carry On* films of the 1960s ('Letter Mr Max! I hopen it, sir? Yes sir! Hokay!...Wery Wery hawful, hisn't it' and 'But ahem! Aha!...Not that it would be a bally imposition I suppose? Eh, eh, ha ha?' respectively). It could, charitably, be asked if these figures are perhaps postmodern caricatures, archetypes of race, class and background reconfigured via the literary equivalent of cartoons. It could, but the question is generously inappropriate because Rushdie's unwitting drift into farce is consistent with his almost maniacal, compulsive preoccupation throughout the novel with transforming every vaguely consensual notion of reality into something manifestly unreal.

The fantastic extrapolations of division and mutual apprehension that Rushdie conceived as a means of capturing the postcolonial experience have, it seems, become an escape route from its very real and very dangerous specificity. Curiously, the vast majority of other novelists who could like Rushdie claim knowledge of the relationship between late-twentieth-century Britain and its postimperial heritage have elected to deal with this in a robustly naturalistic manner.

V. S. Naipaul was born in Trinidad but his family were middle-class émigrés from East India. He won a scholarship to University College, Oxford in the early 1950s and these early experiences of a shifting cultural spectrum would register in most of his fiction. He saw and experienced the Empire – gradually becoming the Commonwealth – not from a fixed perspective; rather he found that different dimensions were continually overlapping with others, variously obscuring and sharpening his vision of their relationships. His acclaimed early novel *A House for Mr Biswas* (1961) is based on his father's experiences in Trinidad, a man attempting to balance the Victorian imperative toward enterprise and self-reliance against a commitment to an Indian tribal legacy that itself has become a ghettoized enclave of the West Indies.

His most intriguing mid-career work is *The Enigma of Arrival* (1987) in which the narrator tells of his experiences after arriving in England from Trinidad in 1950. Prior to this he had assembled his own model of Englishness from a fabric of verbal and visual representations crafted by the likes of Hardy, Wordsworth, Tennyson, Constable and Turner. He arrives not with the naïve expectation of life matching art but more as an inquisitive sceptic, eager as much for shocks as confirmations. What he encounters, however, is something for which he has not prepared himself. Not only is England in rapid retreat form its romanticized self-image, it seems capable neither of noticing nor caring about this. During one episode he rents a cottage in the grounds of a Wiltshire country house and observes with horrified fascination that the owner has, assisted by a questionable illness, immunized himself from any contact with the outside world; he no longer wishes to comprehend, let alone witness, the disappearance of what he once took for granted. It gradually becomes apparent to the narrator that he has, rather by fate than inclination, become a more informed, reflective observer upon postimperial decline than virtually everyone who has grown up in England. Significantly he has ambitions to be a writer, his name is 'Naipaul' and the detail of his arrival and experiences thereafter bear a stunning resemblance to those of his creator. This is not, however, an exercise in postmodern playfulness. It is autobiography, a creative apologia wrapped in a novel: both versions of Naipaul are uniquely dispossessed, both are always at a slight distance from a particular tribal or cultural legacy, and as such each feels able to comment upon the postcolonial experience in a way that is denied to those with more grounded affiliations.

Which brings us to his recent novels, *Half a Life* (2001) and *Magic Seeds* (2004), both parts of the same narrative and each involving Willie Chandran. In the first novel Willie comes from India to London as a student, publishes a book of short stories, marries a woman of Portuguese/African ancestry and after spending 18 years with her in a Portuguese colony in Africa leaves to live with his sister in Berlin. *Magic Seeds* begins with Willie being virtually ordered by his indefatigably radical sister Sarojini to play a part in reclaiming ancient cultures from centuries of European colonialism. Suitably inspired he joins a deranged Khmer Rouge-style guerrilla group in India, rejects them and submits to imprisonment. London-based intellectuals secure his release – in prison he has written a novel about his life – and the rest of the book places him in what was once the capital of the British Empire. Here the novel comes to rest upon its peculiar centrepiece: a man who has witnessed some of the most disorientating and brutal conflicts of the late twentieth century records with choleric despondency the state of Britain at the closing of the millennium. Amongst other things he professes a mixture of lust and contempt for 'council estate women...of plebeian aspect' and notes that everywhere he walks in London the streets seem to have been taken over by 'black people, everywhere, and Japanese; and people who looked like Arabs'. This is Thatcher's Britain but for Willie the vast majority of its population seem content with the lazy residue of postwar socialism: idleness and state-funded indulgence are the endemic features of a cataleptic society. His former acquaintance, Marcus, has become part of the establishment, a diplomat. Marcus's son, Lyndhurst, is half English and is to be married to the scion of an impoverished aristocratic family. The wedding is recorded in magnificently horrific detail, with the last remnants of the English upper classes attempting to be as one with their new postcolonial family – Caribbean bands play and Shakespeare's sonnets are recited. The spectacle is grotesque and Naipaul leaves the reader with an impression that half a century after the British Empire began to disintegrate all that remains is a past and present comingled as dismal burlesque.

There is throughout Naipaul's fiction a residual sense of Britain as having besmirched the self-image it so enthusiastically promoted among its colonial subjects and this is echoed, albeit dissonantly, in an essay by Hanif Kureishi in which he observes that in Pakistan in the 1970s and 1980s 'great pleasure' was taken in England's apparent 'decline and decay': '…strike-bound, drug-ridden, riot-torn, inefficient, disunited, a society which has moved too suddenly from puritanism to hedonism and now loathed itself' (*My Beautiful Launderette and the Rainbow Sign*, Faber, 1986, p. 192). Later in the essay Kureishi states that there must, for the British themselves, be 'a fresh way of seeing Britain', that to avoid 'insularity, schism, bitterness and catastrophe', much 'thought, discussion and self-examination must go into what this "new way of being British" involves' (pp. 101–2). The passage is commendably solicitous but one suspects that a cynical smirk accompanied its composition because his best-known novel involves what comes close to a calculated celebration of Britain's lamentable state. *The Buddha of Suburbia* (1990) can claim to have initiated a subgenre, which I shall call the Assimilated Postcolonial Novel. Naipaul and Rushdie, while very different in the manner and execution of their writing, bring to their work a continual doubling of perspective and affiliation. In their fiction Britain plays an ambiguous role as stranger and confidante, something viewed both from a distance and as a condition. For Kureishi's narrator Karim, and many of his fictive contemporaries, their Pakistani legacy is a curiosity, something that exists and is indeed still capable of generating racist antagonism, but which can for most of the time be treated with affectionate indifference. I use the term 'assimilated' in naming this subgenre not because the likes of Karim attempt to extinguish their sense of difference; rather they make use of it to create a more subtle form of cultural hybridity. *The Buddha of Suburbia*, in tone and style, invests itself

securely within the tradition of British sardonic realism. Karim's narrational mode brings to mind a blend of Justin Cartwright, Julian
Rathbone and Jonathan Coe, with slight echoes of Will Self and
Martin Amis, but Karim, and Kureishi, have access to an indulgence
denied to their white British counterparts. They can manipulate and
exploit political incorrectness. Karim habitually refers to himself and
others as 'Pakis', and in doing so he at once divests the word of its
racist content and treats it with amused contempt. More significantly
Kureishi creates a dynamic between Karim's manner and his racial
background that deliberately undermines the reader's expectations,
particularly and ironically the expectations of white left-leaning
readers. At one point he and his friend Charlie witness a performance
by a postpunk band which, he comments, 'was more aggressive than
anything I'd heard since early Who...Not a squeeze of anything
"progressive" or "experimental" came from these pallid, vicious little
council estate kids with hedgehog hair, howling about anarchy and
hatred' (pp. 129–30). The image of Karim that forms in the mind of
the reader is that of a jaundiced, slightly arrogant figure, reinforced
when he reflects judiciously on the youth culture of London.

> There were bookshops with racks of magazines printed without capital
> letters or the bourgeois disturbance of full stops; there were shops
> selling all the records you could desire; there were parties where girls
> and boys you didn't know took you upstairs and fucked you; there
> were all the drugs you could use...(*The Buddha of Suburbia*, Faber,
> 1990, p. 121)

With his polished manner Karim reminds us self-consciously that he
is superior to the world he inhabits and it is all the more ingenious of
Kureishi to make use of this as a counterpoint to another dimension
of his character. Sentences such as 'there were kids dressed in velvet
cloaks who lived free lives; there were thousands of black people everywhere, so I wouldn't feel exposed...' (p. 121) are slipped, coat-trailed,
into longer passages as reminders that Karim's self-confidence enables
him to treat the fact that he is a second-generation Pakistani with
something close to detachment. He ogles strippers in an East End pub,
dances for entire evenings at the Pink Pussy Club, attends greyhound
racing tracks and is an avid fan of that monument to feral brutality,
Millwall Football Club, 'where I forced Changee [his darker skinned

friend] to wear a bobble hat over his face in case the lads saw he was a Paki and imagined I was one too' (p. 98). That he has chosen to ally himself, and his friend, to a fanbase that thrives on racial intolerance is emblematic of the novel's potency. Throughout Karim's narrative there is a curious blend of accommodation and provocation. His intellectual mindset places him above most of the shallow, predictable characters of his acquaintance but he is not content; he needs continually to remind us, and himself, that he is at once integrated with British society and a class above it. Towards the end he reflects:

> We became part of England and yet proudly stood outside it. But to be truly free we had to free ourselves of all bitterness and resentment, too. How was this possible when bitterness and resentment were generated afresh every day? (p. 227)

He seems to leave the question open but an answer, of sorts, is woven into the novel. The hypothesis of freedom from bitterness and resentment is an abstraction, an absurdity. All that is available, as Karim shows, is a balancing act between being part of England and treating this with aloof amusement.

The Buddha of Suburbia set a precedent and one of its more shameless recent manifestations is Nirpal Singh Dhaliwal's *Tourism* (2006). Dhaliwal's Bhupinder Singh Johal is Karim reborn with extra portions of loathing both for white liberals – who wallow in the 'vague suicidal melancholy' of postcolonial guilt – and their working-class counterparts whose racism is, almost pitiably, a function of their lazy stupidity. Like Karim, Bhupinder, or 'Puppy' as he is affectionately known, exploits his colour and background, reflecting gleefully at one point that slavery and its horrors involved a fortuitous twist upon natural selection. White women, he avers, now tend to be aroused more by the indigenous rough athleticism of black men than the flabby tenderness of the latter's one-time oppressors: 'It's great to know that in his grab for wealth, Whitey created the body his women want to fuck the most'. Wittingly or not the title of the novel perfectly captures its prevailing theme. 'Puppy' functions like someone passing through, with no corresponding affiliation to the things and people he encounters. As a consequence he feels licensed to treat everything – capitalism, art, politics, women, multi-culturalism, homosexuality – with almost equal contempt.

Rather more restrained and circumspect followers of the *Buddha's* trajectory are Zadie Smith, Monica Ali and Andrea Levy. Smith's first novel *White Teeth* (2000) deals with the relationship between races in a way that borders upon the farcical, and whether this is effective, or entirely wilful, remains open to question. Samad Iqbal, a Bengali Muslim, and Archie Jones, a working-class Englishman, form a lifelong friendship when serving together in Europe in World War II. Such an occurrence is not impossible – a small number of Indian troops did land in Europe after D-Day – but in that period and those conditions the odds against such figures having the time and opportunity to recognize in each other temperamental affinities and remain courageously oblivious to differences in appearance and background are long, to say the least. An even greater strain upon credulity is placed when the two of them capture a French scientist, Perret, who is alleged to have worked on the Nazi sterilization programme. They discuss what to do with this individual and Samad convinces Archie that he should kill Perret as a just response to the evil of Nazism and as a symbolic statement regarding Britain's postcolonial destiny. Archie marches Perret into the forest and appears to dispatch him with a gunshot.

The faint suspicion that these characters are ciphers in a clumsy novel of ideas is confirmed when the narrative takes us into the postwar period. Archie marries a Jamaican immigrant whose grandfather was a middle-class Englishman, and, prior to meeting his multicultural bride-to-be, he is prevented from committing suicide by a Halal butcher. Samad's twin sons Millat and Magid are, respectively, a rabid Muslim fundamentalist enthusiastically involved in the public burning of Rushdie's infamous novel and a quintessential Anglo-Indian exhibiting a patrician cultivated manner that more closely echoes the fiction of Waugh and Wodehouse than the actuality of modern Britain.

The novel also contains the equally preposterous Chalfen family. The father, a Jewish scientist, is creator of 'Future Mouse©, a genetic experiment that echoes those of Nazism and reflects the Chalfen's own introspective self-possessed brand of Englishness. Millat regards this as a blasphemous undermining of Allah's concept of nature and attempts to shoot one of the scientists responsible for the programme, only to have the bullet deflected by Archie. And who is the scientist? He is Perret who decades earlier Archie would have killed had his very British sense of decency not intervened.

Smith is a talented writer and is particularly adept at satire, albeit rather heavy handedly (for example, the militant group joined by Millat is called the 'Keepers of the Eternal and Victorious Islamic Nation': KEVIN) but one cannot help but wonder if this novel, which involved such an awkward blend of the baroque and the symbolic, would have found a publisher, let alone generated critical acclaim, had it not been so determinedly fixated upon the theme of multi-culturalism.

In *The Autograph Man* (2002) Smith executes a calculated double take. She avoids an anticipated second chronicle of postcolonialism while carrying forward some of the subgenre's cachet. Her hero is Alex-Li Tandem, half Jewish, half Chinese, who buys and sells the signatures of the famous, from iconic figures of the Victorian age to the likes of Madonna. The implication – never of course made manifest – is that there is some psychological link between Alex as an embodiment of otherwise disparate cultures and his obsession with trophies that combine transience with a trace of permanence. The setting, appropriately enough, is contemporary London which itself carries the 'signatures' of hundreds of races, legacies and past existences.

One suspects that Smith's third novel *On Beauty* (2005) most reflects her temperament and disposition and that the others have been a means to this specific end. At several points the novel announces itself as a modern version of E. M. Forster's *Howards End* (1910). The latter concentrates upon the relationship between the Schlegel family who live from an unearned income and pride themselves upon their cultivated liberalism, and their neighbours, the Wilcoxes, who work in commerce, are pragmatic materialists and have little time for art or associated finer sensibilities. Smith narrows the dichotomy so that both of her families are preoccupied with similar social and cultural issues. Howard Belsey, white English art historian, espouses a collection of radical left-leaning causes, particularly those involving race and gender and one wonders if he has married and put up with Kiki his verbally egregious Africa-American wife as a combined ideological gesture and act of penance. Belsey works – though is, to his bitterness, untenured – in an Ivy League style university, a modest version of Harvard where Smith spent time as Visiting Professor in Creative Writing. Howard's senior colleague and apparent nemesis is Sir Monty Kipps, advocate of reactionary, conservative politics and bitter opponent of all the intellectual pieties embraced by Howard. We know that

Howard's desperate attempts to better Monty's cultural and intellectual positions are doomed from the start for the simple reason that Monty himself is black. In one deft incisive move Smith lays bare the contradictions of an academic and intellectual ruling class. Their conceptions of race are as fixed and hidebound as those of white supremacists; they patronize the cultural-ethnic groups to whom they profess sympathy by expecting them to accord with their own ideological rationale. When a black, Sir Monty, voices opinions that are robustly right-wing and does so with an intellectual strength and independence that transcend racial division, Howard and his ilk are effectively silenced.

This conceit, in which political correctness is rehearsed, choreographed and mirthfully spoiled, runs through all of the novel's many subnarratives. Particularly notable is the contrast, perceptible but never actually mentioned, between the noisy academics who continually debate multi-cultural and Third World issues and the regiment of Haitians and Latin Americans who service their affluent lifestyles. Smith shows us, without having to mention, the indifference of the latter to the former.

In *On Beauty* Smith turns a sharp satirical blade against targets first set up by Kureishi: that the preconceptions regarding race maintained by a predominantly white middle-class intellectual corpus are as absurdly self-obsessed, though rather less offensive, as those of avowed racists. For an example of this one might go to Maggie Gee's *The White Family* (2002). One has the sense throughout the novel of an author tiptoeing clumsily around issues for which she feels beholden, on behalf of her unenlightened kinsfolk, to apologize. The conceit of the title is toe-curlingly simplistic, given that the family represent one-by-one the various shades of racism, confusion and guilt exhibited within the socio-political body of 'white' Britain over the previous five decades. Alfred White, the patriarch, has for half a century been the keeper of Albion Park, making sure that football games are played in the proper areas and remaining alert to untoward goings on in the Gents toilet. One is uncertain of whether to treat such symbolism as embarrassing or unwittingly hilarious but we can remain confident that Alfred will turn out to be a xenophobic bigot. An altercation with members of a black family proves too much for his aged constitution – please note, if necessary, further helpings of allegory regarding Britain 1950–2002 – and the rest of the family are drawn to his hospital bedside. These include Darren, US-based journalist and the conscience of the family, choked with anger at what his father still appears to embody. Shirley, the daughter, endured her father's wrath, often including violence, when she was dating her eventual husband, a Ghanaian who proved to be a success and has left her a wealthy widow: so there, Alfred. Now she is causing vengeful bitterness by conducting a relationship with Elroy, a black social worker. And then there is Dirk, the youngest, a skinheaded accomplice of BNP-type activists. It turns out that his loathing for nonwhites is symptomatic of his own repressed, latent homosexuality. The bitter irony of Alfred having named his son after that matinee idol (Bogarde) who was also by necessity duplicitous regarding his true sexuality, seems fittingly retributive, and procures from the old bigot a moving almost redemptive moment of transformation. The novel is pitiable for two reasons: the type of person requiring improvement via its clunking, evangelistic symbolism would in any event be unlikely to read novels at all, and its flagging up of racial stereotypes is just as divisive – albeit condescendingly rather than offensively – as the predispositions of its more repulsive characters. Ironically only nonwhite writers appear able to set aside the prescriptive mechanisms of political correctness when writing about the complexities of racial difference and idiosyncratic affiliation.

In *Small Island* (2004) Andrea Levy is intent upon provoking comparisons. The novel is set in 1948 and its characters and circumstances could be those of Lamming and Selvon viewed via half a century of hindsight. Gilbert Joseph is a Jamaican who served in the RAF in the war, returns to Britain on the *Windrush*, and is joined soon afterwards by his new bride, Hortense. Hortense is effectively a reworking of Phillips's Leila from *The Final Passage*; both have grown up with an image of England as populated largely by mannered and agreeably polite individuals who spend much of their spare time immersing themselves in the magnificent cultural heritage of the motherland, and both are horribly disappointed. Gilbert bears a close resemblance to Leila's husband Michael, in that each provides their partner with a counterbalance of grim experience, principally involving racism. Parallels with Smith are flagged up in the presences of Queenie and Bernard Bligh, the working-class English couple with whom the Josephs find lodgings, but Levy's interracial counterplot is more complex and unsettling than the friendship between Archie and

Samad, and here we begin to detect the rationale behind the novel's acknowledgements of its predecessors. Levy has each of her four chief characters provide a subjective first-person account of shared narrative and for the first time in the lineage of the British postcolonial novel it becomes almost impossible to disentangle racial stereotypes and preconceptions regarding the history of immigration from undistilled idiosyncrasy and impressionism. Hortense's perception of Queenie carries a good deal of condescending tolerance; she regards herself as a class above her shabbily dressed, ill-educated, and white, landlady. Queenie, meanwhile, does not mind being seen in public with her tenant, partly since she finds her companionship agreeable but principally because Hortense, with her mellow complexion and sharp physiognomy, could be mistaken for a European. These initial pairings of temperament with racial stereotype are deliberately misleading. The more we are drawn into each character's monologue the more they begin to animate the drab landscape of postwar London and become the more intriguing and unpredictable. On several occasions Levy transposes the activities of her invented figures with verifiable events from the period. One of these has Gilbert and Queenie recollect a wartime experience where the US army attempted to impose a segregated seating plan in a cinema. Both became involved in the subsequent riot and while neither is presented as a cipher or exemplar for heroic liberalism we are left with a sense of them having shared a moment that has a manifest and long-term effect upon their respective mindsets. Levy's overall intention in combining subjectivity with documentary realism is to provide a sharper emphasis for the former. London in 1948 is made dispassionately real, yet at the same time Levy's characters move through it and speak to us from it as individuals who develop emotionally despite rather than because of their circumstances. Fictional representations of race and migration procure expectations of polemicism and Levy in *Small Island* acknowledges this tendency by undermining it and her novel is more honest and thought-provoking as a consequence.

In *Brick Lane* (2003) Monica Ali makes use of the same ingredients as Smith, Levy, Kureishi, Rushdie, Naipaul et al. and to her credit comes up with a surprisingly different confection. Nazneen arrives in London in the mid-1980s from Bangladesh; she is 18 and about to enter an arranged marriage with the farcically egotistical 40-year-old Chanu. At the beginning she can barely speak English but as she and the novel mature she moves from an inhibited watchful presence to a figure via whom we are offered a limpid portrait of the Bangladeshi immigrant community. Chanu is a tirelessly refashioned cliché, recalling a legion of characters from Naipaul's Biswas to Levy's Hortense. He nurtures a respect for British culture in which the Royal Family merit the same devotional scrutiny as the Brontës or Thackeray and is appalled by the ways in which his revered motherland has let its aesthetic and moral standards slip. Also he is a tragicomic failure, a corpulent intellectual mediocrity who continually fails his Open University degree examinations and, without a hint of irony, frames and hangs his cycling proficiency certificates instead. Eventually as their daughters are drawn toward a twenty-first century culture of amoral, secular indifference, Chanu's disillusionment with Britain becomes an obsessive desire to reclaim stability, and his own threatened role as patriarch, by returning the family to Bangladesh. In the meantime Nazneen meets Karim, the 'middleman' who supplies and sells the clothes she works on in dismal sweatshop conditions. He is younger, more dynamic than Chanu and handsome, and Nazneen sleeps with him. He is also a militant Islamic fundamentalist and the events of 9 September 2001 prompt Nazneen to look again at these two men who have influenced her life more than anyone or anything else. In the end she is able to move beyond racial or religious prerogatives: the character who began as almost a mute figure in a novel centred upon England leaves it as the only one who can properly understand, through experience, the fact that the two epigraphs chosen by Ali are indivisible: 'Sternly, remorselessly, fate guides each of us' (Turgenev) and 'A man's character is his fate' (Heraclitus).

Hari Kunzru's widely celebrated *The Impressionist* (2002) is the story of Pran, born in Edwardian, colonial India, whose prevailing characteristic is his ability to reinvent himself, something that is partly a consequence of his unusually Caucasian skin colour and bone structure and partly an acquired inclination toward the chameleonesque. Following his ejection from the family home for allegedly betraying his Indian ancestry he re-emerges, first in Bombay as the ambitious playboy 'Pretty Bobby', next as the very English Jonathan Bridgeman, initially in Oxford and then in the African colony of Fotseland, and eventually in Paris as a rootless absentee.

The novel leaves a conspicuous trail of clues as to its influences and intent. Rushdie's prognosis of his 'homeland' as an indivisible

confection of the imaginary, the remembered and the actual is embodied in Pran's obsessive shifts between what he knows, or at least thinks,
he is and the utterly convincing performances that deceive everyone
else. At another level Bhabha's notion of a cultural animus which
disrupts and undermines the 'powerful master discourse' of colonial
history is fictionally enacted. Pran's actual identity is obscured from
everyone else in the book which enables him to drift in an almost
proprietorial manner through fictional scenarios that evoke the fabric
of England and its Imperial legacy. He is a character who features in
thinly disguised versions of the novels of Waugh, Forster and Kipling
while enacting a counternarrative available only to himself and the reader.

The Impressionist bristles with narrative tricks and conceits but at
the same time one detects a vigilant recycling of the mainstays of
postcolonial theory and writing – Bhabha, Said, Rushdie et al. – which
Kunzru no doubt encountered during his English degree at
Cambridge. Perhaps he sensed that working within such shadows
and expectations was a self-limiting exercise because his second novel
Transmission (2004) bears a close resemblance to Smith's *On Beauty*
in that both break away from the familiar topographical nexus of
Britain and its postcolonial legacy. *Transmission* tells the story of the
young Indian computer programmer Arjun Mehta who spends much
of the novel in California, having his fantasies regarding the dream
life of Silicon Valley dashed and taking revenge with the invention
of a mischievous virus 'LeelaO1' dedicated to his other fantasy, the
beautiful, wealthy Bollywood actress Leela Zahir. Like Smith, Kunzru
exploits the ideological currency of location and multiculturalism as
scaffolding for his real objective. Both novels involve a merciless and
often very effective exercise in satire directed mainly against an Anglo-
US bourgeois elite at once satisfied with the current state of politically
correct multiculturalism but just as greedy and exploitative as their
imperialist forebears.

Time and events have granted Rushdie a respected, avuncular status
among writers who address related postimperial topics but while
admired by them the vast majority of his successors have eschewed his
practice, and ordinance, of magic realism as the only discourse suitable
for tales of racial dispersal and realignment. They have chosen realism
instead, and effectively disproved the view that its use involves a sub-
junctive complicity with white, middle-class mores of expression and
representation. An apparent exception is Bernardine Evaristo whose

three principal works *Lara* (1997), *The Emperor's Babe* (2001) and *Soul Tourists* (2005) match an energetic refusal to conform to the usual parameters of time and space with equally dismissive attitude toward the borderlines of literary genre. *Lara* begins with a shrewd picture of life in suburban London during the 1960s and 1970s but this spirals into an epic cacophony of voices tracing Lara's heritage through nineteenth-century Brazil, colonial Lagos and rural Ireland to Islington in the 1950s, where her parents meet. This might bring to mind *Midnight's Children* were it not for the fact that it is a novel in beautifully executed verse. Her characters from the past control and master their media in a manner that recalls the dramatic monologues of Browning. Evaristo effects a balance in each instance between a formal register that is distinctly poetic – usually a combination of blank and free verse – and a robust singularly of presence and circumstance. It might, for some, appear ironic that a cast so diverse in background and affiliation can remain contented and self-possessed within such a robustly Anglocentric genre. The fact that this apparent incongruity never features in appraisals of her work further indicates that the once overarching postulate that orthodox technique and irredentist ideology are complicitly intermeshed is now becoming an irrelevance.

Fate or some agency with a taste for the sardonic has prompted the publication of two novels within months of each other which unwittingly constitute a dialogue. Gautam Malkani's *Londonstani* (2006) is even more blatantly exploitative of its subjects than Dhaliwal's *Tourism* (2006). Malkani's assembly of second- and third-generation Indians appears to have successfully countercolonized the once-capital of the Empire. They have evolved a language of their own – a combination of Cockney, text-message concisions and traces of subcontinental patois – and each of them appears intent on stretching clichés of violent nefarious teenage angst beyond their known limits. Will Self in *The Book of Dave* (2006) comes up with a presence – albeit white and in early middle age – who is remarkably similar. Dave is a London taxi driver who also communicates in the manner of a moderately deranged cell-phone. Improbably he transcribes his rants as a book that is buried with him following his demise in 2002. It is unearthed some decades later, after an apocalyptic flood that wipes out virtually all of London, and becomes what amounts to the scriptural basis for a new religion and culture. The allegory is clumsy and somewhat patronizing – the nasty misanthropic author of the eponymous testament is, apparently, an indication of what most of the population are already on the brink of becoming – but more fascinating is the sense of equanimity that exists between Malkani's and Self's fictional spectacles. Semiarticulate yobbishness is now, it seems, a condition and indeed a discourse which unites the once-colonized with the one-time colonist. That both authors, sophisticated middle-class Oxbridge men, maintain in their work a cautious inscrutably superior distance from their subjects – Malkani by handing over the narration to the unendearing Jas and Self by contrasting his own style and wit with Dave's lack of both – should be taken into account by those tempted to treat either novel as a serious engagement with contemporaneity.

In all of the novels dealt with above the characters and indeed their creators are buttressed by protocols of collective experience, shared histories. The fact that these are relatively recent – post-*Windrush* – and still unfolding lends their novels a healthy and, paradoxically, secure dynamic. These novelists have been granted the twin franchise of postcolonial angst and self-caricature. They can offer a dire portrait of Englishness in all its post-1948 manifestations and at the same time indulge themselves with the likes of Chanu, Hortense or Leila: clumsy, buffoonish figures who if created by male, white, middle-aged writers would be deemed as overtures to racism. One is therefore caused to wonder about the kind of fiction that might be produced if the contrapuntal relationship of a community within a community were not such a reliable leitmotif. Such a hypothesis might seem untenable but, fascinatingly, it informs the work of one of the most enigmatic of the post-1970s generation of 'British' novelists, Kazuo Ishiguro.

More than any other late twentieth-/early twenty-first-century novelist – Evaristo included – he deserves the nomenclature 'poetic', and not because his style is self-consciously arch or layered with conceits: quite the opposite. Ishiguro's prose is precise, transparent, cautiously accessible. Yet his characters, his narrators, imply far more than they actually state. His best known, Booker-winning novel *The Remains of the Day* (1989) has the narrator, the butler Stevens, recounting a past and observing a present, circa 1956. His previous employer, Lord Darlington – served also by Stevens's father as underbutler – is dead and the country seat, Darlington Hall, has been purchased by a rich, condescendingly vulgar American called Farraday, who is intent on preserving the traditions of the English stately home, based mainly on Hollywood representations of the same. Stevens yearns for the almost feudal regime of the prewar years during which Lord Darlington, authentic aristocrat, combined patrician Englishness with an enthusiastic support for Hitler's Germany. Stevens's mentors form in our mind via his hints and clues to their dispositions; they are oblique presences, as much resonant of Stevens's restless state of mind as reliable representations. Standard images of England – from the romantic and rarefied through the nostalgic to the repulsive – are threaded into Stevens's narrative and Ishiguro's great achievement is to leave the reader perplexed as to how exactly this fabric has been generated, whether it is a function of the novel, and by implication its author, or a reflection of the unsettled, distracted mindset of Stevens.

Ishiguro, in all of his fiction, offers acute memorable observations, moments that, strangely, combine involvement with detachment, but these accumulate without any collateral sense of narrative propulsion; the plot develops yet the questions of why, how and to what end it does so remain coyly unanswered.

Ishiguro was born in Japan in 1954 and left for England in 1960 when his father began work at the National Institute of Oceanography. Thereafter he attended primary and grammar schools in Surrey and took degrees at the Universities of Kent and East Anglia. The language of Japan and more significantly its social and cultural fabric made up the entire compass of the six-year-old Ishiguro's existence and this was suddenly exchanged for something, literally, incomparable. Unlike first- or second-generation immigrants from the Indian subcontinent or the Caribbean, Ishiguro could not reflect upon the network of cultural matchings and mismatchings that constitute a collective diasporic legacy. His interfaces were particular and unique and in his novels we encounter a corresponding blend of fascinated observation and puzzlement.

The Unconsoled (1995) is a 500-page Kafkaesque chronicle in which the narrator, a concert pianist called Ryder, arrives in an unnamed European city to be celebrated as a cultural messiah. No-one ever fully explains to him why he has achieved this status nor what exactly it might involve. Instead Ryder appears to accept that all questions are by their nature unanswerable and we follow him through a sequence of related but equally meaningless incidents as if being led up, or down, an Escher staircase.

When We Were Orphans (2000) involves a similarly unreliable narrator, though in the case of Christopher Banks his profession belies his perfidiousness. He is a private investigator who sets out on a personal quest to make sense of his parents' disappearance from the international settlement of Shanghai 20 years earlier. This book's first sentence echoes the thrillers of John Buchan: 'It was the summer of 1923, the summer I came down from Cambridge, when despite my aunt's wishes that I return to Shropshire, I decided my future lay in the capital and took up a small flat at No. 14b Bedford Gardens in Kensington.' The studied cautiously layered syntax reflects Banks's persona but we eventually realize that this disguises an unusual personal history. At school he feared that the other boys would suspect from his speech habits that his background was non-English. So he began to monitor his utterances and even into adulthood he is self-consciously aware of having two pasts, one acquired, one half forgotten. This might explain why his own account of the investigation of his parents' disappearance begins to accumulate inconsistencies. He tells us things which contradict statements that he has already made and eventually we wonder if Ishiguro has lured us, via Banks, into the presence of someone delusional and possibly deranged.

One cannot help but notice parallels between Banks's state of manic self-deception, Stevens's inability to move beyond his class-obsessed script of expectations and Ryder's mordant acceptance of nihilism. Each exists in a world where everything has a double significance; Stevens immunizes himself from it, avoiding its pre-emptive notion of choice, while the others continuously enact and bequeath it to the reader.

Never Let Me Go (2005) is Ishiguro's most bizarre and, paradoxically, characteristic novel so far. Kathy H, the narrator, is 31 and has worked for 11 years as a 'carer' at a recovery centre, where she assists 'donors'. Her exact duties remain obscure, but innocuously so, at least until we begin to learn of Kathy's past. She and her friends from early childhood have been raised in an institution called Hailsham which appears to be a cross between an orphanage and an enlightened public school. At Hailsham Kathy and her peers are made aware, with morbid politeness, of their functional destiny: they are clones, will eventually be dismantled and their organs transplanted. She too will become a donor. The plot might portend an Orwellian presentation of individuals as dehumanized victims, but the fabric of the novel runs against this. Kathy and her Hailsham peers, Tommy and Ruth, move through near-contemporary England – it is set in the 'late 1990s' – like people who have no other inclination than to observe. Kathy scrutinizes office workers, shoppers, commuters, and does so in a way that blends disinterest with compassion. Here the novel turns our conditioned expectations against us. We might assume that the clones will draw our sympathy, perhaps horrified empathy, but instead we find that they become the observers and we, the ordinary normal people who read novels like this, become its mute robotic subjects.

With the exception of *The Unconsoled*, England features in Ishiguro's fictions as an alluring paradox, something always perceived at one remove, at once predictable but because of its distance, enigmatic. It is, however, impossible to extrapolate from this an attitude, let alone an ideology, because a unique autobiographical thread runs through, without diminishing, all of his writing: there is a prevailing sense of a separateness that cannot be shared and must as a consequence be continually re-examined and refashioned.

Only two other recent novelists share Ishiguro's unconventional status as figures with an allegiance to a culture and heritage outside Britain which is at one private and alienated. W. G. Sebald, who died tragically in a car crash in 2001, was born in Bavaria, but spent most of his adult life as an academic in England. In his last novel *Austerlitz* (2002) the narrator is unnamed and only reluctantly discloses that he has set out on a journey through Europe to conduct 'research', a journey which occupies the entire 418-page span of the novel and whose actual objectives become obscured by a general mood of listlessness. Indeed the figure of Jacques Austerlitz, a fellow academic met by the unnamed one, effectively displaces the latter whose already indeterminate presence becomes reduced to providing an occasional 'he said' or 'he added' to Austerlitz's story. This is an account of how, aged five, he was sent to Britain from Prague as the Nazis closed in. His parents didn't escape. He grew up in a vicarage in mid-Wales and seems to have spent much of his life reflecting upon the fact that 'I have never known who I really was'.

All of Sebald's fiction is a meditation upon the impossibility of offering a candid, impartial account of World War II. While there are numerous examples of other writers who have wrestled with a similar unbidden taxonomy of elisions Sebald's difficulties are aggravated by his having apportioned roughly equal amounts of his life to the two nations and cultures which inevitably perceive the same thing in different ways. The novels were written in German but he worked alongside their English translators Michael Hulse and Anthea Bell in a manner that resembled Beckett's translations of his fiction from French to English. He was aware that beyond the particulars of stylistic reproduction the mindset of a specific group of readers would play as significant a part in the generation of meaning as the words on the page. It becomes evident, particularly with a knowledge of Sebald's life, that the unnamed narrator and Austerlitz are versions of the same person or to be more precise embodiments of the same problem. The latter takes over from the former, both prove equally unable to make sense of their past and their current identity and it is possible to imagine the same novel being continually rewritten with the identical package of unaskable, unanswerable questions passed on infinitely from one speaker to the next.

Rachel Seiffert was born in 1971 of German and Australian parents and has spent most of her life in Oxford and Glasgow. By virtue of her family connections she shares with Sebald a double affiliation. *The Dark Room* (2001) though marketed as a novel, is actually a collection of three novellas, each of which involves a mosaic of various shades of guilt, evasion and complicity. Their subjects are Germans who experienced and participated in World War II or are related to those who did. While, unlike Sebald, she writes in English we intuit that she is equally concerned with the ways in which British readers' preconceptions will interact with the narrative. As a consequence she evolves a style that, brilliantly, matches the eloquent collection of detail with the exclusion of anything that resembles an emotive register. The prose comes as close to photographic naturalism as any produced in recent years. Unlike Sebald she does not obscure the specifics of participation in and knowledge of the Holocaust – quite the contrary – but she renders individual stories with such sharp and spare particularity that the reader becomes compellingly, and irrespective of their preconceptions, only a witness.

Chapter 13

Wales

One of the unwelcome side effects of the so-called Scottish renaissance was the creation of what might be termed inverse cultural imperialism, an agenda of expectations in which the relationship between national affiliation and the unallied qualities of fiction became by varying degrees strained, suffocating and specious. With this in mind a comparison between contemporary Scottish and Welsh fiction gives cause for dispirited puzzlement or optimism, depending upon your disposition, because recent Welsh fiction is a tradition as sparsely populated as the more attractive parts of the national landscape. There could be a number of plausible explanations for this. Perhaps Welsh writers feel that by focusing exclusively upon native social, cultural or economic issues they impose an arbitrary inhibiting limitation upon the range of their work or their innate abilities. It could also be argued that Wales has, since the mid-twentieth century, become little more than a version of the fragmented hinterland of Englishness: not so much suppressed by the cultural hegemony of the latter – which has in any event largely ceased to exist – as complicit in a more general mood of cultural disinterestedness. True, Welsh Nationalism with all of its socio-cultural baggage has since the 1960s been a vocal and sometimes influential instrument of a collective will, but the consequences of this for Welsh writing in English have been counterproductive for the simple reason that the Welsh have preserved far more effectively those features of their indigenous culture that in Ireland and Scotland still struggle for survival: Welsh language and literature.

Probably the most celebrated Welsh novel in English of recent years is Trezza Azzopardi's *The Hiding Place* (2000) which offers a largely autobiographical account of childhood in Cardiff's dockland-based Maltese community from the postwar years to the 1960s. As an exercise in unapologetic documentary realism, with notions of benevolent working-class solidarity ruthlessly overturned, it is deserving of the praise it received. One wonders, however, whether if it had been set in London it would have attracted sufficient attention to earn it a place on the Booker Prize shortlist, a rare achievement for a debut novel. Most reviewers and commentators remarked upon its setting, yet shunned the question of whether it presented 1960s Cardiff as significantly different from most other large urban industrialized landscapes. In truth it didn't, but to have pointed this out would have gone against the tendency among the London-based literati to eulogize anything linked with the Celtic mindset, however tenuous that link might be.

Desmond Barry's *A Bloody Good Friday* (2001) is another tale of poor people behaving badly and Erica Woolf's *Mud Puppy* (2000) lights up its grim small-town background with a story of joyous lesbianism. The fact that the former is set in 1970s Merthyr Tydfil and the latter in Newport a generation later is of slight significance.

Novels which force-feed aspects of Welshness into their fabric so that the consequences are unavoidably manifest appear to do so for reasons that are less than charitable. *In and Out of the Goldfish Bowl* (2001), Rachel Tresize's short harrowing tale of child sexual abuse, is curiously double-focused, leaving it uncertain as to whether Rebecca's vile stepfather or the Rhondda valley are more deserving of contempt. John Williams has since 1999 provided a regular chronicle of life in the Cardiff underworld (*Five Pubs, Two Bars and a Nightclub*, 1999; *Cardiff Dead*, 2001; *The Prince of Wales*, 2003) and throughout one has the impression that he is working hard at trying to make his characters more horrible and unpredictable than, say, Irvine Welsh's, without plunging beyond credulity. In *Five Pubs*, for example, we are introduced to Kenny Ibadulla, former rugby prodigy who now owns his own sleazy nightclub and for reasons both nostalgic and financial is branching out as sponsor of Cardiff's first Nation of Islam mosque. The formula seems to be: select a handful of well-rehearsed sociocultural stereotypes, blend and reshape daringly, and see if a patina of idiosyncrasy disguises the originals.

Williams, commendably, is honest about his reasons for undertaking such energetic debasements of the ordinary. The introductory note to *Five Pubs* tells us that 'The Cardiff that appears in this book is an imaginary place that should not be confused with the actual city of the same name'. Given that everything in fiction is an inaccurate version even of its most obvious real counterpart this seems a redundant comment, unless – as one suspects – it also involves an apology and complaint. The Cardiff of the millennium, with the newly opened Welsh National Assembly and the attendant influx of wealth and image-obsessed smugness, is most certainly the capital of Wales but it is not a particularly fruitful location for those with a taste for the dangerous and macabre.

Niall Griffiths shifts his narrative focus a little further north, with an occasional eastward drift. Sometimes he plays upon that curious, uncomfortable relationship between England and Wales, but the latter is most certainly not eulogized as the secure bastion of an ancient national tradition; in terms of his taste for grotesquery and deviance Griffiths makes Williams appear genteel. Ianto, in *Sheepshagger* (2001), is a true original in that there are few if any central characters in fiction who are semiarticulate and whose mindset appears to exist beyond the scrutiny both of the reader and the other unfortunates with whom he shares the dismal environs of mid-west Wales. His first instinct, we are told, was to 'put something where there is nothing, to bring substance upon emptiness'. The precise manner of this involved him, aged five, pushing pebbles into the blank eye sockets of a newborn lamb and there is some irony in the elevated manner of the description because the kind of people who might have pictured Ianto in such updated Blakean terms – English visitors to the locality particularly – are just as likely as the lamb to fall prey to his adult feral rampages.

In Griffiths's *Stump* (2003) the action takes place during a single day, with Darren and Alastair, two small-scale villains from Liverpool (who would in *Wreckage* feature in a work about the curiosities of that city, see p. 189) driving to Aberystwyth. They are the somewhat incompetent hit men charges of gang boss Tommy Maguire. Their target is an unnamed, one-armed man, a recovering alcoholic, living with his rabbit in a cheerless bolthole on the West Wales coast. The novel is too addictively grotesque to submit to the cosy title of allegory yet at the same time the journey of brutal, hapless Darren and Alastair toward their unnamed victim cannot help but involve a resonance of other incursions into Wales from that nation to the east. Intriguingly and very effectively the anonymous narrator peppers his *Pulp*

Fiction-style account with reflections upon holidays of his own spent during his youth in guesthouses along the dishearteningly beautiful route.

Malcolm Pryce's trilogy *Aberystwyth Mon Amour* (2001), *Last Tango in Aberystwyth* (2003) and *The Unbearable Lightness of Being in Aberystwyth* (2005) light-footedly avoids association with any obvious subgenre. The central character, the wisecracking private eye Louie Knight, is a Raymond Chandler offshoot but he is too distracted and incompetent to be taken seriously as a fictional detective and his environment involves a bizarre conglomeration of satiric, magic and hallucinogenic realism. Pryce is a skilled stylist and he has a particular talent for causing parallel worlds to seem as if they belong together within the fabric of the book, yet, when thought about, to appear surrealistically ill matched. The recent war between Wales and Patagonia is treated with insouciance and the cast of druids (real ones), mad nuns, semideranged whelk stall owners, porn stars and academics who populate the texts do so as the literary equivalent of asylum seekers, all suspect and weirdly out of place but with nowhere else to go. Funny as these novels are, one cannot help but ask if they serve any other function and in doing so one is struck by the similarities between Pryce, Griffiths and Williams, irrespective of their more obvious differences. For each, Wales announces itself as a hopeless vacuum, a place with only a fissiparous or mythologized sense of its own identity and as a consequence ripe for the most bizarre experiments with exaggeration and representational hyperbole. Pryce and Griffiths share a fetishistic interest in Aberystwyth, whose nonfictional reputation as cynosure of bad weather, dreary existence and somewhere to take a holiday as a reminder that home was agreeable enough appears to guarantee its value as a blank canvas for their Breughelesque inventions.

In the anthology *Wales Half Welsh* (ed. John Williams, 2004) even the title reeks of apologetic unease, pre-empting as it does Williams's desperate introduction in which he explains first that at least half of the 12 writers included are not Welsh, that as many do not write too much about Wales – unless prompted to do so by commissions for such an anthology – and that in any event Wales itself is, to put it charitably, a fragile mutable subject.

One of those included, James Hawes, was presumably brought in to make up the numbers given that his treatment of Wales in *White Powder,*

Green Light (2002) is that of the shamelessly Anglocentric satirist, involving as he does the dreadful University of Pontypool and the 'Welsh Oscwr Awards'. Similarly Jasper Fforde in *The Eyre Affair* (2001) invents the Independent Republic of Wales not as a political prognosis but as a prospect as laughably absurd and fantastic as his main plot line, a literary detective whose job it is to rescue Jane Eyre from a villain who wants to change the ending of the novel. Barry Pilton in *The Valley* (2005) offers a picture of mid-Wales in the 1980s that blends the patronizing humour of an Ealing Comedy with *Little Britain*'s merciless counterpart. The incomers – principally ecology-friendly dimwits – are as absurd as the stereotypes who make up the indigenous population and the fact that a backlash from the Welsh cultural establishment was not forthcoming indicates on its part a degree of self-conscious insecurity regarding what exactly it might have been defending.

Sean Burke's *Deadwater* (2002) is a Cardiff-based tale of murder and drug-dealing with the routine accompaniment of noirish dilemmas. Stylistically it cuts an uneasy path between the laughable and the unendurable. Consider the following:

> He holds her until they must both vomit ecstatically into the rubbish bag that was itself a sack of vomit. The beer and a little food rose orgasmically like hairs abristle a stroked arm, gentle as lover's shadows flung elegant by streetlamplight on the pavement. And then prone, open eyed, dreaming, he lay with this labile girl, flaxen, limpid, gamine dark, pale and blood and bruise-mottled, and himself wondering where they were no words, no knowing, and the imponderable could be held with clarity and tenderness. (*Deadwater*, Serpent's Tail, 2002, p. 109)

Normally this kind of merciless self-indulgence is parodied by Craig Brown in *Private Eye* and one suspects that we are expected to accommodate it for more than 180 pages because it is interspersed with stern reflections on the recent political and social history of Cardiff, a place that has been obliged to abandon its wonderful carnivalesque past:

> …a Creole community evolving its own way of being, its own ethics of spontaneity, respect and cheerfulness – without need of statute, politician or book – like a city shrived of politics or dignitary and mirthed into its own order by jokers, acrobats and fakirs. (p. 47)

Whether such an image of old Cardiff – an exuberant community combining Bakhtinian hypothesis with bacchanalian excess – is plausible or recognizable is open to question but it is a foolproof ingredient for this type of fiction: load the text with thinly disguised hymns to Marxist sentimentality and the painful hyperbole that makes up the rest might be treated as symptomatic of a sense of loss and therefore acceptable, if not always comprehensible. As Niall Griffiths put it on the cover blurb, '*Deadwater* will haunt me for years'.

Chapter 14

The Troubles

Fiction set in Northern Ireland can claim for itself an unenviably unique status: it can only address one subject. Other narratives may unfold in Scotland, Wales and England and treat the topic of nationalism with disdainful indifference, but during the past three decades not a single novel focused upon Northern Ireland has been able to unshackle itself from a predominant issue, generally referred to as 'the Troubles'. Imagine, if you can, a novel set in Belfast, in Londonderry (or Derry) or any part of the six counties or their peripheral border regions which immunizes itself from the residue of 30 years of violence and the ongoing internecine tribalism of a divided community. It is difficult to conceive of such a hypothetical text because it would by necessity be a postmodern tour de force that can only be treated in the abstract, the equivalent of a Beckettian experiment in which a fictive community of individuals neither speaks nor thinks. Even if one succeeded in realizing this hypothesis it would still be perceived as a novel 'about the Troubles', an appropriately evasive, nihilistic disengagement from a topic that has exhausted rational comprehension.

Brian Moore was born in Belfast in 1921 but spent most of his adult life outside Ireland, observing the Troubles from a distance, and he tells of how the idea for one of his best-known novels, *Lies of Silence* (1990), came to him. He had returned to Belfast to receive an honorary degree from Queen's University and found himself, in the middle of the night, put out into the street from his hotel following a bomb scare. Most of his fellow evacuees treated the event with sanguine resignation but he noted a group of French tourists who stood out because their manner and exchanges indicated a mixture of fear and bafflement. He 'wondered about what it would have been like if they were killed and didn't know who killed them'. This scenario fascinates and horrifies him principally because virtually everyone else in Northern Ireland had evolved a mindset wherein violence and its perpetrators had specific causes. Victimhood had for the denizens of the six counties a historically programmed specificity so he 'made the hero [of *Lies of Silence*] someone like me who doesn't want to be in Northern Ireland, who left it, and just has no desire to go back there, hates the place, and then I'll be able to identify with him . . .' (Denis Sampson, *Brian Moore: The Chameleon Novelist*, Marino Books, 1998, pp. 276–7). This, cogently put, is Moore's programme for dealing with the embedded circumscriptions of writing fiction about Northern Ireland: step outside and only then will your egalitarian distaste for both factions drag itself free from the place's momentum of sectarian affiliation. He creates Michael and Moira Dillon, a middle-class Catholic couple, whose home is occupied by an IRA unit. Dillon is ordered to transport a car bomb to his workplace while his wife is held hostage. Dillon responds with a combination of anger and stoicism, refusing to treat the IRA men as figures within some complex ideological struggle, but rather as instruments of violence who deserve only contempt. Some have perceived the novel as a thriller, and the narrative is certainly programmed to focus the reader's attention on what will happen next, but its conclusion carries with it a depressing metaphor. Dillon recognizes one of his captors and much later decides to testify formally to the police. He is then approached by a Catholic priest who attempts to persuade him that this is a misguided act of betrayal. We never learn of what he has chosen to do because just prior to making the decisive phone call he is shot by the IRA who have been informed of his potential inclinations, and location, by the priest. One cannot help but note the parallels between Dillon's pragmatic life-threatening dilemma and Moore's description of his own as a novelist, a figure who is attempting to reconcile his hatred for Northern Ireland, his wish to no longer be associated with it, with his engagement with the place in fiction. He appears to imply, via Dillon, that writing novels about Ulster involves a brand of realism mercifully avoidable elsewhere, that in representing it you become part of it and there is no escape from its shroud of compulsive evil.

A similar note of bitter cynicism echoes through Robert McLiam Wilson's *Ripley Bogle* (Picador, 1989). Bogle does not have much of

a story to tell. He has alienated himself from his Catholic, Nationalistic background in West Belfast, spent time briefly as a Cambridge
undergraduate and ended up jobless on the streets of London. But
the absence of a robust narrative is amply compensated for by the
presence of Bogle himself, a figure who blends anecdotes from his
Belfast past with rancorous irony. At one point he offers a potted
history of the Troubles. He sums up the 1960s as 'just a lot of jobless
Catholics getting the shit kicked out of them and having their homes
burnt down on Protestant feast days'. Next come the Civil Rights
marches, followed by angry Protestant retaliations. The British Army
is dragged in to protect the Catholics from the 'brutality of their
Proddie countrymen', but following the army's rash behaviour on
Bloody Sunday 'the Catholics grow rather peeved and start extermi-
nating a whole plethora of soldiers, policemen, prison officers, UDR
men, Protestants, Catholics, English shoppers, Birmingham pubgoers
and men who make the mistake of editing the *Guinness Book of
Records*' (p. 83). Later he turns his attention to those intellectual
guardians of Irishness in all its fascinating complexity, 'Americans and
Professors of English Literature. Menace and cupidity. All balls...'
(p. 160) and goes on to aver that the spectacle of grotesquery is helped
along by the Irish themselves:

> What is it about Ireland the Irish love so? What makes them go on so
> endlessly about their country? Is it the pain and the poverty, the death
> and danger? Is it the spite, hatred, treachery, stupidity, vice, inhumanity
> or the comfortless despair? (p. 160)

As a narrator and instrument for his author's justifiable self-esteem
Bogle reminds one of the creations of Martin Amis, a presence who
combines showy syntax and lexical exuberance with an aesthete's
disdain for the world he describes. However, for Bogle, and indeed
Wilson, the bitterness is driven by a self-imposed obligation. By electing to write about Northern Ireland he must continually address the
one issue that informs every dimension of existence there and for the
author and his avatar this is deserving of unmitigated contempt. One
might venture that *Ripley Bogle*, while sharing some characteristics
with other Northern Ireland fiction, obtains an exclusive status of its
own. Bogle wants desperately to escape from the mindset that destiny
bequeathed him by an accident of birth. 'I began to memorise the

ferry timetables for Holyhead, Stranraer and Liverpool [...] My answer would be my exit' (p. 84). One begins gradually to realize that Bogle's manner, the energy that he injects into a narrative without direction, his digressions so poised and replete with loathing for his unasked-for legacy, are not only the novel's animus but also its subject. He wants to escape from the narrative. His anger, his flashy linguistic manner-isms are aids to endurance. The final, short, chapter has him homeless in Trafalgar Square and he asks 'And my quest? What of that? What can we salvage from the butchered shambles of my acid little history?' The question is, it seems, absurdly rhetorical. 'Can you see it? I must admit, I can't? Not at all. Not a sausage. Absolument rien' (p. 272).

In his second novel *Eureka Street* (1996) Wilson's mood seems to lift slightly above energetic despair, but the impression is deceptive. It was written shortly after the 1994 IRA ceasefire and it plays with the idea of Belfast as a place which, almost despite itself, will allow people to indulge themselves and pursue the kind of interests that preoccupy the inhabitants of most other Western cities; where having relationships, making money and, in general, securing a lifestyle that is as agreeable as possible are more important than some overarching political issue. He invents Jake and Chuckie who seem almost by magic to have been provided with hedonistic opportunities that shift them beyond their working-class origins; the latter rapidly becomes a suc-cessful entrepreneur, while Jake obtains a mysterious and generous inheritance. Chuckie takes up with Max, a beautiful American, Jake begins a relationship with an English journalist, Sarah; and Wilson, deliberately and provocatively, is testing the limits of credulity, setting up his two heroes as embodied fantasies and hypotheses. Is this, he asks, what life in Belfast might aspire to if only the place could enjoy itself beyond its state of internecine isolation and reconnect with the rest of the world? Ultimately the question remains unanswered – 'there's room for all kinds of endings and any number of commence-ments' (*Eureka Street*, Minerva, 1997, p. 396) says Jake at the conclusion – but the asking of it is intercut with a theme that Wilson carries over from *Ripley Bogle*. Irrespective of the becalmed particulars of violence the Belfast of *Eureka Street* is still enmeshed in a political and cultural mindset as repulsive as fascism, but far more enduring: the two tribes, so long as they exist, will ensure each other's strength of purpose. Wilson contrasts the optimistic portraits of Chuckie and Jake with images and reflections that provoke recognition beyond the text. Gerry Adams appears as Jimmy Eve, leader of Just Us, a crude translation of Sinn Fein, and there is a memorable passage in which Jake and Chuckie attend an 'Evening of Irish Poetry'. The star is Shague Ghintoss, a mercilessly accurate version of Seamus Heaney. Ghintoss's poems are composed of symbol-laden landscapes – 'hedges…lanes, bogs…and spades' as the narrator puts it – and Wilson choreographs the episode so that it is evident that the audience is pretending to accept these images as unaffiliated while waiting for a signal to indicate that they share with the poet an exclusively Nationalistic agenda.

> In a startling departure, he read a poem about a vicious Protestant murder of a nice Catholic. There were no spades in this poem and only one hedge, but by this time the crowd were whipped into such a sectarian passion they would have lauded him if he'd picked his nose [...] These people gathered close together, snug in their verse, their culture, they had one question. Why can't Protestants do this? they asked themselves. What's wrong with these funny people? (p. 176)

While Wilson's prose boils with infuriation, Glenn Patterson's *Burning Your Own* (1988), *Fat Lad* (1992) and *The International* (1999) represent the North with a little more measure and circumspection. *Fat Lad*, deliberately or not, picks up the central conceit of *Ripley Bogle*, the young intelligent native of Belfast observing the place through the prism of his act of removal. Wilson leaves Bogle in Trafalgar Square but Patterson has Drew Linden return to Belfast from England to take up the post as assistant manager at a new city centre bookshop. The first two chapters involve an ingenious double focus with Drew landing at Belfast International Airport, travelling into the city, and finding, almost to his disbelief, that the place is becoming more like the urban centres of Britain. The chain stores have purchased and rebuilt the larger properties, and refurbished bars offer an air of casual normality that belies the media-generated image of the city as a bombsite. Yet his observations are intercut with his special, endemic knowledge of the place. The brash confidence of the new one-way traffic system is, on the face of things, encouraging but Drew can't help but note that 'Outgoing traffic was now directed onto Dublin Road by an *All Routes* sign just below Hope Street' (p. 17). This accumulation of signs and names, apparently accidental and innocuous, gathers for Drew a darkly comic resonance: 'An Ordnance

Survey Drollery, to be delivered, for preference, in an Ian Paisley voice'. Drew's cautious optimism is founded upon his objective of remaining indifferent to the worst aspects of Belfast rather than any idealistic hypothesis. But the longer he remains in the city the more he recognizes that its fabric of narratives – not just his memories but the intertwined recollections of his family and friends – is at once undesirable and irresistible. At the end of the novel Drew recognizes that there is only one way to deal with the region's capacity to dismantle aspirations to independence, even indifference, its rapacious ability to suck the individual back into its maw of wounded affiliations, and that is to leave. He does so, for a job in Paris. Despite his more affable manner Patterson, with Drew, is as depressing in his prognosis as Wilson: Northern Ireland is possessed of a self-perpetuating malignancy.

Eoin McNamee's *Resurrection Man* (1994) is based upon the grisly career of Lennie Murphy, one of the leaders of the so-called Shankhill Butchers who during the 1980s evolved a special brand of sectarian murder, supplementing the killing of helpless Catholics with an unaffiliated taste for torture and mutilation. Victor Kelly, Murphy's fictional counterpart, is presented with stark objectivity. He enjoys what he does, even indulges in images of himself as a mutant for-God-and-Ulster version of American film noir gangsters of the 1930s and 1940s. Beyond that, however, McNamee does not offer anything close to a psychological profile of Victor, and as far as an ideology which might underpin his murderous, sadistic rampage is concerned, this is merely part of the landscape, a predictable sediment of birth and location.

Irrespective of superficial differences McNamee has a good deal in common with Moore, Wilson and Patterson. The latter ensure that the reader will attach themselves sympathetically to the texture, the narrative focus of the book, for the simple reason that the particulars of violence and their generating ethos of sectarian division are viewed from the outside, by people who wish to remove themselves from both. McNamee engages with the same theme, except that he removes the protection of an intermediary. In *Resurrection Man* we don't visit Northern Ireland via the experiences and perspectives of a Dillon, a Drew or a Bogle. In this novel our encounter is unmediated but the abiding image is the same. Conflict and its hideous consequences are inviolable and compulsive, resistant equally to avoidance and justification. One could add to this list Lionel Shriver's *Ordinary Decent Criminals* (1992) and Colin Bateman's *Divorcing Jack* (1994). Both are comedies but of a type hardly encountered since the period of Swift. Their shared pretext is that to engage seriously with the political and intellectual mindset of Ulster sectarianism is effectively to connive in its brutality. Parody, ridicule, derision, with a helping of caricature are deployed very effectively by Bateman and Shriver as a means of dismantling the self-righteous chain of alleged historical causes, assertions of tribal identity and claims to victimhood by which both sides link killing with a political rationale.

In a 1994 *Guardian* article Ronan Bennett launched an attack upon the position adopted by virtually all of the novelists considered so far (16 July 1994): 'In fiction...the Troubles are thus presented as an appalling human tragedy, devoid of political content. Like any bloody struggle anywhere...it becomes nothing more than a series of repulsive and meaningless massacres'. In Bennett's view Wilson's depiction of extreme Republicanism as both 'inherently ridiculous' and 'fascist' is indicative of a prevailing bourgeois consensus that amounts to anti-Nationalist 'propaganda'. Bennett's complaint reflects a consensus of critical opinion in which novelists of the Wilson–Patterson persuasion are accused of having failed to deal properly, indeed seriously, with the Troubles. Seamus Deane in numerous articles and prefaces written during the 1980s and 1990s provides a theoretical subtext for Bennett's grievances:

> To believe there is such a thing as fine writing and that it is somehow separate from a speech by Ian Paisley, John Hume or Margaret Thatcher, is to show you have truly been brainwashed. It shows that you actually do believe that there is a stable place called 'culture', to which you can retreat from the shouts and cries of the street, from the murder and mayhem that takes place there, and that you can go into that realm of humanist subjectivity in which literature or great art prevails. ('Canon Fodder: Literary Mythologies in Ireland', in Jean Lundy and Aodán MacPóilin (eds), *Styles of Belonging: The Cultural Identities of Ulster*, Lagan Press, 1992, pp. 26–7)

On first reading there appears to be something curious about this passage, given that it is difficult to conceive of how any literary writing which addresses Northern Ireland can fail to engage with politics and violence, but the real target of Deane's ideological invective is actually those texts which treat both as ghastly imponderables, or as Eve Patten puts it, those which follow a 'novelistic obligation to offer consensual (and usually apolitical) liberal humanist comment on the predicament' ('Fiction in Conflict: Northern Ireland's Prodigal Novelists', in Ian A. Bell (ed.), *Peripheral Visions: Images of Nationhood in Contemporary British Fiction*, University of Wales Press, 1995, p. 131). Gerry Smyth explains that the politics of the conflict 'are displaced and defamiliarised through a variety of strategies, the most important of which is the introduction of a degree of *distance* into the novelistic vision'. This can be a literal or 'physical' distance – and here we should recall Wilson's and Patterson's use of their characters' experience of life beyond Ulster as a counterpoint to its peculiarities – or 'discursive' with a particular reliance upon 'irony and parody' (*The Novel and the Nation. Studies in the New Irish Fiction*, Pluto Press, 1997, pp. 116–17).

Rarely, if ever, in the history of the novel has a group of critics (and one can add to this list Terry Eagleton and David Lloyd) treated a contemporaneous trend within fiction as ideologically defective: this might have occurred within the old Soviet bloc but the scenario is purely hypothetical since it is unlikely that such writers would have been published in the first place. At its centre is the predominant thesis that to treat the Troubles in all their blood-strewn internecine complexity as something that can be viewed from the outside – be this via contemporaneous ridicule or modulated nonaffiliation – betrays the proper duty of the novelist's task. The puzzling, and still largely unanswered, question raised by this is of what exactly these critics perceive this task to be. Bennett, Deane, Patten, Eagleton, Lloyd and Smyth all in varying degrees regard Northern Ireland as one of the last of the many twentieth and twenty-first-century manifestations of postcolonialism. Postcolonialism is as much an ideological prognosis as an observed historical process, with colonizer and subject operating according to theses inculcated by figures such as Edward Said and Homi Bhabba. Irrespective of its precise manifestations it is treated by virtually all critics and theorists as having a fascinating, almost inexorable dynamism and the Troubles offer themselves to advocates of postcolonialism as a minimalist conclusion to the vast narratives of the twentieth century. As a consequence if novelists chose to treat them with insouciance then such theorists judge this as an act of betrayal.

What, one might ask, is the alternative to aesthetic impartiality? The most cumbersome is Danny Morrison's *West Belfast* (Mercier, 1989), a righteous justification for Republican violence thinly disguised as literature. The body of the narrative is concerned with how members of the O'Neill family are drawn into what amounts to a struggle for their own identity but the most memorable passage must be the monologue of Stevie, IRA volunteer (pp. 173–7). In this he reflects compassionately upon the similarities between himself and the man he is about to kill, a British soldier. Perhaps they had, as children, stolen the same chocolate bars from similar corner shops, told the same jokes to school friends, listened to the Beatles and enjoyed *Coronation Street*. But he reminds himself that this man, who may well also have a wife and children, is the instrument of colonial oppression; and by some process of self-fulfilling logic Stevie's moment of humanity reinforces his determination as an agency of justice: 'I entertain doubts precisely because they strengthen my single-mindedness, my convictions' (p. 175). Later, when he learns that the man he has killed was indeed married with two children, Stevie makes a bizarre claim. 'I'll think about him more than his commanding officer. I'll maybe even be still thinking about him when his widow has stopped' (p. 177).

This surely answers Deane's call for the sweeping aside of 'humanist subjectivity' and the joining of literature with 'the shouts and cries of the streets, the murder and mayhem that takes place there', yet the novel was treated with tactful indifference by those same critics who railed against the separation of art from the peremptory brutalities of Ulster. Perhaps it was a little too vulgar in its rampant affiliation to the ideology of Republican paramilitarism. One suspects as much because Ronan Bennett himself offered a more sophisticated lesson in how fiction could immerse itself in the complexities of conflict in *The Second Prison* (1991). The three principal characters are Kane, a senior IRA figure, Tempest, his English Special Branch adversary and Benny, the apolitical criminal who becomes Kane's confidante in prison. Unlike Morrison, Bennett makes some pretence toward impartiality, casting Kane and Tempest as subject to a historical vortex that dehumanizes each of them. With clunking irony it is Benny who offers to Kane the shrewdly honed wisdom that he should focus upon freeing himself from the 'second prison', the rituals of hatred and vengeance forged by centuries of antagonism. Kane does indeed attempt to make some claim upon an untarnished ordinary existence but a combination of habituated commitment and merciless circumstance pulls him back into his original life. The novel is deceptive because beneath its patina of compassionate psychology there is a solid political agenda. All of the principal characters are killers and while none is treated as entirely excusable in their actions only Kane is presented as the one who, in the end, finds himself denied the opportunity to choose. Tempest is an agent of colonialism, Benny commits crimes to obtain money, but Kane is a tragic victim of circumstance. Rarely has impartiality been so subtly and ruthlessly abused.

An even worse example of faux-neutrality is Edna O'Brien's *House of Splendid Isolation* (1994). Josie O'Meara resides in a decaying big house near Limerick and is visited continually by reflections on the state of Ireland, North and South. Her father was killed in the 1920s by the Black and Tans but despite sufficient cause to loathe the British she regards the ongoing campaigns by Republicans north of the border as a disgrace to the honourable heritage they profess to espouse. Soon, however, her musings become substantial with the arrival of an unwelcome visitor, the IRA man Frank McGreevy. With grinding predictability Josie's initial feelings for McGreevy of anger and distaste are modulated as she becomes more aware that beneath the media-generated carapace of ruthlessness exists a driven, tormented, almost tragic figure, a man who despite himself is forged by a history of injustice and has no choice but to respond appropriately.

McGreevy is based upon the INLA leader Dominic McGlinchey whom O'Brien visited on several occasions during his detention in Portlaoise Prison when she was planning the novel. McGlinchey was responsible for some of the worst atrocities of the Troubles and when reading of the relationship that develops between Josie and McGreevy one cannot help but suspect that the *House of Splendid Isolation* is a novel born of an amalgam of self-aggrandisement and macabre hero-worship.

Seamus Deane in *Reading in the Dark* (1996) offers a fictional supplement to his numerous commentaries on contemporary Irish writing, particularly regarding the North. The novel covers the period from the late 1940s to the late 1960s, and is set in those parts of Derry where the border is both a tangible presence and a contradiction; it exists, but for many who live next to it – the majority Catholic population of Derry – it ought not to. The central figure is a boy, unnamed, around whom a fabric of stories and rumours form and

never properly unfold. In one instance another boy is killed acciden-
tally by a lorry, the police arrive and because of the collective hatred
for the RUC his unofficial cause of death, within the local community,
has him being run over by a police car. Throughout the novel,
and particularly at the beginning during the boy's childhood, we are
led along narrative paths which indicate but never quite confirm:
what has happened to his late uncle Eddie? Who is the mysterious
McIlhenny? What is the secret that seems to so unsettle his mother?
Are the stories told by the local down-and-out Crazy Joe true, or is
he mad? As the boy matures, the rumours and haunted images become
more concrete. Eddie, his uncle, was shot by the IRA because he
was suspected of being a police informer. The real informer was
McIlhenny, an IRA man who engineered the false case against Eddie
and had been the boy's mother's lover.

The novel trembles with a surfeit of allegory and symbolism. It is
significant, for example, that it concludes as the Troubles begin. Following the first year of violence the boy's mother is rendered speech-
less (and we are never certain if the cause is physical or psychological).
All manner of beguiling interpretive possibilities are made available
here, the most obvious being that the 20 years or so of the novel's
duration is the final incubation period for a broader network of narratives and mythologies. Perhaps the community in which the boy
grows up is a microcosmic version of the tensions that have beset
Ireland since the sixteenth century, given that both seem afflicted by
uncertain mythologies and flawed memories. The image of Ireland
itself as a Mother to those heroic Sons who fight for her freedom is a
widely recognized myth, so perhaps the boy's mother's silence –
inflicted or self-imposed, who knows? – is meant to indicate that the
final period of incubation is at an end, that Ireland, the North, is
experiencing a period of transformation, albeit a horrific one, from
which it might be born into some new destiny. Perhaps. Yet one is
tempted to cite Wilson as an unintended respondent to the novel and
its rich interpretive offerings:

> We Irish, we're all fucking idiots. No other people can rival us for the
> senseless sentimentality in which we wallow. Us and Ulster. The God-
> beloved fucking Irish, as they'd like to think. As a people we're a
> shambles; as a nation – a disgrace; as a culture we're a bore...individ-
> ually we're often repellent. (*Ripley Bogle*, p. 160)

Throughout Wilson's novels one encounters continual asides and reflections which indicate a weary distaste for the task at hand. It is as if for him the relationship between the Troubles and fiction is addictive yet abhorrent, and one can see his point. The novel has since its eighteenth century beginnings been a faithless, quixotic partner to the world from which it feeds itself. It mimics and reflects but it has almost limitless capacities to distort, to create a framework that is subject to the idiosyncrasies of narrators variously amusing, purblind, obsessive, provocatively clever and confidently unreliable. With Northern Ireland these possibilities become circumscribed, hidebound by the nature of their topic.

The 1998 Good Friday Agreement signalled and for some still does signal a moment of irreversible alteration in the fractious history of the relationship between Britain and the two parts of Ireland. The Republic gave up its peremptory constitutional claim upon the six counties and for the first time since partition the entire island of Ireland voted to sanction a single agenda. The IRA proved somewhat reluctant to unambiguously and demonstrably abandon the armed struggle, their Loyalist counterparts continued to kill, albeit principally each other, and the DUP rarely ceased to disparage the Agreement as an act of betrayal, but few would disagree that peace, of a sort, is now the norm.

Glenn Patterson wrote *The International* (1999) in the run-up to and during the months following the Agreement. He approaches contemporaneity with the shrewdness of a seasoned veteran and cautiously avoids, without entirely excluding, optimism. The novel is set in 1967 but it shares none of Deane's atmosphere of apocalyptic incipience. Instead it is overburdened with the kind of feckless confidence that allegedly informed the youth of everywhere from California to Paris during the late 1960s. Danny, the narrator, remembers Belfast in 1967 as a teenager, when slum clearances and motorways seemed to be encroaching on the city's image as a dour industrial conurbation. Television was supplying a daily agenda of excitement – space flight, Jimi Hendrix, the Monkees, the Chinese Cultural Revolution – and suddenly a place that had since its creation seemed a self-obsessed political aberration seemed about to join the rest of the world. And here a dry irony resonates through the title, which both echoes that sense of hope and refers literally to a hotel in central Belfast. The hotel was where the first meeting of the Northern Ireland Civil Rights

Association took place and where four of its Catholic staff were shot dead by Loyalist paramilitaries. Danny is that rare presence in Northern Ireland fiction, a narrator who refuses to be suborned by grim, immutable circumstance. Instead he plays a subtle game with the reader's expectations. He is, as he occasionally reminds us, remembering one period of unsettled optimism from another, and as his manner and idiom become more familiar our uncertainty increases as to whether the blend of nostalgia and cynicism is an honest recollection or a vision of the past modified by the tainted, dystopian prism of experience.

Patterson's two recent novels *Number 5* (2003) and *That Which Was* (2004) were published within less than a year of each other and the suspicion that they were planned as partners is reinforced by their tenor and substance. Their relationship resembles that of two sides of a coin, in that they offer different perceptions of the same indivisible unit. *Number 5* tells the stories of those who pass through a house from when it was built in the 1950s to the present day and Patterson comes close to testing the hypothesis I raised at the beginning of this section: that it is impossible to write a novel about Northern Ireland that is not preoccupied with the Troubles. His demonstrable conclusion is that if you are astute enough, then conceivably you might, but in all honesty, no. He confines the narrative to the interior of a specific house and its inhabitants' perspectives upon the day-to-day minutiae of making a living and looking after the family and shows, subtly, that such a process is by necessity self-conscious of what it excludes. He does not present the residents of Number 5 as apathetic or heedless and nor does he excise all references to the dire situation beyond this particular street, yet at the same time he manages to instil into the sheer ordinariness of his characters something far more admirable than the litanies of bloody heroism and strident victimhood that still overcrowd our perceptions of Ulster.

That Which Was is set where *Number 5* left off, in the post-Agreement present day. Ken Avery has an active, commendably new-mannish sex-life, is a devotee of the Velvet Underground and addicted to stand-up comedians who treat the North with scabrous contempt. He is also a Presbyterian minister whose 'parish' comprises parts of inner Belfast apparently possessed of a revivalist urge to restart sectarian murder on a regular basis. This scenario of improbable tensions and contrasts might in the hands of an ordinary writer drift toward farce but Patterson makes it horribly credible and it becomes the platform for the novel's principal theme, the uneasy relationship between the present and the past, kindled by a particular case of amnesia. A distressed, shifty individual approaches Avery with a recollection of having committed murder. He cannot offer an account of the specifics of the crime or his victim but he is certain both of his guilt and of his memory as having been deliberately damaged via a gruesome surgical procedure inflicted by 'authorities'. Without resorting to cumbersome symbolism Patterson causes this man's story to overlap with a mercilessly detailed portrait of the North as a whole, with Avery as the intermediary. For him, Belfast's recent past seems continually to mutate between states of denial, violent retrieval and grotesquely nostalgic remembrance. Is there a solution? Perhaps, implies Patterson, the best option is for people to be more like the Rev. Ken who accepts what he must, helps when he can and otherwise thrives on his enjoyment of what another, 'Free', Presbyterian Minister would like to ban, particularly on Sundays.

Nick Laird's *Utterly Monkey* (2005) has Danny Williams leave Ulster for a degree in Cambridge and a lucrative career as a lawyer in the City of London, but one should not be deceived by superficial resemblances to Wilson's and Patterson's escapers of the 1980s and 1990s. Ulster pursues Danny, literally, in the figure of his childhood friend Geordie who pitches up on his fashionable London doorstep with £50,000 stolen from Loyalist paramilitaries. Coincidentally, Danny is immediately dispatched to Northern Ireland by his senior, called Vyse, to oversee the privatization and exploitative takeover of 'Ulster Water', there to become involved in a litany of punch-ups, shoot-outs and car chases, all occurring on or around 12 July, the iconic highpoint of the Unionist marching season. He is accompanied on this journey by one Ellen Powell, an athletic, glamorous, black junior colleague who is suitably tantalized by Danny's other life outside the comfortable smugness of London. Ellen's remarkable resemblance to the novelist Zadie Smith, recently married to the smoulderingly handsome 30-year-old Ulster-raised, Cambridge-educated, London lawyer turned-poet-novelist Nick Laird, is purely coincidental. Or, if not, it is an arch flirtation with the novel as a site for clever indulgence. Either way, Laird can claim to have set a small precedent because although Wilson, Bateman, Patterson and Shriver install dark comedy as a remedy for despair, Laird is the first to deal with Northern Ireland in a manner evolved in the US by crime writers such as Elmore Leonard, James Ellroy and Joseph Wambaugh. The latter strike a balance between nonjudgemental realism – including violence, criminality and corruption as the inevitable consequences of a society so dynamic as that of the US – and cynical humour as the provocatively measured response. Similarly Laird presents Northern Ireland, in its muted incompetent savagery, as perversely exciting. One suspects that the novel reflects a broader perception of the province's postceasefire status. The bars, clubs and sectarian murals of Belfast have since 1998 acquired a sexy allure for young people from the rest of the UK who are looking for something more unusual than a weekend in Prague, Amsterdam or Budapest, and Laird's alter ego functions similarly, for the reader, as a temporary escape route from the predictabilities of life. The fact that Loyalist paramilitarism can be treated as pruriently exciting corresponds with the media image of present day Ulster as an awful though relatively harmless version of its past, a consensus that would prompt a cynical shake of the head from Patterson's Rev. Ken.

Louise Dean's *This Human Season* (2005) was published within a few months of *Utterly Monkey*, and is as different from it as two novels on the same topic can be, yet both involve a distinct sense of Ulster as having become, if not quite moribund, then a living museum for those with a taste for the macabre. It is set in 1979 and focuses upon a pivotal moment in the Troubles: the H Block hunger strikes and their consequences. The three main characters are Sean Moran, an imprisoned IRA car bomber involved in the so-called 'blanket protest' for political recognition, Sean's mother Kathleen Moran and John Dunn, an Englishman newly recruited to the Northern Ireland Prison Service but with two decades of experience in military intelligence. The narrative alternates between Kathleen's perspective and John's and incorporates those they share with others on opposing sides of the sectarian and political divide. Dean was born and educated in England. She worked subsequently in advertising in New York and wrote much of the novel at her residence in Provence – having previously researched it by visiting Ulster and amassing more than 250 hours of interviews with people involved with, or who at least recollected, the events of 1979. The intensive research is reflected in the novel's concern with the minutiae of daily life, particularly in Belfast, where even the most mundane aspects of existence are in some way touched by the events at Long Kesh, weekly terrorist incidents and speculations on how the Thatcher government would react to each new development. Dean attempts, with some success, to represent all of her characters impartially, feeding into the plotlines a degree of historical and circumstantial detail sufficient to provide an explanatory logic for the motives and actions depicted. This abundance of documentary objectivity brings to mind Pat Barker's and Sebastian Faulks's fictional treatments of World War I. In the latter, the worthless horror of the events are unsparingly rendered, but our empathy is dissipated by the knowledge that it all happened in the distant past. While Northern Ireland is by no means close to a recognizably stable political settlement, Dean's novel manages to create the impression that the events which animated and sustained sectarian division are memories, bitter and horrifying memories certainly, but at the same time fossilized by the passage of time. Perhaps *This Human Season* indicates, or attempts to indicate, that following the ceasefires, the Good Friday Agreement and subsequent acts of decommissioning the worst of the Troubles can be consigned to recollection. One wonders, however, if an author whose knowledge of the place is the equivalent of that of an anthropologist who then moves on to their next project is entirely trustworthy. The novel is a commendable exercise in documentary realism but its implicit claim to be a realistic diagnosis of Ulster is open to question.

Liam Browne's *The Emigrant's Farewell* (2006) offers an alternative approach to the question addressed in Patterson's *Number 5*, of how or indeed why fiction might disengage from the postceasefire residue of indecisive bitterness. Browne's novel is set in present-day Derry where Eileen and Joe O'Kane suffer the tragic death of their child. Joe becomes obsessed with an apparently innocuous fragment of the city's otherwise tortuous history – he has become a 'research officer' at a local heritage centre – involving the nineteenth-century seaman and shipbuilder Captain William Coppin. Coppin was convinced that he could learn the truth about the vanished Franklin expedition to the North Pole via the spirit of his dead daughter Louisa who, according to Coppin, remained suspended between her previous earthbound state and eternity. The question of whether Joe regards this story either as a means of blocking out his own feelings of despair or as credible evidence that his daughter might too in some way be more than a memory is left tactfully open.

Browne creates a fictional parallel universe in that as we learn of Joe, his loss and his obsession with Coppin so we are invited to locate correspondences with the collective mindset of Derry, a place where, continually, the past is rehearsed and re-enacted, from the Bloody Sunday enquiry to commemorations of the seventeenth-century siege. The fact that Browne pays minimal attention to the particulars of Derry's strife-ridden politics and recent history makes their presence all the more resonant and unsettling. Has Joe become so programmed by a culture which seems to depend so much upon the past as an explanation for the present that he too is becoming a version of Coppin, a desperate pitiable fantasist? Or by asking such questions – and they are inevitably prompted by the novel's setting – are we as readers incapable of disassociating a personal tragedy from our media-inculcated image of Northern Ireland? The novel deals brilliantly with its inescapable context by shifting this burdensome presence toward the reader, a strategy that would not have been available to a pre-1998 novelist and perhaps one that carries a glimmer of optimism for the novel's location.

Chapter 15

Epilogue:
The State of the Novel

Toward the end of the 1970s and during the early 1980s what had previously been a tortuously routine passage of complaints became a crescendo: the novel had turned inward upon its own parochial concerns, become stylistically complacent and self-satisfied and was going nowhere in particular. Over the past two decades, however, such grumbles have been notable for their rarity and the reason for this indicates that we are entering a fascinating stage in the history of the British novel.

Since the 1950s the most vociferous, indignant commentators have been united in a single credo: that innovation and experiment are the lifeblood of fiction and without regular infusions of each the genre will die. Their premise has proved to be self-contradictory, but not for the obvious reasons. What was rarely, if ever, conceded was that the excitement and cachet that attached itself to experimental, postmodern writing was due principally to its marginal status. True, its intrinsic qualities were appreciated among the bohemian sector of the literary establishment and certainly in academe, but the motivating factor for those who argued for the energetic revivification of fiction per se was the accompanying knowledge that this almost certainly would not happen. Advocates of radicalism were like members of the Workers Revolutionary Party, apparently committed to their anti-establishment ideals but secure in the knowledge that such heroic dedication would be sustained by the fact that no-one would ever vote for them. Astonishingly, however, widespread changes in the landscape of fiction have occurred since the 1980s, though not in the manner previously envisaged and campaigned for.

The history of the novel, at least prior to the 1980s, involved to a great extent a struggle between those authors who could not help but incorporate into a story a self-conscious reminder of how peculiar and unusual it is to write stories – a founding principle of modernism – and those who treated the re-creation of the world in a book as a thoroughly guileless act of craftsmanship. Numerically and in terms of mid-to-low cultural popularity the latter were by far the more predominant, and while extreme embodiments of both still exist the sense of there being a bipolar conflict between them has ceased. Competition for aesthetic and intellectual pre-eminence has segued into a middle ground where techniques that once secured difference are now part of a shared taxonomy of devices, all infinitely adaptable and acceptable. In short, the history of the novel, insofar as it was sustained by a bifurcation of radical versus conservative, postmodern versus countermodernist, is over. Ali Smith, Jeanette Winterson, David Mitchell, Nicola Barker, Iain Sinclair et al. are still heirs to the likes of Joyce, Woolf, Beckett and B. S. Johnson but their techniques have become as domesticated as that cosy monument to modernism, affectionately termed 'the Gherkin', that is now as agreeably familiar a part of the London skyline as the dome of St Paul's. The author-in-the-text, that gesture which was once the badge of avant-gardism and warned of serious questions regarding the nature of representation, is now a hoary routine, a version of which occurs even in the diaries of Bridget Jones. Martin Amis blunts its ground-breaking edge and uses it instead as a foil for his stylistic versatility and addiction to black comedy – radicalism has been suborned to populist exigency. When Ali Smith has her swimming champion describe her final suicidal dive into oblivion in the lift shaft in *Hotel World* we are back again with that old reliable, the interior monologue, the linguistic record of that which never would, never could, be spoken, patented by Joyce. In the hands of Smith, however, it is a little more polished and reader-friendly. As the character's chest collapses and its contents plunge into her throat, she reflects: 'For the first time (too late) I knew how my heart tasted' (p. 6). Joyce, radical purist as he was, would never have allowed Molly Bloom such a wonderfully grotesque, well-crafted conceit, but Smith has one eye on the market, on the reader who wants to be impressed and entertained rather than merely confounded.

And then there is the more extravagant version of the author-in-the-text conceit, the book that toys with our registers and expectations and continually raises the question: am I or am I not a novel? Andrew O'Hagan, Nicola Barker and Iain Sinclair are all practitioners but while the method still evinces an echo of fearless unorthodoxy – once again returning us to the apparently vexed issue of whether fiction and truth may be interchangeable – its cultivated clubbability makes it as shocking as the maze in the country-house garden is frightening. Magic realism returns faithfully and comfortably in the fiction of Salman Rushdie in much the same way that Kingsley Amis's penchant for droll bitterness was always a trademark feature of his; in each case it is not so much a sense of surprise that accompanies its discovery in the novel as that of familiar reassurance.

Experimental writing, by its nature, always needed a monolith, an established cultural behemoth, against which it could pit itself and, as a consequence, maintain its identity as a constantly changing, dynamic entity. This obsession with reaction and reinvention enabled the post-modernists to obfuscate embarrassing inconveniences and sustain a myth: fundamental issues – such as the writer's skill as a stylist or imaginative acuity as a storyteller, or lack of each – could be sidelined by righteous celebrations of the unfathomable and unprecedented. In the light of this it is possible to perceive the effective conclusion of the history of the novel as beneficial to the genre as a whole. The battle between countermodernists and postmodernists is over, the former have become more flexible and the latter more market-orientated and both now face the pitiless spotlight of evaluation. I will complete this book with some reflections upon those scrutineers of fiction who treatments of it tend to neglect: its readers.

'Novels are in the hands of all of us; from the Prime Minister to the last-appointed scullery maid' wrote Trollope in 1870 ('On English Prose Fiction as Rational Amusement', from *Four Lectures*, ed. Morris L. Parrish, Constable, 1938, p. 94). The ghastly class system upon which Trollope based his image of fiction as the only classless literary genre has, if not completely disappeared, then at least mutated. What is also the case is that the distinction between the precious sphere of high culture, guarded by modernism since its inception, and the tastes of the ordinary reader, is also dissolving. David Mitchell, celebrated innovator, is discussed by readers' groups convened for Channel Four's *Richard and Judy* afternoon shows; the Internet now enables readers with no professional connection with writing or publishing to become critics, with publishers and individual authors regularly installing websites as the equivalent of unsupervised seminars. All this is to the good for fiction, allowing the consumer, the person without whom the novel would cease to exist, a voice alongside those who generally control the atmosphere of fiction writing, the literary establishment and the publishing industry. Criticism, once annexed exclusively by practitioners of literature and members of the intellectual elite, is becoming democratized, yet there is one group of critics, academics, which seems indifferent to this.

At the 2005 annual conference of the Modern Language Association of America, playwright and novelist Ariel Dorfman offered a beguiling paper, based, he claimed, on personal experience. He told of how CIA agents had recently detained him in a windowless room in Washington DC airport. One of his interrogators, the silent one, bore a disturbing resemblance to Trotsky, while the other, more loquacious, agent tortured him with endless questions and accusations designed to at once depress and unsettle him. Dorfman quoted from memory the interrogator's verbal assaults, comprising the kind of syntactic contusions and lexical hieroglyphics made fashionable by the likes of Derrida, Lacan, Lyotard, Foucault and so on and taken on as a routine critical dialect by many literary academics in the US and the UK. Disturbingly, most of Dorfman's audience failed to appreciate the joke and appeared confused by being offered a discourse that they recognized as their own within a most unusual context. The darkly comic image of intellectual inaccessibility allied with isolation from the world at large seemed beyond their comprehension.

Dorfman was not just playing games. His escape from Pinochet's Chile, under fear of imprisonment, and his grandparents' experience of the European pogroms testify to his commitment to the duty of writers as witnesses to the actualities of the world in which they live. What irritated him and prompted him to deliver his lecture was the apparent disjunction between the extensive fabric of what we might term literary culture – comprising writers, readers, publishers et al. – and the institutions, universities, wherein literature is studied intensively.

The lexicon, mannerisms and intellectual hauteur of literary theory are now endemic features of the critical writing of all but a small minority of academics. As a quasi-discipline in its own right theory has much to recommend it – challenging as it does routine preconceptions regarding issues such as identity, language, race and gender – but at the same time its own preoccupations have effectively alienated it both from its alleged subject, literature, and the body of individuals who are that subject's lifeblood, intelligent ordinary readers. This has occurred for two reasons. First, the language of theory has become as reflexive and self-referential, as immune from the routines of ordinary exchange, as that of the texts it tends to idolize. Secondly, the absorption of theory into academic criticism has all but immunized the latter from that most contentious, subjective feature of talking and writing about literature: an inclination to offer an opinion on whether or not the novel or the author are any good. The reasons for this are many and various, but most obviously the theoreticians' perception of the reader and author as the subjects or constructs of specific ideological conditions and discourses undermines the notion of being able to recognize aesthetic value or quality as intrinsic features of anything. This has, however, completely separated academic criticism from that broader fabric of exchanges involving newspaper critics and the readers themselves, where evaluation – the recognition of what is or is not fiction of quality – is the central issue.

Newspaper reviewers can be ruthlessly judgemental and can sometimes allow their private tastes and affiliations to trespass upon measured assessment but in general the review itself will be an accessible, often entertaining, exercise. Even if the reviewer loathes their subject their writing will be sharp and amusing enough to draw the reader into a culture of rebarbative exchange. It is at this level that such fundamental issues as whether the novelist is skilled at their craft can be properly addressed. Consider, for example, Martin Amis's comments on Michael Crichton's *The Lost World* (in *The War Against Cliché*): 'The characterization has been delegated to two or three thrashed and downtrodden adverbs [...] Malcolm seems to own "gloomily"; but then you irritably notice that Rossiter is behaving "gloomily" too, and gloomily discover that Malcolm is behaving "irritably". Forget about "tensely" and "grimly" for now. And don't get me started on "thoughtfully"'(p. 222). Amis makes use of his own skills as a stylist to pinpoint the inadequacies and excesses of Crichton's endeavours. Similarly, after reading a weary passage by D. M. Thomas he offers hilarious, disingenuous concern 'that the writer's face is about to flop onto the typewriter keys; the sentences conjure nothing but an exhausted imagination' (p. 145). One is aware that here is a novelist well attuned to the peculiarities and demands of good writing making use of them to signal their negligent scarcity in the work of his peers. Similarly, when D. J. Taylor offers the image of Amis himself as 'the author running into the room to arrange the chairs before the characters arrive' (*After the War*, Chatto, 1993, p. 292) we know that Taylor the critic is raising his game to deal with Amis the novelist. Which would you rather read as a commentary upon a novel, the above, or, 'This movement, "by analogy", offers the glimpse of synechdotal singularity, by which the other remains other rather than merely the subject of difference' and 'In Jungian individuation, deconstruction of the ego occurs also by reading archetypal images as fictional, metaphorical, provisional, culturally coloured manifestations of plural psyche not open to conquest, divination or specificity'? One could, with appropriate background reading and intellectual exertion make sense of these but surely and most significantly they indicate that the relationship between academic criticism, which they typify, and the pure pleasure of reading and thinking about fiction has become tenuous, to say the least.

Academia, with its hidebound theoretical obsessions, lags far behind the novel, which is now part of a transparently public discourse. Perhaps the clogged impenetrability of literary theory will eventually disperse and enable – no, oblige – academic critics to tackle literature on its own ground, to be as amusing, as thoughtfully available and shiftlessly elegant as their subject; to evaluate and assess the qualities of fiction rather than treat it as a springboard for intellectual prating. I hope so, but I doubt it.

LIBRARY, UNIVERSITY OF CHESTER

Select Bibliography: Recommended Further Reading

Bentley, N. (ed.), *British Fiction of the 1990s* (London: Routledge, 2005).

Connor, S., *The English Novel in History: 1950–1995* (London: Routledge, 1996).

Craig, C., *The Modern Scottish Novel: Narrative and the National Imagination* (Edinburgh: Edinburgh University Press, 1999).

Eagleton, M., *Figuring the Woman Author in Contemporary Fiction* (London: Palgrave, 2005).

Gasiorek, A., *Post-War British Fiction: Realism and After* (London: Edward Arnold, 1995).

Head, D., *The Cambridge Introduction to Modern British Fiction, 1950–2000* (Cambridge, UK: Cambridge University Press, 2002).

Kennedy-Andrews, E., *Fiction and the Northern Ireland Troubles Since 1969: (De-)constructing the North.* (Dublin: Four Courts, 2003).

Lane, R. J., Mengham, R., and Tew, P. (eds.), *Contemporary British Fiction* (Cambridge, UK: Polity, 2003).

Leader, Z. (ed.), *On Modern British Fiction* (Oxford: Oxford University Press, 2002).

Lee, A. R. (ed.), *Other Britain, Other British: Contemporary Multicultural Fiction* (London: Pluto, 1995).

MacDougall, C., *Painting the Forth Bridge: A Search for Scottish Identity* (London: Aurum, 2001).

Mengham, R. (ed.), *An Introduction to Contemporary Fiction: International Writing in English since 1970* (Cambridge, UK: Polity, 1999).

Monteith, S., Newman, J., and Wheeler, P., *Contemporary British and Irish Fiction. An Introduction Through Interviews* (London: Arnold, 2004).

Rennison, N., *Contemporary British Novelists* (London: Routledge, 2004).

Stevenson, R., *The Last of England. Vol. 12, The Oxford English Literary History, 1960–2000* (Oxford: Oxford University Press, 2004).

LIBRARY, UNIVERSITY OF CHESTER

Taylor, D. J., *After the War: The Novel and English Society since 1945* (London: Chatto and Windus, 1993).

Todd, R., *Consuming Fictions: The Booker Prize and Fiction in Britain Today* (London: Bloomsbury, 1996).

Waugh, P., *Harvest of the Sixties. English Literature and its Backgrounds, 1960–1990* (Oxford: Oxford University Press, 1995).

Werlock, A. H. P. (ed.), *British Women Writing Fiction* (Tuscaloosa and London: University of Alabama Press, 2000).

Index

Ackroyd, Peter 82–3
  The Great Fire of London 82
  Hawksmoor 82
  The House of Doctor Dee 82
  Milton in America 82–3
  Notes for a New Culture 25, 83
Adams, Gerry 229
Ainsworth, William Harrison: *Jack*
  Shepperd. A Romance 104
Ali, Monica 206, 210–11
  Brick Lane 210–11
Amis, Kingsley 7–9, 10, 12, 16, 26,
  116, 117–18, 119, 164, 176,
  184, 244
  Lucky Jim 7, 35, 117–18, 164
  Take A Girl Like You 119
Amis, Martin 12–18, 24–5, 37–8,
  41–3, 76–8, 107, 141, 146–9,
  184, 246–7
  Dead Babies 13, 14
  The Information 41–3, 147–8, 184
  London Fields 16–17
  Money 13–15, 36, 146–7
  Night Train 107
  Other People 16
  The Rachel Papers 12

  Time's Arrow 25, 84
  The War Against Cliché 148, 246
  Yellow Dog 76–8, 149
Armitage, Simon 143
  The White Stuff 145–6
Arnott, Jake 104–5, 108–9
  He Kills Coppers 105
  The Long Firm 104–5
  Truecrime 105, 108–9
Attlee, Clement 27
Austen, Jane 132–3
Auster, Paul 107
  City of Glass 107
  Ghosts 107
  The Locked Room 107
Azzopardi, Trezza: *The Hiding*
  Place 219–20

Baddiel, David: *The Secret*
  Purposes 99
Banks, Lynn Reid: *The L–Shaped*
  Room 117
Barker, Nicola 54–7, 76, 243, 244
  Behindlings 55–6
  Clear 56, 59
  Love Your Enemies 54–5

Barker, Pat 84–6
  The Eye in the Door 84–5
  The Ghost Road 84
  Regeneration 84–6
Barnes, Djuna: *Nightwood* 137
Barnes, Julian 48–50, 95–6, 107,
    141, 143, 180–3
  Arthur and George 95–6, 107
  England, England 50, 180–3
  Flaubert's Parrot 48–9
  *A History of the World in 10^1/$_2$
    Chapters* 49
  Love etc 50, 143
  Metroland 48
  Staring at the Sun 84
  Talking it Over 49–50, 143
  see also Dan Kavanagh
Barry, Desmond: *A Bloody Good
    Friday* 220
Barry, Sebastian: *A Long Long
    Way* 97–8
Barstow, Stan 9
Bateman, Colin: *Divorcing Jack* 231
Beaudrillard, Jean 66–7
Beauman, Sally: *The Landscape of
    Love* 138
Beckett, Samuel 5–6, 7, 71, 243
  Malone Dies 5
  Molloy 5
  The Unnameable 5
  Waiting for Godot 7
  Watt 5
Bennett, Ronan 91–2, 231, 233
  Havoc in its Third Year 91–2
  The Second Prison 233–4
Berger, John 6, 67–8, 69, 71, 78,
    163
  The Foot of Clive 6
  Here is Where We Meet 67–8, 69
Bergonzi, Bernard 25–6

Beveridge, Sir William 27
Bhabba, Homi 198, 212
Billingham, Mark 106
  The Burning Girl 106
  Sleepyhead 106
Birch, Carol: *Turn Again Home* 189
Black, Lawrence: *Hit List* 102
Blacker, Terence: *Fixx* 33
Blair, Tony 38–39, 188
Blanchard, Stephen: *Wilson's
    Island* 46
Blincoe, Nicholas 61
Bly, Robert 148
Bolt, Rodney: *History Play* 93
Boyd, William 84, 88–9, 141–2, 176
  Brazzaville Beach 141
  An Ice-Cream War 88
  The New Confessions 88–9, 142
Boyt, Susie: *Only Human* 135–6
Bradbury, Malcolm 35
  Cuts 35
  The History Man 35
Bragg, Melvyn 26
Braine, John 9, 116, 184
  Stay With Me Till Morning 10
Briscoe, Joanna: *Sleep With Me* 185
Brooke-Rose, Christine: *Such* 6
Brookmyre, Christopher 106
  *All Fun and Games Until Someone
    Loses an Eye* 106
  Quite Ugly One Morning 106
Brookner, Anita 126–7
  Altered States 127
  Hotel du Lac 126–7
  Leaving Home 127
  Lewis Percy 127
Brown, Craig 223
Brown, Dan 91
Browne, Liam: *The Emigrant's
    Farewell* 240–1

Browning, Robert 90
Buford, Bill 26
Burgess, Anthony vi, 9
   A Clockwork Orange 52
   Enderby 9
   MF 9
   The Wanting Seed 52
Burke, Sean: *Deadwater* 223–4
Burley, W. J. 108
Burns, Alan: *Celebrations* 6
Byatt, A. S.: *Possession* 90

Cain, James M 102
   Double Indemnity 102
   The Postman Always Rings
      Twice 102
Carry On films 200
Carter, Angela 119–20, 123, 127
   The Magic Toyshop 119
   Nights at the Circus 119
   Wise Children 119
Cartwright, Justin 30–1, 71–3, 186,
   204
   Look at it This Way 30–1, 41
   The Promise of Happiness 71–3, 186
Caute, David 6
   The Confrontation 6
   Veronica, or the Two Nations 33
'chick lit' 132–4
Clark, Candida: *A House of*
   Light 185–6
Clarke, Susanna: *Jonathan Strange*
   and Mr Norrell 93
Close, Ajay 134
Coe, Jonathan 39–40, 43–5, 47,
   143, 184–5, 204
   The Closed Circle 44–5, 143,
      184–5
   The Rotters' Club 43–4, 143
   What a Carve Up! 39–40, 43

Cooper, William 7
Craig, Cairns 161, 174–6
Crispin, Edmund 100
cummings, e. e. 175
Cutler, Judith: *Power Games* 105

Darling, Julia: *The Taxi Driver's*
   Daughter 187–9
Dean, Louise: *This Human*
   Season 239–40
Deane, Seamus 231–2, 233, 234–5
   Reading in The Dark 234–5
Deighton, Len 111
   Funeral in Berlin 111
   The Ipcress File 111
Derrida, Jacques 65–6, 245
Dexter, Colin 100–1
Dhaliwal, Nirpal Singh: *Tourism* 205
Diana, Princess 156–7
Dibdin, Michael 33–4, 108
   Back to Bologna 108
   Dirty Tricks 33–4
Dickens, Charles 17, 81
Dorfman, Ariel 245
Drabble, Margaret 26, 117–18,
   187–8
   The Millstone 117–18
   A Summer Birdcage 117–18
   The Witch of Exmoor 187–8
Dunant, Sarah 105
   Birthmarks 105
   Fatlands 105
   Under My Skin 105
Dunn, Nell 117
   Up the Junction 117
   Poor Cow 117
DUP 236

Eagleton, Terry 66–7
Ealing Comedies 223

Eco, Umberto: *The Name of the Rose* 91
Eliot, George 4
Eliot, T. S. 163
Ellis, Ron 106
Ellroy, James 102, 105
  American Tabloid 102, 105
  The Cold Six Thousand 102, 105
  White Jazz 102
Elton, Ben: *Inconceivable* 145
Evaristo, Bernardine 212–13
  The Emperor's Babe 213
  Lara 213
  Soul Tourists 213

Faber, Michel 93, 171–2
  The Crimson Petal and The White 93
  Some Rain Must Fall 171
  Under the Skin 171–2
Fairbairns, Zoe 124
  Stand We at Last 124
Falconer, Helen 134
Faulks, Sebastian 86–7, 98
  Birdsong 86–7
  Charlotte Gray 98
Fforde, Jasper: *The Eyre Affair* 223
Fielding, Helen 131–3, 135
  Bridget Jones's Diary 131–3
  Bridget Jones: The Edge of Reason 132–3
Forster, E. M.: *Howards End* 207
Forster, Margaret 125–6
  Georgy Girl 125–6
  Is There Anything You Want? 126
  Shadow Baby 125
  Significant Sisters, The Grassroots of Active Feminism 1839–1939 126
Forsyth, Frederick 111

Fowler, Christopher 108
Fowles, John: *The French Lieutenant's Woman* 10, 82, 96, 162
Fraser, George MacDonald 81
Frayn, Michael 74
Freely, Maureen 127
French, Nicci 106
  The Land of the Living 106
  The Memory Game 106
Friel, George 161
Fukuyama, Francis: *The End of History and The Last Man* 87–8
Fyfield, Francis 105

Galloway, Janice: *The Trick is to Keep Breathing* 175
Gee, Maggie 41, 208–9
  Grace 41
  The White Family 208–9
Gerard, Nicci: *Solace* 140
Gilbert, Geoff 164–5
Gilbert, Sandra and Gubar, Susan: *The Madwoman in the Attic* 117
Golding, William 9, 59–60, 81
  Lord of the Flies 59–60
  The Spire 81
Good Friday Agreement, the 236
Gray, Alasdair 137, 161–3, 171, 172, 174
  The Fall of Kelvin Walker 163
  Lanark 161–2, 174
  McGrotty and Ludmilla 163
  1982 Janine 137, 162–3
Greene, Graham 9, 110
  The Confidential Agent 110
  Our Man in Havana 110 ·
Griffiths, Niall 189, 221–2
  Sheepshagger 221
  Stump 221–2
  Wreckage 189

Hamilton, Patrick: *Twenty Thousand Streets Under the Sky* 137
Harris, Martyn: *Do It Again* 34–5
Harvey, John 108
Hawes, James: *White Powder, Green Light* 222–3
Head, Dominic 155
Heaney, Seamus 229
Heawood, Jonathan 157
Hensher, Philip: *Kitchen Venom* 155–6
Heyer, Georgette 81
Highsmith, Patricia 102
    Strangers on a Train 102
    The Talented Mr Ripley 102
Hill, Reginald 100–1
Hinds, Archie: *The Dear Green Place* 170–1
Hines, Barry 75
HIV/AIDS 154–7
Hollinghurst, Alan 114, 151–4
    The Folding Star 152–3
    The Line of Beauty 114, 153–4
    The Spell 153
    The Swimming Pool Library 151–2, 156
Hornby, Nick 143–4
    About a Boy 144
    Fever Pitch 143
    High Fidelity 143–4
    A Long Way Down 50
Howard, Elizabeth Jane 10, 74, 187
    Something in Disguise 10
Hume, John 231
Huxley, Aldous 6

INLA 234
IRA 44, 226, 228, 233, 234, 235, 236, 239
Irvine, A. S.: 'A Novel' 70

Ishiguro, Kazuo 214–17
    Never Let Me Go 216–17
    The Remains of the Day 214–15
    The Unconsoled 215, 217
    When We Were Orphans 216

Jacobson, Howard 149–50
    Coming from Behind 150
    The Making of Henry 149–50
    Who's Sorry Now 150–1
James, Bill 103–4
    Pay Days 103
    Roses Roses 103
    You'd Better Believe It 103
James, Henry 76, 94–5
James, P. D. 100–1, 108–9
    The Murder Room 108–9
Jenkins, Simon 165
Johnson, B. S. 6, 45, 47, 58, 175
    Alberto Angelo 6
    Travelling People 6
    The Unfortunates 6
Josipovici, Gabriel 6
    The Inventory 6
    Words 6
Joyce, James 3, 4–5, 7, 71, 75, 77
Judd, Alan 111
    Legacy 111

Kavanagh, Dan (pen name for Julian Barnes) 107
    Fiddle City 107
    Putting the Boot In 107
Kelman, James 163–5, 171, 172, 173, 174–5, 176
    A Disaffection 174–5
    How Late It Was, How Late 163–5
    You Have to be Careful in the Land of the Free 176

Kennedy, A. L. 74–5, 78, 136–7, 172
  Paradise 74–5, 137, 172
  So I Am Glad 136–7, 172
King, Daren 75
  Boxy An Star 75
  Tom Boler 75
Kingsley, Charles 81
Kinnock, Neil 38
Kunzru, Hari 211–12
  The Impressionist 211–12
  Transmission 212
Kureishi, Hanif 203–5
  The Buddha of Suburbia 203–5
  *My Beautiful Laundrette and The
    Rainbow Sign* 203–5

Labour Party 27, 38–9, 188
Lacan, Jacques 245
'lad lit' 143–6
Lamming, George: *The
  Emigrants* 192–3
Laird, Nick: *Utterly Monkey* 238–9
Lanchester, John 53–4
  The Dept to Pleasure 53–4
  Mr Philips 54
Larkin, Philip 7, 113, 184
  Jill 184
Lawton, John: *Blue Rondo* 108
Leader, Zachary 173
Lean, Frank 106
Le Carré, John 110–12
  Absolute Friends 111
  The Constant Gardner 111
  The Honourable Schoolboy 110
  The Little Drummer Girl 110–11
  A Perfect Spy 110
  The Russia House 111
  Single and Single 111
  Smiley's People 110
  Tinker, Tailor, Soldier, Spy 110

Lessing, Doris: *The Golden
  Notebook* 10, 118–19
Levy, Andrea 206, 209–10
  Small Island 209–10
Litt, Toby 58–61, 70
  Corpsing 58–9
  Deadkidsongs 59–60
  Ghost Story 60
  New Writing 13 (ed) 70
Little Britain 223
Lodge, David 3, 17, 27, 78, 94–5
  Author, Author 94–5
  Changing Places 35
  Nice Work 35–6
London, Jack: *John Barleycorn* 137
Lott, Tim: *White City Blue* 144–5
Lowry, Malcolm: *Under the
  Volcano* 6
loyalist paramilitaries 230–1,
  237–8
Lyotard, Jean-François 195–6,
  245

Maitland, Sarah 124
  Virgin Territory 124
Major, John 38, 39
Malkani, Gautam:
  Londonstani 213–14
Mantel, Hilary 75–6, 78
  Beyond Black 75–6
Marlowe, Christopher 93
Mars-Jones, Adam 36, 154–5
  The Darker Proof 154–5
  Monopolies of Loss 154–5
  The Waters of Thirst 155
Martin, Andrew: *The Blackpool High
  Flyer* 93
Maugham, W. Somerset 8, 165
McCrum, Robert 26
McDougall, Carl 161, 173

McEwan, Ian 18–25, 142
  The Cement Garden 20–21
  The Child in Time 24, 36–8
  The Comfort of Strangers 18–19
  First Love, Last Rites 142
  In Between the Sheets 142
  The Innocent 21–2, 84
  Saturday 22–4
McIlvanney, Liam 173
McIlvanney, William 161
McNamee, Eoin: *Resurrection
  Man* 230–1
McWilliam, Candia 57–8, 174
  'The Only Only' 57–8
  Wait Till I Tell You 57
Millett, Kate: *Sexual Politics*
  116–7
Milton, John 175
Mitchell, David 62–3, 64, 70, 78,
  243, 244
  Black Swan Green 63
  Cloud Atlas 62
Moore, Brian 225–6
  Lies of Silence 225–6
Morrison, Blake 7
Morrison, Danny: *West Belfast* 233
Mount, Ferdinand 74, 78
  Heads You Win 74
Murdoch, Iris 9–10
Murray, John: *Jazz etc* 189

Naipaul, V. S. 201–3
  The Enigma of Arrival 201–2
  Half a Life 202
  A House for Mr Biswas 201
  Magic Seeds 202–3
Naughton, Bill: *Alfie* 116
Neate, Patrick: *City of Tiny
  Lights* 108
'New Puritanism' 61

Nicholson, Geoff: *Bleeding
  London* 45–6
Norfolk, Lawrence 70, 84
  In the Shape of a Boar 84
North, Sam: *The
  Unnumbered* 189–90
Nye, Robert 83–4
  Falstaff 83
  Faust 83
  The Late Mr Shakespeare 83
  The Memoirs of Lord Byron 83

O'Brien, Edna: *House of Splendid
  Isolation* 234
O'Hagan, Andrew 56–7, 76, 244
  Personality 56–7, 69
Orwell, George 14
Overall, Sonia: *The Realm of
  Shells* 93

Paisley, Ian 231, 238
Paisley, Janet: *Not for Glory* 168
Parks, Tim: *Goodness* 32–3
Parsons, Tony 143, 145–6
  The Family Way 145–6
Patten, Eve 232
Patterson, Glenn 229–30, 236–8
  Burning Your Own 229
  Fat Lad 229–30
  The International 229, 236–7
  Number 5 237, 240
  That Which Was 237–8
Paxman, Jeremy: *The English. A
  Portrait of the People* 160
Pears, Ian 91
  The Dream of Scipio 91
  An Instance of the Fingerpost 91
  The Portrait 93
Peck, Dale: *Hatchet Jobs: Writings on
  Contemporary Fiction* 70

Phillips, Caryl 193–5, 209
  The European Tribe 193–4
  The Final Passage 193–4, 209
  A State of Independence 194–5
Picardie, Justine: *Wish I May* 139
Pilton, Barry: *The Valley* 223
Porter, Henry 111–12
  Empire State 112
  Remembrance Day 111
  A Spy's Life 111–12
Pound, Ezra 163
Priestman, Martin 103
Pryce, Malcolm 222
  Aberstwyth Mon Amour 222
  Last Tango in Aberystwyth 222
  The Unbearable Lightness of Being in Aberystwyth 222
Pym, Barbara 19

Quinn, Ann: *Berg* 6

Rabinovitz, Rubin 7
Rankin, Ian 100–1, 103
  Knots and Crosses 103
Rathbone, Julian 31–2, 204
  Nasty, Very 31–2
Raven, Simon: *Places Where They Sing* 10
Read, Piers Paul: *A Married Man* 34
Rees, Simon 74
Rendell, Ruth 100–1, 106
Richards, Ben: *Don't Step on the Lines* 45
Richardson, Dorothy 3, 4–5, 116
Roberts, Michèle 124–5, 133–5
  Daughters of the House 124–5
  Fair Exchange 124
  In the Red Kitchen 125
  The Looking Glass 124

Reader, I Married Him 133–5, 155
  The Visitation 124
Rogers, Jane: *Mr Wroe's Virgins* 93
Rossetti, Christina 90
Rowbotham, Sheila: *A Century of Women* 130
Rushdie, Salman 26, 195–201, 212–13, 244
  Grimus 26
  Haroun and the Sea of Stories 199
  Imaginary Homelands 195–9
  Midnight's Children 195–6
  The Satanic Verses 195–8
  Shalimar The Clown 199–200

Said, Edward 212
Sampson, Denis 226
Sands, Sarah: *Playing the Game* 139
Saunders, Kate 133–4
Saussure, Ferdinand de 65
Scottish National Party 167
Scurr, Ruth 157
Sebald, W. G. 217–18
  Austerlitz 217–18
Seiffert, Rachel 218
  The Dark Room 218
Self, Will 51–3, 155–6, 213–14
  The Book of Dave 213–14
  Cock and Bull 51
  Dorian. An Imitation 155–6
  How The Dead Live 76
  My Idea of Fun 51–3
  The Quantity Theory of Insanity 51
Selvon, Sam 193
  The Lonely Londoners 193
  Moses Ascending 193
  Moses Migrating 193
Seymour, Gerald 111
Sharp, Alan 161

Sillitoe, Alan 9, 10, 116, 184
  Guzman Go Home 10
  *Saturday Night and Sunday
    Morning* 9, 184
Sinclair, Iain 68–70, 76, 243
  Downriver 68
  London Orbital 69
  Slow Chocolate Autopsy 69
  White Chappell, Scarlet Tracings
    68
Sinclair, May 116
Smith, Alexander McCall: *The
    Sunday Philosophy Club* 108
Smith, Ali 58, 70, 72–3, 172, 243
  The Accidental 72–3, 172
  Hotel World 58, 172, 243
  New Writing 13 70
Smith, Zadie 206–8, 212
  The Autograph Man 207
  On Beauty 207–8, 212
  White Teeth 206–7
Smyth, Gerry 232
Snow, C. P. 7, 10, 26
  The Sleep of Reason 10
Spark, Muriel 9, 169–71
  The Prime of Miss Jean Brodie 169–71
Stace, Wesley: *Misfortune* 94
Sterne, Laurence 12, 195
Stevenson, Talitha: *Exposure* 139–40
Storey, David 9, 116, 184
Sutherland, John 25
Swift, Graham 107, 177–80
  Last Orders 178–9
  The Light of Day 179–80
  Waterland 177–8, 179
Swift, Jonathan 161

Tarantino, Quentin 165
Taylor, D. J. 36, 74, 96, 247
  Kept. A Victorian Mystery 96

Tennant, Emma 127–9, 132, 133
  The Bad Sister 127–8
  *Emma in Love: Jane Austen's
    Emma Continued* 129
  Faustine 129
  *Pemberley or Pride and Prejudice
    Continued* 129, 132
  *Two Women of London: The Strange
    Case of Ms Jekyll and Mrs
    Hyde* 128–9
Thatcher, Margaret 29, 34, 38, 39,
    43, 47, 155–6, 197–8, 202,
    231
Thatcherism 29–46 passim, 47–8,
    52, 90, 114, 154, 163
Thorne, Matt 61
  All Hail the New Puritans 61
  Cherry 61
Thorpe, Adam 89, 96–7, 98, 180
  Nineteen Twenty–One 96–7
  The Rules of Perspective 98
  Ulverton 89, 180
Tóibín, Colm: *The Master* 94–5
Tremain, Rose: *Restoration* 89–90
Tresize, Rachel: *In and Out of The
    Goldfish Bowl* 220
Trollope, Anthony 244
Trollope, Joanna 187
  The Best of Friends 187
  Next of Kin 187
Turner, Jerry 127

Vine, Barbara *see* Rendell, Ruth

Wain, John 7–8, 10, 116, 184
  Hurry on Down 7
  A Winter in the Hills 10
Walter, Natasha 127
Walters, Minette 106
  The Shape of Snakes 106

Wambaugh, Joseph 102
  The Choirboys 102
  The New Centurions 102
Warner, Alan 168–71
  Morvern Callar 168–9
  The Sopranos 169–71
  These Demented Lands 169
Waters, Sarah 93, 98–9
  Affinity 93
  Fingersmith 93
  The Night Watch 98–9
  Tipping the Velvet 93
Waugh, Evelyn 9, 13, 16, 154, 176, 206
Weldon, Fay 119–21, 130–1, 135,
    137–8
  Big Women 130–1
  *The Life and Loves of a She
    Devil* 119–21
  Mantrapped 137–8
Welsh, Irvine 165–8, 171, 172
  Filth 175
  Porno 167–8
  Trainspotting 165–7
Wilde, Oscar 94, 156
Williams, Gordon: *Big Morning
    Blues* 137
Williams, John 220–1, 222
  Cardiff Dead 220–1
  *Five Pubs, Two Bars and a
    Nightclub* 220–1

  The Prince of Wales 220–1
  Wales Half Welsh 222
Williams, Nigel 74
Wilson, A. N. 186
  A Jealous Ghost 186
  Wise Virgin 186
Wilson, Robert McLiam
  Eureka Street 228–9
  Ripley Bogle 226–8, 235–6
Wingfield, R. D. 100–1
Winterson, Jeanette 121–3, 127,
    129–30, 133, 243
  Art and Lies 123, 129
  Lighthouse Keeping 121, 122
  *Oranges Are Not the Only
    Fruit* 121, 122
  The Passion 121, 122
  The PowerBook 121, 122,
    127
  Sexing the Cherry 121
  Written on the Body 121, 122
Wolfreys, Julian 70
Woolf, Erica: *Mud Puppy* 220
Woolf, Virginia 3, 4–5, 115–16, 123,
    129–30, 144–5, 163
World War I 84–7, 96–8
World War II 98–9, 181–2, 206,
    209, 217–18

Zaveroni, Lena 56–7